How Mongolia Matters: War, Law, and Society

Brill's Inner Asian Library

Edited by

Michael R. Drompp
Devin DeWeese
Mark C. Elliott

VOLUME 36

The titles published in this series are listed at *brill.com/bial*

How Mongolia Matters: War, Law, and Society

Edited by

Morris Rossabi

BRILL

LEIDEN | BOSTON

Cover illustration: Portrait of Chinggis Khan. Calendar from Blue Banner Publishers (Tsutsumi 2012).

The Library of Congress Cataloging-in-Publication Data is available online at http://catalog.loc.gov
LC record available at http://lccn.loc.gov/2017006128

Typeface for the Latin, Greek, and Cyrillic scripts: "Brill". See and download: brill.com/brill-typeface.

ISSN 1566-7162
ISBN 978-90-04-34338-2 (hardback)
ISBN 978-90-04-34340-5 (e-book)

This book is printed on acid-free paper and produced in a sustainable manner.

The authors would like to dedicate this book to Morris Rossabi for his contributions to the study of Chinese and Inner Asian History

Contents

List of Illustrations

Contributors

Christopher Atwood
(Ph.D. Indiana University) is Professor of Mongol History at the University of Pennsylvania and has written *Young Mongols and Vigilantes in Inner Mongolia's Interregnum Decades* (Brill) and *Encyclopedia of Mongolia and the Mongol Empire* (Facts on File).

Bettine Birge
(Ph.D. Columbia University) is Associate Professor of East Asian Languages and Civilizations at the University of Southern California and is the author of *Women, Property, and Confucian Reaction in Sung and Yuan China, 960–1368* (Cambridge University Press) and a forthcoming book on Yuan law to be published by Harvard University Press.

Michael Brose
(Ph.D. University of Pennsylvania) is Professor of History at the University of Wyoming and author of *Subjects and Masters: Uyghurs in the Mongol Empire* (Western Washington University Center for East Asian Studies).

Pamela Crossley
(Ph.D. Yale University) is Professor of History at Dartmouth College and has written *A Translucent Mirror: History and Identity in Qing Imperial Ideology* (University of California Press) and *The Manchus* (Blackwell).

Johan Elverskog
(Ph.D. Indiana University) is Professor of Religion at Southern Methodist University and author of *Our Great Qing* (University of Hawaii Press) and *Buddhism and Islam on the Silk Road* (University of Pennsylvania Press).

Jargalsaikhan Enkhsaikhan,
an attorney specializing in international law, was formerly Mongolian Ambassador to Austria and Ambassador to the United Nations and focused on developing nuclear-free zones during his tenure as Ambassador.

Yuki Konagaya
received her training at Kyoto University and is currently Director of the National Institute for the Humanities and Professor at the National Museum of Ethnology in Japan. She has written extensively on Mongolian nomadism and on twentieth-century Mongolian history.

James Millward
(Ph.D. Stanford University) is Professor of Chinese and Central Asian History at Georgetown University and has written *Beyond the Pass: Economy, Ethnicity, and Empire in Qing Central Asia, 1759–1864* (Stanford University Press).

David Morgan
(Ph.D. University of London) is Professor of History Emeritus at the University of Wisconsin and author of *Medieval Persia, 1040–1797* (Longman) and *The Mongols* (Blackwell).

David Robinson
(Ph.D. Princeton University) is Professor of History at Colgate University and is the author of *Martial Spectacles of the Ming Court* (Harvard University Press) and *Bandits, Eunuchs, and the Son of Heaven: Rebellion and the Economy of Violence in Mid-Ming China* (University of Hawaii Press).

Introduction: Myths about Mongols and Inner Asians

Morris Rossabi

Myths enshroud the study of Mongolian and Inner Asian history. Until the 1980s, popularizers and highly specialized scholars generally wrote the principal works concerning these mostly steppe peoples. Both had significant flaws. Popularizers wrote, in racy prose, about the thirteenth and fourteenth century Mongols, in particular, as barbarians who plundered, maimed, raped, and killed both enemies and innocents during their so-called rampages in Eurasia. On the other hand, some scholars, explored, in great detail, inscriptions or texts in Mongolian, Persian, Chinese, and other languages, examining specific words with only scant references to the larger contexts of Mongolian history and culture.

In the 1980s, several works on Mongolian history sought to reassess the Mongols' significance in world history, emphasizing their contributions to civilization while not ignoring the destruction and damage they wrought. A new group of specialists described the Mongols' often successful efforts to establish governments in China, Russia, and Iran and the Middle East, their contributions to trade, and their general lack of religious discrimination against the peoples they subjugated. However, popularizers, who sought notoriety, not to mention sales of their books, were, as one biographer of Chinggis Khan has explained, "writers who soft-pedal the casualties caused by the Mongols and stress instead their enlightened attitude to women ... their transmission of culture and the arts, and, even, their role as fount and origin of the Renaissance ... are fanciful and far-fetched."[1]

These purveyors of "fanciful" assertions who had scant knowledge of Mongol history and who were unable to consult Chinese, Russian, Persian, Korean, or any other primary sources, also portrayed Chinggis Khan as an apostle of democracy and an advocate of equitable international relations. They virtually deified Chinggis, which gained plaudits in a modern Mongolia, afflicted by disastrous economic and environmental difficulties since the 1990s. Seeking to restore their pride, some Mongols have depicted Chinggis as the father of the Mongols and have named the capital city's airport, a rock band, a beer, and a vodka, among others, in his honor.

1 As cited in *The Times Literary Supplement* (November 27, 2015), p. 31.

 | DOI 10.1163/9789004343405_002

The overturning of these myths is essential if an accurate portrait of the role of the Mongols and Inner Asians in history is to be produced. The essays in this book have undertaken the task of dispelling some of these myths. Careful sifting of the sources, analyses of their biases, and explications of phrases and passages in the primary texts have been used to understand motivations and actual events. In each case, philological exercises offer insights into and resolve controversies about Mongol history and culture.

An impediment to challenging these myths is the general paucity and, in some cases, non-existence of Mongolian and Inner Asian texts. Written languages in Central and Inner Asia developed much later than the scripts, alphabets, and characters of the sedentary civilizations. The sources about the Mongolians and Inner Asians often reflect the views of their enemies, which prevents a totally accurate perception of events. In his essay, Johan Elverskog seeks to remedy this lacuna by translating a Mongolian work describing the battle of Tumu, in 1449, during which Esen, a prominent Mongol leader, captured the Chinese Ming dynasty Emperor. Accounts of this battle have relied exclusively on Chinese sources. Elverskog offers a seventeenth-century Mongolian portrait of this incident. The text has its own agenda: that is, the view that the Mongols required unity under a legitimate ruler if they were to prosper. Despite its political message, which reflects the disunity that plagued the Mongols at its appearance in 1662, the text represents one of the few Mongolian perspectives on their pre-modern history.

Study of terminology yields insights into policies and historical events. James Millward explores a phrase often used by the Manchu Qing dynasty rulers of China to describe relations with foreigners, especially the Inner Asians whom they incorporated into their empire. He asserts through a study of Chinese and Inner Asian language texts that a term often translated as "pacify," implying a violent and repressive policy, actually meant "cherishing people from afar," which truly depicts the Qing's attitude toward the Inner Asian peoples. This philological analysis appears to confirm the view of the so-called New Qing Historians that the Qing was a true Inner Asian dynasty in embracing and, on occasion, adopting or tolerating the beliefs and values of Tibetans and Mongols.

Christopher Atwood, David Morgan, and Michael Brose examine the sources carefully to question, in part, myths about the thirteenth-century western sphere of the Mongol empire. Atwood explores the conflict that arose between the Golden Horde of Russia and the Il-Khanate of Persia and the Middle East concerning the territory Chinggis Khan granted to Jochi, his eldest son. Much after Chinggis' death, the Il-Khans asserted that Jochi and his Golden Horde descendants had not been granted the entire western region. Atwood demonstrates that Jochi had indeed collaborated with other Mongol leaders in campaigns in Inner Mongolia and China, so he could not claim those regions as his exclusive domains. However, Jochi had the sole responsibility for battles along the Syr Darya River and in Kazakhstan in Central Asia. Atwood's comprehensive exploration confirms that Jochi and the Golden Horde had been granted the major responsibility in the west. David Morgan challenges the popularizers who minimized the Mongol pillaging of Persia and the Middle East and emphasized only the positive aspects of the Mongol invasions and rule. He shows that the Mongols inflicted tremendous damage in Persia and the Middle East, though the thirteenth and fourteenth century Persian accounts exaggerated the destruction. Michael Brose rescues the Qipchak peoples from oblivion. Contrary to the conventional wisdom, the Qipchaks retained their identities even after the Mongol conquests. A special Qipchak Guard played important roles in the struggles for succession in the Mongol Yuan dynasty.

Bettine Birge and David Robinson show that the Mongols had greater influence on China than commonly believed. The traditional interpretation was that the Mongols scarcely contributed to Chinese civilization, and indeed many Mongols were attracted by Chinese civilization and actually became Sinicized. Birge reveals that aspects of Mongol criminal and marital law and inheritance practices often prevailed during the Mongol Yuan dynasty and then affected the Ming (1368–1644) and Qing (1644–1911) dynasties. The Mongol practice of a criminal's payment to the bereaved family in restitution for the damage it incurred often served as a legal precedent in the Ming and Qing. Mongol limitations, through the institution of the levirate, on the property rights of women, which had earlier been affirmed in the Song (960–1279) dynasty, dovetailed with the rise of Neo-Confucianism, which, in general, undermined the status of women. An emphasis on widow chastity and thus dependence on the dead husband's family also subverted the position of women. David Robinson describes the influence of the Mongols on the Ming dynasty, especially during the reign of the Yongle (1403–1424) emperor who initiated five major campaigns against them forty years after they withdrew from China. The Chinese historical accounts portrayed his forays into the steppes as extraordinary victories and are truly mythical representations. Frequently moving around in their own territories, the Mongols, for the most part, eluded the emperor's forces, and, contrary to the myths perpetuated in the Chinese histories, no major battles took place. Nonetheless, the Ming produced poetry and songs commemorating the transparently mythical victories over the Mongols, although the Chinese did not totally stigmatize the peoples of the steppes in these works, as they wished to integrate them into China.

Pamela Crossley, Yuki Konagaya, and Ambassador Enkhsaikhan Jargalsaikhan provide factual appraisals relating to both the traditional and contemporary Mongols. The steppe peoples were quintessential horse riders, and their cavalries offered an advantage over all their enemies. Crossley describes the riding patterns, including isolation of the horse's flank from the rider's leg, which provided such leverage. Her fine technical analysis avoids the generalities and myths about Inner Asian horses. Yuki Konagaya writes that the deification of Chinggis Khan, through songs and portraits, did not, as many specialists on modern Mongolia as well as journalists have assumed, originate after the fall of socialism in Mongolia in 1990. She shows that that the Japanese played a major role in boosting Chinggis' image. Trying to whip up Mongol nationalism in the 1930s in order to detach Inner Mongolia from Chinese control, the Japanese latched on to Chinggis and.encouraged Mongols in Inner Mongolia to feature him in rituals and festivals, setting the stage for his deification. Ambassador Enkhsaikhan Jargalsaikhan brings modern Mongolia into focus, with a description of the country's relation to nuclear energy and power. Surrounded by two countries which have nuclear weapons, Mongolia seeks to be in the midst of a nuclear weapon free zone. Yet as Ambassador Enkhsaikhan points out, the nuclear weapons tests by China and the Soviet Union and then Russia have been conducted near Mongolia, and he questions the assurances of the two powers about the safety of the Mongolian homeland. He also worries about the deposits of nuclear waste near Mongolia's border and about the myths regarding Mongolia's own peaceful use of nuclear energy for generation of electricity. Mongolia has substantial reserves of uranium, but Ambassador Enkhsaikhan wonders whether Mongolia has the expertise and proper equipment to extract it safely.

The Mongol Empire and Inner Asian History have often been portrayed inaccurately. Sensationalism has frequently plagued the depictions of the Mongol eruption into East, Central, and West Asia and has emphasized their so-called barbarism and the destruction they wrought. The late twentieth century witnessed a reappraisal which stressed the Mongols' contributions to cultural, religious, and scientific exchanges during the height of the Mongol Empire. The originators of this revised version did not exculpate the Mongols' killings and destruction, but non-specialists focused exclusively on the Mongols' contributions and exaggerated their attributes to include democracy and an influence on the European Renaissance. Post-1990 Mongolia, the era after almost seventy years of communist rule, has also elicited overabundant praise for the development of "democracy" and, at the same time, nostalgia for the so-called benefits of the communist era. This book seeks a balanced version of Mongol and Inner Asian history and society.

I should mention that the essays in this volume were written in respect of my career.[2] I am truly humbled and honored that such distinguished scholars devoted considerable effort and time to contribute to a so-called festschrift. Yet, as I read the essays, I found a common theme that went beyond the often disparate papers in a conventional festschrift. Each dealt with myths about the Mongols and the Inner Asian peoples that needed to be questioned. This particular motif, which clearly emerged from the papers, deserved closer attention than a group of essays lacking unity. I am pleased that the volume started as a festschrift, but I think it has a broader significance, and I trust that the reader will agree.

We are indebted to Dr. Marleen Kassel for conceiving of this work, to Joanna Jellinek for editing the essays, and to Professor Bettine Birge for the title of her chapter, which inspired the title of the book.

---

2 For my own assessment, see Morris Rossabi, *From Yuan to Modern China and Mongolia* (Leiden: Brill, 2014), pp. 3–15.

CHAPTER 1

Sagang Sechen on the Tumu Incident

Johan Elverskog

The Tumu Incident of 1449,[1] when the Oirat ruler Esen captured the Ming emperor fifty miles north-west of Beijing, was a watershed in Chinese history.[2] One scholar has even claimed that it changed forever the Ming intellectual world.[3] Yet, as with much else about the Ming period, little is known about this particular episode from the Mongol-Oirat point of view. Indeed, since we have no extant sources from this period it is impossible to know what they actually thought about the episode, including why it happened, let alone how they understood its subsequent fallout on both sides of the Great Wall.

Even so, from what we do know, it is certain that in the decades leading up to the Tumu Incident Esen had become one of the most powerful rulers—if not *the* most powerful—in eastern Eurasia, but was not descended directly from Chinggis Khan, making him ineligible to assume the title of "Khan." And clearly the capture of the Ming emperor played a role in Esen's fateful decision to proclaim himself Khan, which in turn the Mongols saw as a gross violation of the Chinggisid principle and which drove them not only to unite, but also, ultimately, to overthrow the century-long reign of the Oirat.

Of course, little is known about how these events actually played out, much less how they were understood at the time by both the Mongols and the Oirats.

---

1 I began my academic career with an interest in Tibet. Thus, upon graduating from college, I set off for India and Nepal. Of course, not much there conformed with the Shangri-la myth that had initially inspired me, so in short order my interests shifted from seeking enlightenment to trying to make sense of Buddhism as a world historical reality. A key factor in this intellectual reorientation was my discovery, one afternoon in a Katmandu bookstore, of Morris Rossabi's *China and Inner Asia: From 1368 to the Present Day*. The book hit me like the proverbial icepick, and soon it was saturated with yellow highlighter and I was looking for graduate programs where I could learn to do similar work. The rest, as they say, is history. I would therefore like to present my translation of a short piece about a pivotal moment in Chinese-Inner Asian history as a small token of appreciation to Professor Rossabi, who has, quite literally, played a key role in making me who I am today.

2 F.W. Mote, "The T'u-mu Incident of 1449," in *Chinese Ways in Warfare*, eds. Frank Kierman Jr. and John K. Fairbank, 243–272 (Cambridge: Harvard University Press, 1974).

3 Chu Hung-lam, "Intellectual Trends in the Fifteenth Century," *Ming Studies* 27 (1989): 9.

 | DOI 10.1163/9789004343405_003

Nevertheless, we do know how later Mongol historians of the seventeenth century were to remember them, as evidenced in the Mongol chronicles. And on the basis of these works we need above all to realize that the Tumu Incident was understood very differently in Mongol historiography than in the Chinese tradition. Moreover, as with other episodes of post-Yuan history in Mongol sources—such as the Legend of Muna Mountain,[4] the Yongle Legend,[5] and the Story of Zhu[6]—the account of the Tumu Incident is less about what actually happened in 1449, and more a commentary on contemporary political and social realities. In particular, the need for a powerful state led by a legitimate ruler was felt by Mongols, not only during the Mongol-Oirat civil war, but also in regard to the seventeenth-century civil war that ushered in the Manchu conquest.[7]

With a view to encouraging a greater appreciation of these elements of Mongol historiography I would like to present here a translation of the account of the Tumu Incident and its broader imbrication with the fall of Esen as found in Sagang Sechen's *Precious Summary* or *Erdeniin Tobchi*, a major history of the Mongols written in 1662.[8] The story begins right after Toghan, Esen's father, has killed the Mongol ruler Adai Khan, and then, while trying to receive the royal blessing from in front of the Chinggis Khan shrine, is instead killed by the spirit of Chinggis Khan.[9]

---

4 Johan Elverskog, "The Legend of Muna Mountain," *Inner Asia* 8, 1 (2006): 99–122.

5 Henry Serruys, "A Mongolian Version of the Legend of the Mongol Ancestry of the Yung-lo Emperor," in *Analecta Mongolica: Dedicated to the Seventieth Birthday of Professor Owen Lattimore*, eds. John G. Hangin and Urgunge Onon, 19–61 (Bloomington: Indiana University, 1972); Hok-lam Chan, "The Demise of Yüan Rule in Mongolian and Chinese Legends," in *Altaic Religious Beliefs and Practices*, eds. Géza Bethlenfalvy and Alice Sárközi et al., 65–82 (Budapest: Akademiai Kiado, 1992).

6 Johan Elverskog, "The Story of Zhu and the Mongols of the 17th Century," *Ming Studies* 50 (2004): 39–76.

7 Johan Elverskog, "Sagang Sechen on the Qing Conquest," in *The Black Master: Essays on Central Eurasia in Honor of Professor György Kara on his 70th Birthday*, eds. Stéphane Grivelet, Ruth Meserve, Ágnes Birtalan, Giovanni Stary, 43–56 (Wiesbaden: Harrassowitz Verlag, 2005).

8 Saγang Sečen, *Erdeni-yin tobči* (*Precious Summary: A Mongolian Chronicle of 1662*), *vol. 1*, eds. M. Go, I. de Rachewiltz, J.R. Krueger, and B. Ulaan (Canberra: Australian National University, 1990), 54r19–60v21.

9 On this episode and the broader role of the Chinggis Khan cult in Mongol rulership see Johan Elverskog, *Our Great Qing: The Mongols, Buddhism, and the State in Late Imperial China* (Honolulu: University of Hawai'i Press, 2006), 52–54.

In this way Adai Khan and Toghan Taishi both passed away, one after the other, in a single year [1438]. In that same year Toghan's son Esen, born in the Ding-Swine year [1419], at the age of thirty-two in the Uu-Horse year [1450], ascended the throne in front of the [representation of the] Lord [Chinggis]. In accord with the pronouncement of his father, he slew Möngkebei of the Mongoljin. On that same day, he gathered the two—the Forty [Mongols] and the Four [Oirat]—and they rode out on campaign against the Chinese. Then one night Esen Khan dreamed as follows:

I myself was being born again,
and everyone was saying, 'Now who will rear him?'
'Who other than Lady Akhadalai,
Wife of Alima Chingsang [(who is)]
The son of Arugtai Taishi of the Asud?'
That is what I dreamed they were saying together.

When he said, "Interpret this dream," the Oirad Shiraikhan Bishuun said: "It means that you will seize the Great Ming Khan of China, and will have Aliman Chingsang of the Asud guard him."

Subsequently, passing through the Datong region [Esen] captured the Great Ming Jingtai Khan,[10] and said, "This was the dream omen." And having Aliman Chingsang guard him, he issued an order saying, "Care for him in the warmth of the place of the Six Thousand Üjiyed."

On the return journey, he declared, "If any person tells my mother before I do, '[Esen] captured the Great Ming Khan,' that person will be killed." When he arrived and embraced his mother, [Esen] said, "Dear Mother! I have [now] really been born again of you!" When his mother said to her son, "My dear! They say that you have captured the Great Ming Khan," he asked, "Who said that?" She said, "Böke Sürsün of the Yüngsiyebü happily told me!" Then Esen Khan, not heeding the advice of his mother, slew Böke Sürsün and had him hung from a bent tree.

Then the elite of the Mongols and Oirats said to one another, "When [Esen] set out on the great campaign, he killed a person and [now] when decamping he kills a person. What good is there in this bloodshed?"

Further, the Mongols said,

10 The emperor captured at Tumu was Zhentong (正統, reigned 1435–1449, and then after Tumu reigned as the Tianshun 天順 emperor, 1457–1464), thus the name given here is clearly a confusion with the Jingtai emperor (景泰, reigned 1449–1457), who was installed after Zhentong's capture.

Previously he killed Möngkebei.
Now he has killed [Böke] Sürsün.
If it continues like this, then
He will kill all us Mongols.

Then one after another they all turned away [from Esen].

In agreement with these words were: the first of the three sons of Ajai Taiji, Taisung Taiji, born in the Sim-Tiger year [1422]; the second, Agbarji Taiji, born in the Güi-Rabbit year [1423]; and the youngest, Manduulun Taiji, born in the Bing-Horse year [1426]. Thereupon Taisung at the age of eighteen in the Gi-Sheep year [1439] became Khan himself, and he appointed Agbarji to be Jinong when he was seventeen and Manduulun Taiji was fourteen.

When the three brothers rode out, they fought the Four Oirats at a place called Black Türin. At that time, saying, "Let us struggle for the circle of the great battlesite," they sent out two good men to meet each other. The Mongols sent out Baatar Süüsitei, and the Oirats sent out Baatar Guulinchi. Thereupon they asked each other their names and who they were, and they jointly sang forth their names. And when they heard each other's names they said. "We two were once here in a time of peace as sworn brothers. Remember how we sat here one day drinking and saying to one another: 'If the Forty [Mongols] and the Four [Oirat] ever split, who else but you and I will come to this fight? If it happens so that we two meet at that time, what will you do to me?'"

Guulinchi said, "I am a good shot, and though you bear armor, I will shoot you through!" Then Süüsitei said, "I am a good swordsman, and I will slash you from top to crotch!"

Baatar Süüsitei had put on two layers of armor, and when they met one another, he approached and cried: "You, man, who shoots from afar, take precedence and shoot first!" And when Baatar Guulinchi shot first, he shot through the two layers of Süüsitei's armor, and going through his body [the arrow] stuck in the back of his saddle. Yet, when he raised [himself] up and sat forward, Süüsitei slashed and cut Guulinchi from top to bottom.

Thereupon twilight approached, and the [Mongols and Oirats] said to each other, "Let us meet at sunrise." That night they spent the night watchful of each other. The Four Oirats were upset and considerably frightened, saying, "Shall we give in now, or what shall we do?"

Abdula Sechen of the Telenggüs said, "The Mongols are shortsighted; let me go and heap invective on them. If I come back, I expect recognition! If I die, take care of my children." And departed.

He proceeded, saying to himself, "It is known that Taisung Khan is clever, and Agbarji Jinong is dumb; let me try and trick him. But poisonous Kharguchag, the son, will surely figure it out; how can I trick him? Be that as it may, let fate decide!"

Entering the Jinong's tent, he said, "Jinong, if you take us together, then we will surrender; but if you and the Khan divide us, why should we surrender to you? If it be done by you thus, it would be better for us all to die on our spear points. Esen Taishi sent me to say [the foregoing]. Furthermore, the Khan, your elder brother is always deprecating you, we have heard it said:

'Though an elder brother sit and eat,
He is giving it to his younger brother.'"

That very evening they sat and spoke among themselves, and the Jinong said: "These words of Abdula Sechen are true and correct. My elder brother the Khan earlier made me Jinong, but when sending me to the Right Tümen he had everything loaded onto a single blind black male camel, and sent me off. Now, on the journey he appropriated my groom, Alagchud Chaghan. Why should I ally myself with him and call him 'brother'? Let me now instead unite with the Four Oirats and drive him away!"

His son Kharguchag Taiji spoke as follows:

It is said, 'If one protects his in-laws, he will fail,
If one protects his blood-relatives, he will rise higher.'
It is said, 'If one protects his relatives by marriage, he will grow weak;
If one protects his Khan, he will be admired.'
Esen Taishi is my father-in-law;
For the sake of your name, my own father, do I speak.
Instead of trusting the word of a stranger,
As soon as the enemy attacks, it would be better to slash him.

Thereupon the Jinong said, "(Be) you a child or a man, you are ranting nonsense." And that night he left with Abdula Sechen, as well as Khutubagha of the Solonggod and Möngke of the Khonichuud, and linked up with the Four Oirat.

The next day, when he went with the Oirat forces, his elder brother Taisung Khan was killing relentlessly, yet when that army was in a desperate fix and beaten, the Khan spoke as follows:

Greatly have you been admired, Baatar Süüsitei!
Whilst I watched, the heavenly orb revolved,
And Agbarji Jinong was deceived by Abdula Sechen.
Greatly despoiled and ruined has been my beloved name.

Taisung Khan then fled on his wild bay horse, and headed for the Kentei Mountain by crossing the Kerülen River.

Previously, he had divorced and returned his wife named Altangaljin, who was the daughter of Chabtan of the Khoorlad, and as he fled in this manner, he met Chabtan of the Khoorlad.

Her father Chabtan said:

> It is said, "The person one hates (is the one whom)
> One meets on a narrow defile,"
> Let me slay him.

But his daughter said,

> The fault (of the divorce) was mine;
> If one harms a Borjigin, misfortune will accrue.
> But if we support him in his distress,
> Will that not be advantageous sometime (in the future)?

Though she so warned her father, he did not agree. Taisung Khan, having ruled from the Gi-Sheep year [1439] for fourteen years, departed this life at the hand of Chabtan in his thirty-first year, the Sim-Monkey year [1452].

Agbarji Jinong then united with the Four [Oirat], saying, "Yesterday my upstart son Kharguchag said,

> As regards this outsider in distress,
> let me efface the ancient enmity by pursuing and slashing him to death.

I was apprehensive and made him stop with a warning."

But all the Oirats and Mongols were secretly deriding him, and laughing together,

> This Jinong of ours
> Is really no Jinong at all!
> He is a colossal ass!
> So let us bray like you!

Which is why they say that Agbarji Jinong had become an ass.

Later, when the Oirats were talking amongst themselves, they said, "This Jinong is like a head of livestock. Kharguchag Taiji is surely one who can take revenge. How can one keep a fox in one's saddlebag? There are many enmities between the Forty and the Four. When one thinks about revenge, how can we let them stay alive? Let us slay both, father and son."

Thereupon, Esen Khan, who hated his son-in-law, said: "Although his father is wrong, he pursued his elder brother and joined up with us. The son is a good man (worthy) to become a comrade. What will be accomplished by killing them?"

Abdula Sechen replied,

A father (i.e. Agbarji Jinong) who pursues his elder brother,
And slanders his own son is
A person who has no understanding of family and relatives.
How can we let foreign enemies become comrades with us?
We may not treat his son (Kharguchag Taiji) as a man;
Truly it is a dangerous evil.
Is he not on the point of carrying out his obnoxious words?

He spoke, all approved of it, and they made a plan. Thereupon, Abdula Sechen went and reported as follows to the Jinong:

We two, the Forty [Mongols] and Four [Oirats]
Have become solely your subjects.
Now Jinong, our lord, you should be Khan!
Bestow (your) Jinong title on our Esen Taishi!

The Jinong said, "These words of yours are correct, let it be so!" Then, after they had gone, Kharguchag Taiji said:

As the sun and moon are in Heaven,
The Khan and Jinong are on Earth.
There are Taishis and Chingsangs among the descendants of [Chinggis],
Thus, how can one give one's name to another?

Thereupon his father, the Jinong, was angry and disapproved, and his son Kharguchag Taiji spoke as follows:

It is contrary to custom to speak against one's father and Khan;
I speak on behalf of the beloved name and jade state [of the Borjigen].
You want to lay down your dark head (i.e. to die);
You want to exterminate all your Mongols?

Thereupon the Forty and the Four were assembled and Agbarji ascended the throne, and made Esen Taiji the Jinong.

At once the Four Oirat devised a scheme, and constructing two big tents one behind the other, they dug a large hole within the back ger and covered it with felt. Then, while they prepared for a stupendously great feast, the evil Abdula Sechen went and said to [Agbarji]:

Jinong, you are now Khan over the Forty and the Four,
And you have bestowed on our favorite the title Jinong.
And having honored (us) exceeding well,
Your nephew Esen Jinong is preparing a feast of rejoicing,
And has sent me to invite his Uncle the Khan.

At once he went, and arriving they said, "Let us sing aloud, proffering goblets and seat you: the Khan first, then older and younger brothers with their comrades are to enter two at a time in a single file."

Thus they seated numerous others far off, and then summoned the Khan with four comrades, and then the Taijis with two comrades at a time. And as soon as they had the first enter there was singing, and as everyone sang in a loud voice, they seized them firmly in turn, slew them, and cast them into the hole in the back tent. They assassinated thirty-three plumed ones (i.e. nobility).

Kharguchag Taiji was cautious and had his groom, Inag Gere of the Naiman go and look in secret. He then came and said, "There are no people to be seen, but from the left side of the back tent blood is flowing."

Saying, "Let's lie down (= i.e., give up);
Let's lie down and die (= give up and be killed);
Let's die (= try to escape even if we die),"

Kharguchag Taiji took his groom Inag Gere and fled.

Thirty good men of the Oirat came in pursuit, and as they were coming close [Kharguchag and Inag] took refuge at the Onghon ravine. Then when Silbis Baatar of the Oirats, called Türin, clad in double armor, came through the pass, Inag Gere shot, and shot through the layered armor, and he fell and rolled down the slope. Then Cheleg Türgen of the Turghuud dressed himself in three layers of armor, seized a lance and came through the pass. Inag Gere said, "Against him I cannot avail; Taiji, you shoot him!" When the Taiji let him pass and shot him in the heart, [the arrow] pierced the three-fold armor and protruded out from the back. Thus when Cheleg Türgen fell, those at the back fled.

Then they said to one another, "Should we go on foot?" And then when night had fallen Inag Gere went and stole the black horse of Esen Khan, named Buura Khabsag, and his bay-blazed mare called Eremeg Sirgagchin. He had the Taiji ride the black horse, and Inag Gere rode the bay mare. Then, saying, "The Togmog princes, descendants of Jöchi, are our relatives," they proceeded to the Togmogs. On the way they encountered a rich man named Ag Möngke of the Togmog, and he and the Taiji became friendly, and he dwelt with him a while. He then dispatched Inag Gere saying, "Go and determine whether Esen Taishi is alive; and how things are going with the Forty and the Four; and also if there is a way, and if no man has married her, try to bring my wife Secheg."

In the meantime Esen had become Khan, and was ruling the Forty and the Four.

Later, when the rich man organized a hunt, ten antelopes passed by, and the Taiji shot all but one, which made Ag Möngke's younger brother, Yagsi Möngke, extremely jealous. Whereupon he shot and killed [the Taiji], saying "It was an accident."

Thereupon his groom, Inag Gere, came and encountered Ag Möngke's herdsman on the outskirts and asked [about the Taiji]. And when he said, "Your master was slain in such and such a way," Inag Gere killed him and then went back, driving off a herd of horses. When he met with Secheg Biiji at her place, he explained what had happened and as they wept together he said, "The Togmog have slain my lord, and they having ill-treated me, I revolted and came here." He then went and met Esen Khan.

Then Secheg Biiji said, "Though people may be saying 'Let your father [Esen] present you to a man!,' until I hear personally of Kharguchag's death, I will not go unto a man," and because she continued to say so, when three months had elapsed from her parting from Kharguchag in her seven-month of pregnancy, she gave birth in that same Sim-Ape year [1452]. Her father Esen Khan said, "If this child of Secheg's be a girl, let it live; if it be a boy, kill it!" His daughter hearing this drew and tied back the child's testicles and thus displayed him. The people observing said, "It is a girl."

Thereupon, after they had departed, Secheg Biiji placed in a cradle a girl, daughter of one called Old Lady Odoi of the Chakhar, and left her there. She then went to her great-grandmother, Samur Günji, and when she had related these events, the Günji had the boy brought to her, named him Bayan Möngke, and had him suckled and cared for by Kharagchin Taibujin, wife of Solonggas Sanggaldur.

Then when Esen Khan, her grandson, said, "Let's kill this child," the grandmother Samur Günji said, "Do you mean to say that when he grows up and becomes a man, you're afraid he will carry out some sort of revenge? He may be my younger relative, but is not he also your grandson? If my son Toghan were alive, he would say as follows, 'Esen, you have sired a grandson; now let him be!'" When she rebuked him in this way, her grandson was fearful and left without a sound. He then said:

> I have said, 'I will cut off the descendants of the Borjigin,'
> But my grandmother [who is a Borjigin] does not agree.
> Now I will kill him, concealing it from the Günji.

Inag Gere heard this and told the Günji, whereupon she said, "If there is a trustworthy man [to be found], we should probably send the child to the Mongols." Inag Gere replied, "One Ögedei Taibu of the Oirats has told me, 'I have been leading a detachment for thirteen years, and have well given my considerable strength. Yet during this time Esen has shown me no favor.' I shall try to find out what he actually means," and departed.

"Baatar Ögedei, if you are seeking honor, Esen is saying to everyone that he wants to kill Secheg Biiji's three-year-old child. If you make known to the Günji that you will bring this child to the Mongols, what doubt is there that this deed will be key to your own person, as well as your future generations, not to mention the Mongols."

Ögedei Taibu approved of these words and and went to the Günji and said, "Your Esen is trying to kill this child; let me deliver him to the Mongols, your maternal in-laws." The Günji was delighted, and said, "If these words of yours are true, it is very good." And thus they sent off the child, having it delivered by these four: Ögedei Taibu of the Oirat's Goolun Minggan, Bulai Taishi of the Mongol Kharachin, Bayantai Mergen of the Sartuul, and Eselei Taibu of the Khonggirad.

In the meantime, Orochu Süüsi of the Uruud presented his own daughter Sikhir to [be the wife] of Bayan Möngke, and saying, "Let us deliver (him) to his remaining relatives," took him into his care and stayed there.

At that time, Alag Chingsang of the Right Wing of the Oirats, and Temür Chingsang of the Left Wing, these two came and said, "Esen Khan, you have become Khan of the Forty and the Four, now present your Taishi title to Alag Chingsang." Esen said, "I do not understand what you mean by this; I have previously given it to my own son."

The two grew very angry and said, "By the schemes of Abdula Sechen, by the cleverness of Batula Baatar, by the energy of Nigitei Mergen, you have taken the Mongol state and put yourself in a fine position. But now, you two, father and son, just try to keep together the state of the Forty and the Four." And at once a force came riding and attacked. And as they took and rounded up women and children, folk and cattle, Esen Khan proceeded to depart in flight. Then while Esen Khan was fleeing by himself, one called Baghu, son of Böke Sürsün, slew him, and then hung him on a tree upon Kökei Mountain.

Thereupon Aliman Chingsang of the Asud gave a wife named Molo to Great Ming Jingtai Khan, who had been captured by Esen, and re-naming him Chaghan Seüse, made him to be a servant. Thereupon these people suffered a jud [i.e. disastrous winter] epidemic with much pestilence and plague. One night while Chaghan Seüse lay sleeping, a maidservant of Aliman Chingsang, when she rose to milk the cows, saw a reddish-yellow beam emerging from his eyebrows; thereby perceiving that he was one to be lauded. She told this to her lady, Akhadalai, and then gradually everyone saw it and marveled together.

This person is a man of great destiny.
Since after taking him in custody, everything went awry,
And now he has displayed signs different from ordinary men;
Let us deliver him back," they said to one another.

When they returned the Great Ming Jingtai Khan, he bestowed unsurpassed treasure, and presented the title "Great Imperial Favor of Daidu" to the six thousand Üjiyed. From the wife of that Jingtai Khan taken by the Mongols, who was named Molo, there came the descendants of Jüü Daasa, and the fact that he is said to be Talbai Tabunang of the Asud is certain.

Thereupon, hearing that Esen Khan was no more, the minor queen of Taisung Khan, Samur Taikhu, who had produced a son called Markörgis, born in the Bing-Tiger year [1446], rode out when he was seven years old. His mother, Samur Taikhu, girded herself with a sword, and went on campaign with an infantry force with horses and oxen. They attacked the Four Oirat on the Könggei and Jabkhan [rivers], and taking great booty and spoils, they returned home. They then made Markörgis Taiji, at seven years of age, Khan. When they gave him the title Ükegtü Qa'an, and while they were organizing the remaining Mongols, at the age of eight, in the Güi-Hen year [1453], he was murdered by Doolang Taiji of the Seven Tümed.

Back when they had returned Queen Altaaljin of Taisung Khan, she had left behind her three-year-old Molan Taiji, born in the Ding-Snake year [1437]. He was now sixteen years old, and Chabtan had been rearing him, saying "He is my daughter's son." But in that same year Chabtan was slain, and thus Khabchir of the Khoorlad took him into his house.

Suddenly these people suffered a great calamity, and when they asked the soothsayers, because these said, "The misfortune is due to mishandling a Borjigin," they said to one another, "If this be true, then it must be so," and were afraid. And thus Dakhatai Taibu of the Kemjigüd and Moltai of the Khoorlad, delivered him to Prince Molokhai of the Ongli'ud.

Thereupon everyone said, "You are the one to establish the state of the great nation; thus now be Khan!" They then had him mount his yellow-hued horse, and he implanted the Golden Vajra, and when they brought him before Lord [Chinggis], at the age of seventeen in the Güi-Hen year [1453] they put him on the throne.

Then Khutubagha of the Solonggas came before Molan Khan and said, "Prince Molokhai is approaching with his wife Samandia, and with his troops, to take aim at you."

Molan Khan said, "He once did well for me; now why should he be doing evil?," and did not believe it. When he sent other people to see about this, Prince Molokhai was holding a hunt on his territory and [the messenger], seeing the dust, turned back midway. And when he came and said, "It is true; dust was rising up," [Molan] said, "If this be so, let us go meet him," and taking his forces rode out to meet them.

This same Khutubagha then slipped away and to [Molokhai] said "Molan Khan is approaching on campaign, saying he is going to kill you and take your nation." Prince Molokhai did not believe it, saying, "I have only helped him, not harmed him, thus how can he be riding against me?"

"If [you think] I am lying, see for yourself by sending out a reconnaissance."

Then Prince Molokhai said, "It is surely false. Let me go up on high and see for myself," and went out and rode onto a height and looked out at the horizon. He put on his armor and poured libations to the heavenly deities, and said respectfully:

Supreme Heaven, Eternal One, you know!
You Second, the Holy Lord [Chinggis], know!
I have rendered service to your royal descendant;
And in return he does evil towards me.

Deign to render your command, which will
Graciously distinguish white from black, namely
(A member) of your own Imperial family, Molan Khan, and
Prince Molokhai who has become his subject.

Although there were few, when they fought, Molan Khan was slain. Molan Khan, beginning with the Güi-Chicken year [1453], ruled two years, and at the age of eighteen, in the Ga-Dog year [1454], died.

At once Mönggöchei, the queen of Molan Khan, said in her weeping and wailing:

Oh Khutubagha, who has separated me from the Lord Khan,
And has thus besmirched my lovely and good name!
Oh Khutubagha, who has separated me from the Lord of All,
And has thus destroyed the established state!
Oh Khutubagha, who has separated me from Lord and Khan,
And has brought a rift between father and Molokhai.

Hearing her lament, Prince Molokhai also mourned for Molan Khan, and cut out Khutubagha's tongue and killed him.

Since [Molan] Khan had died without descendants, his uncle, Manduulun by name, born from an Oirat wife of Ajai Taiji in the Bing-Horse year [1426], and thirty-eight years of age in the Güi-Sheep year [1463] became Khan. When he rode out to take revenge for Ükegtü Khan, he slew Doolang Taiji, descendant of Khachigin, and subjected the Seven Tümeds.

Thereupon, as regards the grandson and younger brother, when the father-in-law Orochu Süüsitei, and the four noblemen from before, delivered the two, Bayan Möngke Taiji and Sikir Beiji, the paternal great-uncle, Manduulun Khan, was very happy and at once declaimed, "Let him be a seed of the Borjigin fruit," and re-named Bayan Möngke as Bolkhu Jinong. Then, to take revenge for Molan Khan, he rode against Prince Molokhai. Prince Ünebolad, son of Baatur Süüsitei of the Uruud, went at the fore with his cinder-coloured horse, and killed Prince Molokhai at Three Pass Ravine.

Thereupon the brothers Manduulun Khan and Bolkhu Jinong concluded a peaceful alliance, and readied the Six Tümen.

CHAPTER 2

What did the Qianlong Court Mean by *huairou yuanren* 怀柔远人? An Examination of Manchu, Mongol and Tibetan Translations of the Term as it Appears in Chengde Steles, as a Defense of "New Qing History"

James Millward

In 1998, the journal *Modern China* hosted an exchange stimulated by the publication of James Hevia's *Cherishing Men from Afar*. Joseph Esherick used his review of Hevia's book to mount a critique of "postmodern (or poststructural or postcolonial)" approaches to history. Within this broad critique, Esherick suggested that Hevia had mistranslated certain key phrases and thus misinterpreted the Macartney embassy and Qing handling of it. In his response, Hevia defended his translations as consistent with his overall interpretive approach; that is, with "the historiographic, theoretical and methodological issues around which the book is organized." Hevia argued, in essence, that his use of glosses like "cherishing" (for *huairou*) and "centering" (for *fengjian shizhong*) arose from a contextual analysis of the ritual processes he was explicating, one that was closely based on sources, but not on rote citation of dictionary definitions.[1]

That discussion, initially animated by the impending impact of "postmodernism" or "cultural studies" in the field of Chinese history, seems dated now. "Theory" has come more or less to stay, among some scholars, while "empiricism" and even philological approaches to sinology have been neither displaced nor discredited. And we are fortunate that the obscurantist writing style which for a while seemed de rigueur for Anglophone scholars enamored of French theory never took firm hold among historians of China.

The immediate concerns of the 1998 debate may be behind us, but, in another way, the question of Hevia's interpretation of *huairou*, enmeshed as it was in his broader argument about the Manchuness of the Qing, the importance of Tibetan Buddhism in the Qianlong court, the role of Mongols in the Qing imperial project, the analogousness of Qing and British empires and

1 Esherick, "Cherishing Sources from Afar," 135 and 141, and Hevia, "Post-polemical Historiography," pp. 319, 323, 327 notes 4 and 5.

 | DOI 10.1163/9789004343405_004

similar topics, remain sharply relevant today. Though not often labeled as such, Hevia's *Cherishing Men from Afar* was one of the first sallies in the broad revision that has come to be known as the "new Qing history." And in the second decade of the twenty-first century, following a delay of a decade or so while some English-language works were translated into Chinese and read by PRC scholars, a heated, at times vituperative, debate has broken out in the PRC over the "new Qing history" / *Xin Qing Shi*. Of particular concern to many PRC scholars is the issue of sinicization and whether the Qing ruling elite can properly be called "Chinese": some Western scholars, myself included, have described the Qing empire as "more than just China," and talked about China as "part of the Qing empire," thus challenging the implicit logic of nationally-tinged dynastic history in which each new dynasty is simply another reincarnation of a pan-historical entity called "China." These reinterpretations, questioning the "Chineseness" of the Qing, are often viewed in China as direct challenges to PRC sovereignty in Xinjiang and Tibet, among other grave sins. I was myself recently accused of "entirely occupying the standpoint of the Zunghar separatist forces."[2]

While challenging the old, simplistic "Qing = China" and "Manchus = Chinese" equations riles up some of our PRC colleagues, the "new Qing history" revision is no longer especially new in Anglophone Qing history circles, and raises few eyebrows outside the PRC. But some time ago, when it remained controversial, I attempted to demonstrate a philological "proof" of sorts, namely, to try to show through analysis of words in different languages of the realm, how in its ideological thinking, concretely demonstrated in language, the Qing court was not simply "Chinese," but functioned on different registers when dealing with these different constituencies: the Chinese, the Manchus, the Mongols, and the Tibetans. I was inspired to do this by the ostentatious polylingualism of the ideological pronouncements by the Qianlong emperor himself, for example in his preface to the *Xiyu tongwen zhi* 西域同文志, in which he lists the words for "heaven" in the dynastic language (*Guoyu* 国语 = Manchu), in Han language, in Mongolian, Zunghar, Tibetan, and Turki, before unsubtly implying that it was his own "great unity" (*datong* 大同) that unified the names and made everyone recognize Heaven when they saw it.[3] And of course, the Qing deployed this polylingualism when it inscribed momentous writings on stone steles in cities, temples, and frontier sites. If Chinese alone did not suffice for the imperial rhetoric of the Qing, then it would seem that non-Chinese

2 Li Zhiting, "Xin Qing shi."

3 See discussion in Millward, *Beyond the Pass*, p. 199.

versions of Qing writings were worth looking at. And indeed, increasing numbers of scholars of China have been productively doing so over the past few years.[4]

Looking for simple evidence of the Inner Asian sensitivity demonstrated by the Qing's centralized pluralism, I analyzed the freighted keyword *huairou* 怀柔 as translated in three Qing languages. I have never until now published the result of that analysis, but the new *furor* over "new Qing history" in China suggests that this analysis might be still of use.

First, to refresh our memories: Esherick challenged Hevia's use of "cherish" to translate the verbs *huairou, huai* or *rou*. In so doing, Esherick drew upon the Chinese *locus classicus*, the *Doctrine of the Mean* (*Zhongyong*), and "commentators and dictionaries from the Tang dynasty on." Although Esherick acknowledged that James Legge, in his edition of the *Four Books*, translated *huai* in the *Zhongyong* text as "cherish," Esherick's main point was that Hevia overstressed the term's softer sense at the expense of its tougher meanings, namely, "pacify, cause to submit." In other words, according to Esherick, Hevia's *huairou*="cherish" is too much velvet glove, not enough iron fist, and overall Hevia is wrongly "intent on countering the notion that the Qing excluded foreigners prior to its 'opening' in the Opium War, replacing it with a benevolent and compassionate incorporation of foreigners into the Qing realm."[5]

But why should sinology (i.e. classical Chinese philology) serve as the sole method through which the meaning *huairou yuanren* in Qing times is to be established? There is a fine irony to those efforts to translate *huairou yuanren* into English. Back when Chinese was routinely described as fiendishly ambiguous, Western students of the classical language were advised to consult Manchu translations of Chinese texts as a guide to the actual meaning of ambiguous Chinese expressions. Legge himself did not think much of this practice, and few today would consult the Manchu translation to find out what the Chinese ancients meant (though they might well consider doing so to find out what people in the Qing era *thought* the Chinese ancients meant).[6]

In this case, we do not so much want to know what the Chinese ancients meant as what the Qing court meant when it used ancient Chinese terms. And

---

4 Here it is necessary to credit Morris Rossabi, along with Joseph Fletcher, who, many years before the "New Qing History," first put "China" and "Inner Asia" together in the scholarly crosshairs and titles of their works.

5 Esherick, "Cherishing Sources," pp. 143–44. Elman and Huters ("*Maga'erni shituan*") went on to critique Esherick's critique, and Zhang Longxi to defend it ("*Shenme shi 'huairou yuanren'*"), all on sinological grounds.

6 (Möllendorff, *A Manchu Grammar*, p. v; Gertraude Roth Li, *Manchu*, p. 3).

as valuable as knowledge of the classical Chinese texts themselves are as background, neither the language nor circumstances of the Zhou dynasty, nor even those of Zhu Xi's time when the late imperial Confucian canon was laid down, are identical to those of the eighteenth century Qing. When the Qianlong emperor (and/or ministers and secretaries in his stead)[7] used the term *huairou*, he did so in a contemporary context, to serve a contemporary political purpose, even as it alluded to the valorized classical concepts. The founders of the United States (Qianlong's contemporaries) were well educated in their own Greco-Roman classics, and from the image of George Washington as a latter-day Cincinnatus to the architecture of Washington, DC, the history of the early US republic bristles with allusions to the ancient Mediterranean world. But to understand how early American leaders understood democracy, power, or the notion of "the people," would we rush to Liddell and Scott's Greek lexicon?

One obvious way to get at what the Qing court meant by the term *huairou* is to analyze what it did when *huairou*ing a guest—this is precisely what Hevia's study of guest ritual, with its discussions of Qing "interdomainal relations" in general (including those with Liu Qiu, Southeast Asia, Tibetan lamas, and others in addition to Macartney), does in great detail. However, if one wants, like Esherick, to investigate what the Qing court meant by *huairou* through philological means, then we do have more direct evidence than the classical referents themselves: namely, the Qing's own translations of the Chinese term *huairou* into the other languages of the empire.

The passage from the *Zhongyong* cited by Esherick as the *locus classicus* reads 柔遠人, 則四方歸之。懷諸侯, 則天下畏之, *rou yuanren, ze sifang gui zhi; huai zhuhou, ze tianxia wei zhi. Huairou* is thus a compound, here broken down and its two parts defined one by one. Legge renders this passage as "By indulgent treatment of men from a distance, they are brought to resort to him from all quarters. And by kindly cherishing the princes of the States, the whole

---

7 There is a valid argument that the high Qing emperorship was more the production of a group of high ministers and ideologues than the work of the emperor personally. The Qianlong emperor could not alone have produced all of the writings that went out under his name (tens of thousands of poems, edicts, rescripts, prefaces, stele inscriptions); it is possible that much of this material was produced by ministers and others involved in shaping the imperial persona and ideological expression of the reign (see Bartlett 1991 for an argument on the influence of the Grand Council over Qianlong in important policy matters). Nevertheless, the Qianlong voice is so clear in many of these materials, including the stele essays discussed below, so idiosyncratic in its self-satisfaction or high dudgeon at critics in the bureaucracy, that it seems justifiable to refer to an individual, rather than a corporate author. My general points in this essay hold in any case.

kingdom is brought to revere him."[8] The Manchu translation of this passage, in the *An dulimba* (*Zhongyong*) section in the *Han i araha ubaliyambuha duin bithe* (*Imperially commissioned translation of the* Four Books), translates the Chinese verb *huai* 柔 with the Manchu verb *hefeliyembi*, meaning "to carry at the bosom" (literally, at the "belly"), "to cherish," "to embrace," "to conceal in one's clothes" or "to be pregnant."[9]

The same text translates *rou* 柔 by the Manchu verb *bilumbi*. Because only these terms, and not *huai* or *hefeliyembi*, appear in the Chengde stele I analyze below, I will discuss *rou / bilumbi* at more length. The Manchu term *bilumbi* is also glossed in Chinese in the late eighteenth-century *Wuti Qingwen jian* (Five-script mirror of Qing language)[10] as *fuyang, fuyu* (both of which mean to rear, foster, nurture) and *qie rou pian* (cut meat into thin slices). The standard Manchu lexicons and dictionaries of later date expand, while drawing on, these basic Qing period definitions of *bilumbi*:[11]

> 1. 愛撫する *aibu suru*; 撫育する *buiku suru*; 手 で 撫でる *te de naderu;* 2. 肉 お 薄く 切る *niku o usuku kiru* (Haneda, p. 43)
>
> 1. *streicheln, hätscheln, liebkosen;* 2. *liebenswürdig sein, sich annehmen, sorgen für;* 3. *besänftigen, beschwichtigen;* 4. *Fleisch in kleine Stücke schneiden* (Hauer, p. 94)
>
> 1. to stroke, to rub, to nourish, to caress, to fondle; 2. to cut meat into small pieces (Norman, p. 30)

---

8 *Zhongyong*, chapter 20; Legge, *The Four Books*, 1:409–10. Esherick translated it as "Treat men from afar flexibly, and they will resort to you from the four quarters; embrace the feudal lords and all under Heaven will submit to you."

9 *An dulimba* (*Zhongyong*): pp. 17b–18a, in *Han i araha ubaliyambuha duin bithe*, 1755. I am grateful to Chu Mi Wiens for locating this volume in what was then a largely unsystematized and recently relocated Manchu collection at the Library of Congress. Definitions from Norman, *A Concise Manchu–English Lexicon* p. 127 and An, *Man-Han da cidian*, p. 1003. I do not provide as full a treatment of *hefeliyembi* as I do of *bilumbi* because only the latter verb is used in the stele passage discussed below.

10 This dictionary, compiled ca. 1785–94, provides equivalents of Manchu words in Tibetan, Mongolian, Turki (in Arabic script) and Chinese. The citations here are from section #11, *renyi* 56b / 1437; #13 *shengchan* 13b / 1693; #28 *boge* 22a / 3908 (Tamura et al., 1966). Neither *rou* nor *huairou* appears in its political sense in this dictionary. English equivalents of the Chinese glosses here are from *Mathews' Chinese–English Dictionary.*

11 The Haneda definitions follow the *Wuti Qingwen jian* closely; Haneda's entry cites the relevant entries from this Qing dictionary.

1. 抚 *fu*, 抚慰 *fuwei*, 安抚 *anfu*, 抚育 *fuyu*, 抚养 *fuyang*. 2. 摸 *mo*, 抚摩 *fumo*, 摸弄 *monong*. 3. 切成薄片 *qie cheng bo pian* (An, p. 423)

I. 1. 抚摩 *fumo*. 2. 抚养 fuyang, 抚育 *fuyu*. 3. 安抚 *anfu*. II. 切成薄片 *qie cheng bo pian* (Hu, p. 91)

It is also worthwhile looking at meanings of various forms of the verb and derivations from the stem:

bilun: pacification; 绥 *sui*, 绥抚 *suifu*
bilungga: peaceful, pacified; 安抚的 *anfu de*, 抚育的 *fuyu de*
bilukan: on the sly, secretly; 悄悄地 *qiaoqiao de*
bilukū: one who deceives using sweet talk; a confidence man; 好奉承的 *hao fengcheng de*, 善于起哄的 *shan yu qihong de*

The Qianlong court, especially in its dealings with people from afar, was multilingual. No less cognizant of the classical attestations of a term like *rou yuanren* than scholars are today, the Qianlong emperor—or his court—faced a greater problem of "translingual practice"[12] than we do: because so many of his grand pronouncements relating to men from afar, especially Inner Asians, were literally writ in stone—carved multilingually on steles—he had to render them not just into Manchu, but into at least three other languages for tetraglot inscriptions.[13] How did he do so?[14] The answer could possibly help explicate what the process of *huairou* was supposed to be about, and what the term meant to the Qing rulers who deployed it.

One such text in which the term *rou yuanren* appears is the "Tuerhute quan bu guishun ji" 土尔扈特全部归顺记 (Record of the entire Torghut *aimagh's* return to allegiance), which was inscribed in Manchu, Chinese, Mongolian,

12 The term is Lydia Liu's. Liu, *Translingual Practice*.

13 Namely, into Manchu, Mongolian, and Tibetan. The term *rou yuanren* or *huairou* may appear in Qing sources—such as steles—simultaneously produced in Uyghur (Turki) and Oirat / Zunghar (Western Mongolian) as well, but I have not found any attestations in these languages. I welcome readers bringing further examples to my attention.

14 As far as translation of stele inscriptions goes, the emperor theoretically could compose in or translate into Chinese, Manchu and Mongolian, and presumably at least reviewed the translations of major essays himself. (My thanks to Pamela Crossley for information on the Qianlong emperor's facility in Mongolian). Although the emperor also studied Tibetan (as well as Uyghur), he had apparently achieved only a basic conversational ability by the time of the Panchen Lama's visit to Chengde in 1780—nine years after the date of the stele essay I discuss here.

and Tibetan on a stele erected in front of the Putuozongcheng Miao, or Potala temple, one of the principal temples of the Tibetan Buddhist temple complex ringing the Bishu shanzhuang ("Mountain Villa to Escape the Heat") at Chengde (Rehe, Jehol), the summer and fall hunting retreat from Kangxi through Jiaqing reigns, and site of Macartney's audience with Qianlong and many other such diplomatic encounters with Tibetan lamas, Mongol princes, and Muslim luminaries from the West.

This particular stele (one of many in the area) commemorates the return of the Torghuts, a western Mongol group who had migrated westward to escape rising Zunghar power in the late sixteenth and early seventeenth centuries, eventually finding new pastures along the Volga. In 1771, after the Qianlong campaigns had eliminated Zunghar power in Central Asia, a group of some 50,000–70,000 Torghuts (known in Russia as Калмыки, Kalmuks) returned to Qing territory in northern Xinjiang. Pursued en route by Tsarist forces, the Torghuts suffered great loss of human and animal life during their harrowing trek across central Eurasia.

Though now nearly forgotten in Western historiography, the Torghuts' return was a momentous event in Qianlong times, and remains significant to PRC historians today. The Qianlong emperor viewed the Torghuts' voluntary and unanticipated submission to the dynasty as a major accomplishment of his reign and the ultimate vindication of a century of Qing policy toward Inner Asia, including his own Xinjiang campaigns. The emperor overruled his anxious ministers and resettled the nomads within his realm, bringing the Torghut leaders to Chengde for festivities and enfeoffment amidst great fanfare. The massive Potala temple at Chengde, although initially constructed to commemorate his own sixtieth (1770) and his mother's eightieth (1771) birthdays, was thereupon also dedicated to the Torghuts, who were ritually received in a Buddhist ceremony in the temple hall on its roof.[15] A contemporary painting recreates this scene: in the painting, Buddhist deities hover beneficently over the ceremony on auspicious green clouds.[16]

The emperor wrote two essays describing the Torghuts' return and the relief operations carried out by the Qing. These were carved on stone steles mounted

15 Sven Hedin, *The Chinese Lama Temple* and *Jehol, City of Emperors*; Ma Dazheng and Ma Ruheng *Piaolu yiyu de minzu*; Millward, "Qing Inner Asian Empire and the Return of the Torghuts."

16 The painting is "Qianlong Receiving the Torghuts." Screen painting, color on silk; height 164.5 cm, width 114.5 cm. Palace Museum, Beijing. Gugong bowuyuan, *Qingdai gongting huihua*, p. 234. See also Zito, *Of Body and Brush*, pp. 23, 25, and fig. 4.

by the Chengde Potala gate.[17] The term *rou yuanren* appears in the first of these essays, in a sentence within a passage linking the Torghuts' return in 1771 to Qing Inner Asia policy since Kangxi times:

> The Mountain Villa was built by my Imperial Ancestor [the Kangxi emperor] as a place to *rou* people from afar. Soon after fêting Cereng and his men, the Western Regions were thereupon pacified (*pingding*). Now, not many years later, we have this matter of the unexpected and unsummoned coming to allegiance by the Torghuts. With this, all the Mongol lineages are subjects (*chen*) of the Great Qing.

Qianlong thus attributes the surprise arrival and allegiance of the Torghuts to his successful pacification (N.B.: *pingding*, not *anfu*) of the Western Regions (Xinjiang) through military means, which in turn was originally facilitated by the practice of *rou yuanren* at the Bishu shanzhuang, which the Kangxi emperor established. It was at the Bishu shanzhuang, in Chengde, where the emperor entertained and enfeoffed the prominent Dörböt[18] *taisha* Cering[19] and his followers upon their defection to the Qing in 1754, before putting them on the front lines in the campaigns against the Zunghars in the Altai and Yili regions. (Amursana was a still more important Zunghar defector received in identical fashion at Chengde, but the emperor chooses to omit mention of him here, no doubt because Amursana later rebelled.) Note that the emperor defines the Bishu shanzhuang precisely as a place to *rou* people from afar, and then mentions hosting Cereng there; the explicit "pacification" (*pingding*) took place elsewhere, but was closely related to preliminary groundwork accomplished at the Mountain Villa.

In Chinese, the key sentence reads:

> 夫此山庄，乃我皇祖所建，以柔远人之地 *Fu ci shanzhuang, nai wo Huangzu suo jian, yi rou yuanren zhi di* (This Mountain Villa was built by my Imperial Ancestor as a place to *rou* people from afar)

17 Franke and Laufer *Epigraphische Denkmäler aus China*, II, *Tafeln* pp. 63–70; Qi, *Waibamiao beiwen zhuyi* pp. 60–82.

18 The Dörböts were one of the western Mongol tribes that composed the Zunghar federation before it began to disintegrate in the 1750s.

19 *Taisha* is a title. Manchu and Mongol = Cering (I have used C for the Č sometimes used in transcribing Mongol), Chinese = Ce-ling, and Tibetan = Tshe-ring. In English, he is often referred to as Tsereng; Hummel calls him Tseren ([1943–44] 1970:10).

Here is the sentence in the parallel Manchu version, with a quite literal translation:

> *Ere halhūn be jailare gurung serengge mini han mafa i ilibufi goroki niyalma be* ***bilure*** *ba.*
>
> This Palace to Avoid the Heat, caused to be built by my Khan-grandfather, [is] a place to *bilumbi* men from afar.

Bilure, the last word in the long clause modifying *ba*, "place," is the imperfect participle of the verb *bilumbi*, which is here, like in the Manchu *Zhongyong*, used as equivalent to *rou*.

Now, to discuss the definitions of *bilumbi* listed above. The Manchu term replicates quite closely the nuances of *rou*. One set of basic meanings involves touching, working with the hands. The Manchu verb also means handling in a more abstract sense: *fuyu* and *fuyang* today can refer to the nourishing or fostering of people—the ideal way in which the Party treats the children of revolutionary martyrs, for example. This is little different from "cherish." On the basis of the Manchu definitions of this term and of *hefeliyembi* (the Manchu equivalent of *huai*), then, there is nothing wrong with Hevia's translation of the term *huairou yuanren* as "cherishing men from afar." Had he been more literal-minded, he might legitimately have gone even further and entitled his book "Embracing and Stroking Men from Afar"—and might thus have increased book sales.

But all is not sweetness and light here. Our lexicographers do indeed give the verb *bilumbi* the meaning "pacify, pacification," especially in words derived from conjugated forms of the verb and in compounds. There is a cynically manipulating hand (if not exactly an iron fist) in this caressing glove. Interestingly, this sense of "pacification" for *bilumbi* does not appear in the *Wuti Qingwen jian*; perhaps this sense, together with the negative connotations involving secrecy and trickery, evolved later in parallel with *rou*?[20]

Taken in sum, the nuances of *bilumbi* seem to stop short of violence; the calm, or pacification, is that achieved through blandishments (perhaps not entirely sincere), not forceful coercion. I would argue that the definition "cutting meat" is for our purposes distinct (it is listed as a separate entry in the

20 The basic meanings of "to stroke, caress," and even, in one Evenki dialect, "to grease," are represented in cognates of this word in all Tungusic languages; the earliest root is *bul-*. Manchu is, however, the only Tungusic language to attest these negative meanings. Personal communication, James Bosson, 5/9/00.

dictionaries), and not semantically linked to the other meanings; one might argue that this sense could subtly infiltrate the others, but no matter what one thinks of Qianlong, he was more diplomatic than to to offer to "slice men from afar." He had other words for that action.

But what of the other languages of the empire? Let us now examine the Mongol text of the Torghut stele inscription.

> *Ene qalağun jailaqu ordun kemegci minu qağan ebüge ecige–yin baiğulju, qoladaki kümün–i* ***nomuğadqaqu*** *ğajar mön bolai.*
>
> This "Camp [or, Palace] to Avoid the Heat," caused to be built by my Khan-Grandfather, is a place to *nomuğadqaqu* men from afar.

For the verb *nomuğadqaqu* we have these definitions:

> 1. rendre doux, docile, soumettre à la discipline; 2. dompter, subjuguer; 3. élever, donner une éducation, civiliser; 4. instruire, éclairer (par la religion), convertir (à la religion) (Kovalevskii, pp. 690–691)
>
> 1. To appease, pacify; to subjugate, conquer; to convert; to tame (as animal) (Lessing, p. 591)

Nomuğadqaqu has nothing to do with "caressing," "cherishing" or "fostering." This term has overall a harder edge than either Chinese or Manchu equivalents, and gives the sense of a more direct and forceful process. Related words (*nomuğadqal* = appeasing, pacification, conversion; *nomuğadqasi* = indomitable, untamable) are likewise generally in line with these sharper nuances.[21] But here, too, there is a softer side, albeit metaphorically different from those of *rou / bilimbi*: the Mongol definitions involving instruction, illumination, and conversion in a religious sense.

---

21 This root carries the same mixed connotations in modern Mongolian. Номхон далай, for example, is the Pacific Ocean. Bulag Uradyn writes, "'Nomohan' can refer to both people and animals. A *nomohan mal* = tamed, quiet, well-behaved livestock. *Nomohan hun* = somebody polite, who obeys rules—a virtue indeed. But too much *nomohan* can be disadvantageous: a *nomohan* person is easily bullied. Still, even Mongols—a nomadic pastoralist people—privilege the domesticated (men and animals), and think people from afar, animals at large, are wild (*jurilig*), and need to be tamed, domesticated, made to obey rules. A nomadic civilizing mission?" Personal communication, 4 May 2000.

The Tibetan equivalent, quite close to the Mongolian in meaning, further highlights these religious connotations of the gloss on *rou*:

> ... *tsha byol pho brang zhes bya ba 'di, nged kyi yab mes rgyal pos bzhengs pa thag ring po'i mi rnams* ***'dul ba'i*** *gnas yin*
>
> This "Palace Where the Heat Turns Aside" is a place built by my royal paternal ancestor to *'dul ba* people from afar.[22]

The parallel of *rou* in this sentence, *'dul ba*, has the following definitions:

> 1. to subdue, conquer, vanquish; sometimes even to kill, to annihilate. 2. to till, to cultivate, waste land. 3. to tame, bring under right discipline; and so, Buddhistically, to convert. (Das, p. 686)
>
> 1. 调制 *diaozhi*, 教化 *jiaohua*, 训练 *xunlian* (as of a wild horse), 制伏 *zhifu* (in Buddhist texts), 调伏 *diaofu* (Zhang Yisun, 1405)

The other principal meaning of the word *'dul ba* is as a noun, "discipline," the Tibetan equivalent of the Sanskrit *vinaya*. The *Vinaya* is the first of the three "baskets" of the *Tripitaka*, and the first section of the Kangyur (bKa' 'gyur). It contains the monastic code of discipline, the rules governing the *sangha*, or community of monks or nuns. The Mongolian *nomuğadqaqu* is also used for *Vinaya* ("*nomuğadqaqu-yin aimagh*" = "the *nomuğadqaqu* or *Vinaya* division [of the Tripitaka]").[23]

The translation of the thirteen-volume Tibetan *'dul ba / Vinaya*, and of the Tibetan Tripitaka as a whole, into Mongolian and Manchu was the foremost example of Qianlong era patronage of Tibetan Buddhism. The mammoth translation enterprise was supervised by the Qianlong emperor's childhood playmate, classmate and, later, personal lama: the second Jang gya (lCang–skya) Khutukhtu, Rol pa'i rdo je (1717–1786).[24] Indeed, the translators who handled the translation of Buddhist texts, including some Chinese-to-Tibetan

22 My great thanks to Susan Meinheit of the Library of Congress for generous assistance in transcribing and translating this Tibetan passage.

23 Das, *A Tibetan–English Dictionary*, p. 687; Ling, *A Dictionary of Buddhism*, p. 266; Rawski, *The Last Emperors*, p. 254; Kovalevskii, *Mongols'sko-russko-francuzskii slovar'*, p. 691.

24 Wang Xiangyun, "Tibetan Buddhism at the Court of Qing"; Elizabeth Bernard, "The Qianlong Emperor and Tibetan Buddhism."

translation, may well have been involved in the preparation of the Tibetan and Mongol texts of the Torghut essays and other polyglot steles at Chengde.

While clearly conveying a coercive, even violent sense of physical subjection, the term *'dul ba*, like *nomuğadqaqu*, also denotes cultivation and conversion. As an equivalent to *vinaya*, its overtones suggest discipline in the positive sense of a Buddhist monk voluntarily obeying rules in order to avoid karmically consequential transgressions.

Let us consider the implications of this Qing translation of *rou yuanren* in Mongolian and Tibetan. Both Mongolian and Tibetan terms simultaneously suggest, on the one hand, externally imposed control, and on the other, voluntary acquiescence to a superior moral state. It was once a commonplace of Chinese studies that Chinese rulers wished to become, or at least to be viewed as, exemplars of such superior virtue that "barbarians" would come over to be converted and do so *of their own accord*. This is of course from the Qing standpoint precisely what the Torghuts did, a fact explaining why the Qianlong emperor celebrated the event as one of the paramount achievements of his reign. (The first Torghut essay begins with the emperor's discussion of the difference between *guixiang* 归降, to surrender after rebelling, and *guishun* 归顺, to submit voluntarily without first having been subjected to force.) In their apparently spontaneous submission, the Torghuts were remarkable in Qing experience, especially in comparison with other Oirat (western Mongol) groups. With their people near starvation and under assault from the Kazakhs, the Torghut princes' sincerity in seeking asylum with the Qing was unquestionable.

Sinologues once took this notion of "coming to be converted," "to become civilized" (来化 *laihua*, 向化 *xianghua*) as pertaining to attraction to a *sinic* center of Chinese or Confucian culture.[25] Indeed, that these Chinese concepts regarding the interaction of Chinese and non-Chinese peoples arise from foundational texts of the Confucian canon (the Doctrine of the Mean, the Tribute of Yu, the *Zhouli*, and so on[26]) would seem to suggest as much. Yet this is not the cultural frame the Qianlong emperor employs. The overtones in the Tibetan and Mongolian texts here concern conversion to Tibetan Buddhism, which was the more salient moral system in the context of Qing Inner Asia, and the patronage of which was a major element in Qing policy. The cultural content of

25 For my critique of the utility of the notions "Sinocentrism," "The Chinese World Order" and "tribute system" in regard to the Qing, see Millward, *Beyond the Pass*, pp. 6–10, 197–203. Hevia's refiguring of the model is in *Cherishing Men from Afar*, chapter 2, "A Multitude of Lords" *et passim*.

26 See Millward, 1998: Chapter 5 for a discussion contrasting the *Yugong* model with the non-sinic center of the Qing imperium.

civilization, the very nature of the destination to which the Torghuts are coming, differs in the different languages of the stele text.

Is this shift just an artifact of translation, a regrettable, unintentional or unavoidable distortion of the author's original meaning? I think not. First of all, there is no particular reason to assume that the Chinese text was primary in the author's mind, or indeed that any of the three non-Tibetan texts is the "original": the Qianlong emperor was nearly trilingual in Manchu, Chinese and Mongolian, and would likely have been aware as he wrote of equivalent terms in each language, regardless of which he initially composed in. Such simultaneous awareness of source and target languages would likewise have been the case, as is likely, were these essays handled by a committee of writers and translators rather than by the emperor himself; such a group, charged as it was with the translation and public presentation of the emperor's words, would be experts and would not take the work lightly.

A second point: one of the key arguments of "new Qing history" has been that the Qing emperorship, especially in the Qianlong reign, showed different ideological faces to different "constituencies" of empire (Han, Manchu, Mongol, Tibetan, Turki). Somewhat more subtly, moreover, the roles of Buddhist *Chakravartin*, incarnation as the Bodhisattva Manjushri, Confucian sage, filial son and so forth were not so much masks strategically donned and doffed to suit one audience or another, but a multifaceted persona presented *as a package* by an emperor who deemed himself a universal monarch.[27] There is thus no reason to understand the conversion / submission that was the goal of the process of *rou / bilumbi / nomuğadqaqu / 'dul ba* as exclusively Chinese / Confucian, on the one hand, or Tibetan Buddhist on the other; to do so is to miss the point of the "cosmopolitanism" or "centralized pluralism" of the Qianlong era in which the emperor and imperium itself, and not some autonomous moral system, stood as central pillar.[28]

Thus, while the Qianlong emperorship (individual or corporate) was well aware of the Chinese classical attestations of terms like *huairou* or *rou yuanren*, it was also familiar with the semantic fields of parallel terms in other languages of the Qing empire. Moreover, close at hand and closely engaged in Inner Asian matters were such figures as Rol-pa'i rdo-je, Sung Yun,[29] and other lamas and

27 See Crossley, "Review Article"; Crossley, *The Manchus*, pp. 112–117; Hevia, *Cherishing Men from Afar*; Rawski *The Last Emperors*; Millward, *Beyond the Pass*, pp., 197–203.

28 Crossley, *The Manchus*, p. 116.

29 Song Yun, a Mongol of the Plain Blue Banner, was then an interpreter; in 1772 (the winter of the Torghuts's arrival) he was appointed clerk in the Lifan Yuan, beginning a rise to prominence in Qing frontier and foreign-relations postings that would have him

linguists as versed in Tibetan and Mongolian literature as the emperor was in Manchu and Chinese. We may safely conclude, then, that the Manchu, Mongol, and Tibetan terms used as equivalents of *rou yuanren* were not casually arrived at. Their meanings and nuances—as much or more than those of the Chinese term *rou yuanren* which was standard Confucian boilerplate—illuminate the emperor's precise thinking, and point us towards what the Bishu shanzhuang was designed to do, in the very words of the people it was doing it to.

To recap the results this exercise in lexical triangulation: From one point of view, my methodology here is extremely limited. The whole problem of translation and especially the "equivalents" of words found in bi- or multi-lingual dictionaries open a nest of theoretical and epistemological problems.[30] Even those not overly concerned with the deconstructionist's quandary of whether equivalents across languages even exist may still argue that bilingual dictionary definitions give only a limited sense of what words mean in context. While this is undoubtedly true, I have attempted to mitigate these drawbacks by consulting multiple dictionaries and focusing on semantic fields rather than individual definitions. Moreover, my main point concerns not the equivalency, but rather the differences between the words and range of possible connotations in the parallel versions of the emperor's essay.

The wide cast of this net leaves us with another problem, however. Far from narrowing down the meanings of *rou yuanren* or eliminating the ambiguities of the Chinese term, this exercise has in fact left us with a still broader semantic spectrum: stroking, massaging, soothing, fostering, cultivating, cherishing, manipulating, appeasing, converting, taming, subduing, pacifying, vanquishing. We are seemingly further from what the term "really means" in Qing official discourse than we were when we started!

But let us consider further. There is a bifurcation of the semantic field; the nuances of the Chinese and Manchu terms are surprisingly close to each other, as are those of the Tibetan and Mongolian words, but a gap separates the two pairs. The underlying metaphor of the Chinese and Manchu terms involves working with the hands, stroking, caressing, and by extension soothing and manipulating in a more abstract sense. These terms, on their face, do not describe violent coercion, but rather a winning of hearts and minds over to the Qing camp, with the result that pacification occurs. In the Mongolian

---

escorting Macartney through the Garden of Ten Thousand Trees in 1793. It is pleasing and not improbable to speculate that Song Yun was somehow involved with the Torghuts or in coming up with the Mongol translation of *rou yuanren* (Hummel, *Eminent Chinese*, p. 691; Gao, *Zhongguo minzushi renwu cidian* p. 302).

30 Lydia Liu, *Translingual Practice*, pp. 10–20.

and Tibetan terms, on the other hand, more muscular concrete associations with subduing and taming animals or reclaiming wasteland are extended to denote the subjection of something wild to a proper discipline akin to that of monks; the goal is a taming of unruly behavior and conversion, as to Tibetan Buddhism. The equation of *rou / bilumbi* with *nomuğadqaqu / 'dul ba* is thus not at all direct or intuitive. In selecting their words, the translators chose to switch from one metaphorical register to an entirely different one. Perhaps most significant, they chose to replace a classical allusion from a fundamental, well-known Chinese text, to one from a fundamental, well-known text of Tibetan Buddhism. Like any good translation, this one thus departs from the literal meaning of the original in order to retain its spirit, while at the same time unabashedly adding something quite new. The sophistication of these translations compels us to recognize the self-consciousness and creativity with which the high Qing state could simultaneously draw upon and depart from Chinese culture. This is a far cry from an "immobile empire," hewing hidebound to ancient Chinese tradition. This Manchu-led court was indeed "Sinicized," to the extent that it could work masterfully with the linguistic, cultural and political resources of the Chinese tradition, but was not bound by or restricted to these resources. Moreover, the issue of translation within the various languages employed by the Qing empire is key to showing how Inner Asia is relevant to understanding not just Qing foreign and intercultural relations with Inner Asia, but Qing foreign relations as a whole. This was the great value (perhaps somewhat lost in all discussion of "postmodernism") of Hevia's insight in reconsidering the Macartney Mission through an Inner Asian lens; translation and Inner Asian frontiers are also key to Matthew Mosca's recent return to the original Fairbankian question of nineteenth-century Qing maritime relations and the British; Mosca now considers the Qing on the southeast coast with a purview that takes in Tibet and Xinjiang, as the Qing court itself did.[31]

But is there any core sense of the term *rou yuanren* left, after the semantic register-shift in the translation to Mongol and Tibetan? Perhaps most remarkably, though the four terms *rou / bilumbi / nomuğadqaqu / 'dul ba* differ significantly in nuance, each encompasses similar ambiguities between soft and hard, spontaneous and induced approaches to achieving the accommodation of those people from far away. The same ambiguity that has sinologists arguing over what *rou* and *huairou yuanren* mean in Chinese is actually present in all four languages! Such a result can only be intentional. This in turn raises a question: Why would the Qing choose to replicate the ambiguities of a Chinese term in the other languages of the empire? Again, the ambiguity between iron

31 See Matthew W. Mosca, *From Frontier Policy to Foreign Policy*.

fist and velvet glove, over which modern historians have argued, must have been incorporated by design. Although "flexibility" per se is not to be found among the literal definitions of these words, the *idea* of flexibility arises from the very duality and ambiguity of the terms themselves in four languages—just as it emerges from the fine-tunable orchestration of guest ritual by the Qing in its reception of lamas, Mongol princes, Kazakh sultans or European emissaries.

I suggest, therefore, that *rou* and its translations *bilumbi* / *nomuğadqaqu* / *'dulba* are intentionally ambiguous—or perhaps "semantically rich" would be a better way to put it. The imagery of caressing as well as of taming, and the resonances with the *Zhongyong* as well as with the *Vinaya* create a range of connotations, not amenable to simple definition, that seem calculated to keep foreigners off-balance. The meaning of *huairou* as the Qianlong court envisioned it is not written in the Chinese classics; only close analysis of the events, texts, contexts and languages of the Qing itself, an Inner Asian as well as Chinese empire, helps us understand its contemporary force. The proposition that to understand and appreciate the Qing, we must see it as more than China—a proposition so controversial in China in the early twenty-first century—is evident in words written in stone in four scripts in the eighteenth.

CHAPTER 3

Jochi and the Early Western Campaigns

Christopher Atwood

Ever since Peter Jackson's seminal article of 1978, it has been recognized that conflict over who owned the West was perhaps the single most important factor in the break-up of the Mongol empire.[1] The descendants of Jochi, Chinggis Khan's eldest son, claimed dominance in the western region, one which the establishment of Hülegü as the Il-Khan in the West negated. Even before Hülegü's creation of a new khanate, the Jochid family had felt their rights as first among equals in the West had been under pressure, as Peter Jackson has demonstrated.

Like many other conflicts in the Mongol empire, this conflict too was fought in the field of historiography. The West was the leading edge of the Mongol conquests and the Jochid family claimed to have been given that leading edge as their patrimony by Chinggis Khan (Juvaini/Boyle, 42). The other families could thus challenge that claim by arguing that the grant of the West carried with it the duty to continue the expansion of the empire by force. If the Jochid family had been remiss in that duty to fight in the West, then their claim to the associated privileges was weakened. As a result, the role of Jochi in the early history of the empire was subject to a systematic challenge. The standard accounts of the rise of Chinggis Khan, whether the *Secret History of the Mongols* or the *Veritable Record of Chinggis Khan*[2] post-dated this re-writing of history and enshrined the resulting criticism of Jochi's supposed inability in the standard historical accounts. Enough has been left, however, particularly in biographical sources, to enable Jochi's real role to be more accurately reconstructed.

1 It is a pleasure to present this work in appreciation of the scholarship of Professor Morris Rossabi, whose works have touched ably on nearly every aspect of the Mongol empire.

2 This work is now lost, but its text may be more or less completely established by comparison of 1) Rashīd al-Dīn's "History of Chinggiz Khan," which was translated from its Mongolian version, and 2) the text of the "Campaigns of Chinggis Khan" (*Shengwu qinzheng lu*) and the first chapter of the Basic Annals of the *Yuan shi*, which were taken more or less verbatim from its Chinese translation. For the correspondences for the sections relevant to this paper between the "Campaigns of Chinggis Khan" and the Rashīd al-Dīn's history, see the Appendix.

 | DOI 10.1163/9789004343405_005

The “Standard Narrative” on Jochi’s Campaigns

What I will call the “standard narrative” of Jochi’s role is found in three works written in the reigns of Möngke and Qubilai Qa’an: the *Secret History of the Mongols*,[3] the *Veritable Record of Chinggis Khan*,[4] and Juwaynī’s *History of the World Conqueror*. Although these works differ sharply in style, coverage, and many points of detail, they share a number of emphases and partisan assertions, marking them all as historiography of the 1251 Toluid revolution. Together, these works in Mongolian, Chinese, and Persian languages set the basic lines of Mongolian imperial historiography in the Toluid realms of Yuan China and Ilkhanate. According to these works, Jochi conducted the following major campaigns: (1) together with his younger brothers Chaghadai and Ögedei he campaigned on the right wing in North China, first against the cities in what is now the Höhhot-Datong area and then along the Taihang Mountains in Hebei and up into Shanxi province (VR §39.2, 39.8); (2) on his own, Jochi subdued the forest peoples in what is now central and southern Siberia (SHM §239; VR §48); (3) during the great campaign against Khorazm, Jochi took several cities along the Syr Darya (VR §51.2; Juvaini/Boyle, 86–91); and finally 4) he participated in the siege of Ürgench, albeit under the command of his younger brother Ögedei (SHM §258; VR §51.2–51.3). In another version, Jochi only dispatched soldiers to the siege of Ürgench (Juvaini/Boyle, 124). After this final campaign, Jochi returned to his homeland and hunted, implicitly leaving the conquest of the Qipchaqs to generals like Sübe’edei (SHM §262; VR §51.3; Juvaini/Boyle, 90, 139–40).

This “standard narrative” had important implications for the legitimate extent of Jochi’s rule. The implications are explicitly spelled out in the case of the Siberian campaign: having conquered the Forest Peoples there all on his own, they were to be his sole patrimony (SHM §239). The same would be true by implication of the Syr Darya cities, Jand, Yangikent, and Barchin. On the other

3 I have explained my reasons for dating this work to the era of Möngke Qa’an in Atwood, 2007a and 2007b. I do not see that the arguments in de Rachewiltz, 2008 actually address the points I have made or in any way demonstrate an Ögedeid political *Sitz im Leben* for the work.

4 I study this work and establish its text in my forthcoming critical edition of the “Campaigns of Chinggis Khan” (*Shengwu qinzheng lu*). To anticipate the conclusions that will be presented there, this work was compiled bilingually, but with Mongolian as the primary language. Research for it was begun under Wang E 王鶚 in 1261–1268, but it was mostly written under the direction of Qorghosun and Yelü Zhu 耶律鑄 in 1273–78. The Chinese version was presented to the court in 1287 and lightly edited before receiving final form in 1303. The *Veritable Records* of Chinggis Khan and Ögedei were again lightly edited and combined to form the “Campaigns of Chinggis Khan” during the reign of Ayurbarwada Buyantu Qa’an in 1317–1320.

hand, he campaigned in Inner Mongolia and North China with his brothers, so while he had his own share in the cities there, it was not the exclusive patrimony of any branch of the family (cf. Rashīd al-Dīn/Boyle, 146; *YS* 2.35).[5] By the same logic, since he had not played the leading role in the siege of Ürgench, this too, should presumably have been the shared property of the three brothers, like the cities of North China. Finally, since the "standard narrative" has him dallying in the hunt after the fall of Ürgench rather than completing the conquest of the Qipchaqs and other people of the western steppe, it would be hard to see this area as by right his exclusive patrimony.[6] Only after death, did his son Batu complete the conquest, and that with the assistance of the whole family. Presumably then, the whole family should also have enjoyed the rich grasslands of the western steppe. In other words, the standard account would justify a Jochid domain including only central and southern Siberia, up to Lake Baikal, and roughly southern, eastern, and central Kazakhstan. The Khorazmian heartland of Ürgench and the steppe from the Aral Sea westward should presumably have been the joint property of branches of the Chinggisid descendants, like North China.

In reality, however, Jochi's patrimony, as assigned to him and his descendants by Chinggis Khan, was explicitly recognized as including Khorazm and the western steppe (Juvaini/Boyle, 42; Jackson, 1978, 208–12). But the size of this patrimony rankled, particularly among the Chaghadaids of Central Asia, who saw themselves as inhabiting a "miserable little *ulus*" (Rashiduddin/Thackston, 521) by comparison. The "standard narrative" thus nourished a sense of grievance against the Jochid family, for what it historically implied were unmerited rewards.[7] Indeed, many of the more elaborate histories in the "standard narrative" portrayed an outright conflict between Jochi and his father, one only aborted by Jochi's premature death (Rashīd al-Dīn/Boyle, 118–19). One may ask: if Jochi was actually so lackluster a commander as portrayed in the "standard narrative" (and even a bastard as was rumored), why did his father grant him so much territory?

---

5 On the granting of revenue appanages in North China, see Allsen, 2001; Matsuda, 1996, 2008, 2010.

6 That Jochi was culpable in neglecting to finish the conquest is explicitly stated in Rashīd al-Dīn/Boyle, 118. In light of this statement, the claims that Jochi simply returned to the northern steppe after the conquest of Ürgench (*VR* §51.3) or the Syr Darya cities (Juvaini/Boyle, 90), without any mention of battles there, amounts to an implicit criticism. (By contrast, cf. Jūzjānī/Raverty, 1101, 1283, which explicitly mentions Jochi warring against the Qipchaq and other peoples there.).

7 This can be seen in the accounts of the execution of the Chaghadaid Büri by Batu; see Jackson and Morgan, 144–45 and references.

Yet examination of accounts produced outside the "standard narrative" and pre-dating it shows that this question is not well posed. In fact, these accounts demonstrate that, in addition to the campaigns already discussed, Jochi led without the help of his brothers the successful first great campaign against the Qipchaq in western Kazakhstan, and that he was the undisputed leader of the siege of Ürgench.[8] In this light, the resulting extent of Jochid patrimony is much more understandable. The question then becomes, when and in whose interests did the "standard narrative" that denied Jochi's primary role in these campaigns come to predominate the history of the early campaigns? Before concluding with thoughts on the answer to this question, I will document Jochi's role, first in the Chem and Irghiz river battles in western Kazakhstan, and then in the siege of Ürgench.

The Chem River Battle

The Chem River campaign was the first Mongol campaign after the Chinggisid unification of the empire to cross Kazakhstan westward. In it, an expeditionary force was sent to pursue fugitive Merkid from northern Mongolia who had fled west to their old Qipchaq allies after defeat by Chinggis Khan. An expedition sent by Chinggis Khan pursued them. The main Merkid leaders were killed or captured in battles on the Chem River (the present-day Zhem or Emba) and elsewhere before the Mongol force returned home.

In the "standard narrative," this campaign is attributed entirely to Sübe'edei. The clearest description is given in the *VR* §44, where the following description is placed in the Year of the Cow:

> His Majesty sent the great general Sübe'edei Ba'atur with carts having iron-shod wheels[9] to wage war on the Merkid and to combine forces

---

8 Whether he "led" this campaign in the sense of the being the actual decision maker is a moot point. It may be doubted, given their ages, whether any of the princes was actually the real commander in these early campaigns. But that he was present and was treated as the titular leader is clear in the sources pre-dating the "standard narrative".

9 "iron-shod wheels": translated as *tieguo chelun* 鐵裹車輪 in the *Shengwu qinzheng lu*. Rashīd al-Dīn expands this: "He ordered many carts to be made for the army and reinforced with iron spikes so that they would not break down on the rocks." These carts are mentioned in *SHM* as a classic attribute of Sübe'edei, §§199 and 236. There he is called *temür telege-tü*, a phrase glossed as *tie chezi you de* 鐵車子有的 "having an iron cart" and translated as *yige tie che* 一個鐵車 "one iron cart."

> with Toquchar who had previously been sent to wage war in the west as a vanguard with 2,000 cavalry. Upon reaching Chem River, they met Merkid's chief Ghodu, gave battle, and completely destroyed them before returning.[10]

In the Chinese version of the *VR*, whose text was incorporated into the *Shengwu qinzheng lu*, the Year of the Cow was specified more exactly as *ding/chou* 丁丑 (1217), a date that accords more exactly with the evidence. The *SHM* following its well-known tendency to compress protracted military conflicts into a single year (see Yosida, 2005, 30–93), took this Year of the Cow to be that of the initial conquest of the Merkid, that is, 1205. The Secret Historian also compressed the geographical range of the conflict by replacing the Chem River with the Chui (the present-day Chu or Shū)[11] and cited *in extenso* the text of Chinggis Khan's instructions to Sübe'edei at the time of his dispatch (*SHM* §§199, 236).

The "standard narrative" greatly confused the issue, however, by reduplicating the battle on the Chem in its account of the submission of the Uyghurs. Under the Year of the Snake (1209), the *VR* §37.1 wrote:

> At that time, that Toqto'a of the Merkid was hit by an arrow and died. Toqto'a's four sons Ghodu, Chila'un, Majar, and Tüseken,[12] since they were unable to properly bury his entire corpse, accordingly cut off his head, crossed the Irtysh, and were about to take refuge in the Uyghur kingdom. They first sent Beken as an envoy to the Ïduqut. The Ïduqut

10 This translation is from the *Shengwu qinzheng lu*, which here inherits the text of the *VR* unaltered, but with reference as well to Rashīd al-Dīn's Persian paraphrase.

11 That the *SHM*'s source originally did not have Chui but Chem is implied by the statement in §198 that the fleeing Merkid "went past the Qangli and Qipchaq" (*Qanglin Kibcha'ud da'arin yörchiju'ui*). Such a path would take them far beyond the Chui which was to the southeast of Qangli territory.

12 Rashīd al-Dīn's version of this list is confused by his attempt to harmonize it with names of Toqto'a's sons, which he derived from other sources. Rashīd al-Dīn knew from other sources of a son of Toqto'a called Qultuqan Mergen and he tried to identify this Tüseken with him. Tüseken's name was written in Persian as Tūzkan, and since *t* and *m* are not dissimilar in Persian and *r* and *z* differ only in the absence or presence of a dot, he evidently thought Tüseken had been confused with the word *markān* (Mongolian *mergen* "sharpshooter"), to which he adds the note: "Markān—that is, good archer, they called him 'archer' because he was such." Also, Rashīd al-Dīn glosses Ghodu (*qūdū*) as a brother, and the other three as sons, an understanding of Toqto'a's family history he evidently derived from other sources.

> killed him and when the four men arrived they fought a great battle with the Uyghurs on the Chem River.[13]

The Uyghur king then sent a message to Chinggis Khan telling him how he had fought the hostile Merkid. As mentioned, the Chem River refers to the Zhem or Emba in western Kazakhstan. Certainly, the Uyghurs could not have undertaken a battle on their own initiative in western Kazakhstan at this time. A similar toponym, Cham, does appears in Uyghur territory in the name of Cham-Balïq "Cham City," roughly present-day Changji 昌吉 city. This would imply that the Cham River is the modern Santun 三屯 river flowing from the Tianshan mountains into the desert of the Junggar Basin. But in reality, the account of the surrender of the Uyghurs was radically rewritten in a new version following Möngke Qa'an's purge of the Uyghur realm (Atwood, 2013). I argue that in this revised version, the participation of a Uyghur contingent in the Chem River battle against the Merkid in western Kazakhstan after 1217 was rewritten as a battle undertaken by the Uyghurs themselves in 1209. The existence of a Cham-Balïq and perhaps even a Cham River in Uyghur territory would make it more plausible to say that a battle against Merkids took place at the Chem~Cham River even before the Uyghur king submitted.

The earlier version of the Uyghur submission to the Mongols, summarized in Juwaynī (Juvaini/Boyle, 44–48), knows nothing of this earlier battle in Uyghur territory. In Ouyang Xuan's biography of the Uyghur Selengge or Xie 偰 family there is also no battle but only a brief altercation with a minister in the Uyghur kingdom with Toqto'a Beki, who decoyed him into a private encounter and chopped off his head (Ouyang/Chenghua, 11.4b–5a; Ouyang/Tang, 11.322–23). Thus there was no earlier large-scale battle of the Uyghur forces against the Merkid.

But Juwaynī also adds that after submitting to the Mongols: "when the [Mongol] army set out against Küchlüg [of the Qara-Khitay], the *idi-qut* [i.e. Uyghur king] received orders to present himself with warriors from the Uyghur country. In obedience to this command, he joined Chingiz-Khan with three hundred men and rendered him assistance. When he returned from that campaign, he was allowed to have a retinue of his tribe, family, and servants" (Juvaini/Boyle, 46). This probationary campaign with a small force, probably placed in the vanguard as *ba'atud*,[14] was then followed by participation of

13 Again, this translation is from the *Shengwu qinzheng lu*, which here inherits the text of the *VR* unaltered, but with reference as well to Rashīd al-Dīn's Persian paraphrase.

14 On the institution of *ba'atud* "heroes" as convicts or former enemies doing probation as front-line warriors, see Juvaini/Boyle, 53 and the *Hei-Da shilue* in Xu, 2014, 108. In early

much larger forces in campaigns against the Khorazm-Shah and the Tangut. In the post-purge version of the submission of the Uyghur king, the probationary campaign was omitted and only the more honorable large-scale participation in campaigns against the Khorazm-Shah and the Tangut is mentioned (*YS* 122.3000; Huang Wenbi, 1983, 459).

Juwaynī says that the Uyghur unit was sent against Küchülüg Khan, another refugee from the Mongol conquest who had usurped the throne of the Qara-Khitay empire. The campaign against Küchülüg Khan under Jebe Noyan took place at the same time as the campaign against the Merkid remnants under Sübe'edei Ba'atur (see *VR* §§44, 47) and the two were often confused, especially since Jebe and Sübe'edei were later to campaign in the West together. But while there is no corroboration of a Uyghur role against Küchülüg Khan, a commander named *Alichu~A'rchu* 阿里(~尔)出, is specifically said to have been selected by Sübe'edei as his vanguard (*YS* 121.2976; Wang Yun, 519b, also cited in Su Tianjue/Yao, 24).[15] This name does not appear elsewhere in that form, but may be taken to be a garbled version of Barchuq-Art (Chinese *Ba'rzhu-A'rte* 巴而术·阿而忒), the personal name of the Uyghur king. Together with the identity of the location as the Chem River, this allows us to see that the battle in *VR* §37.1, otherwise geographically incoherent and historically dubious, is actually a displaced reference to the Uyghurs' probationary participation in the campaign described in *VR* §44. The post-purge version moved this participation in the Chem River battle into the main narrative of the submission to amplify the idea of the Uyghur king's precocious loyalty and to eliminate the distasteful idea that he had ever been on probation.

Once this misplaced Uyghur-centric version is eliminated, the real story of the Chem battle and its important aftermath can be seen in both East Asian and Perso-Arabic sources, albeit with a number of inconsistencies that need to be ironed out.[16] The most important account is in the biographies of the famous Mongol commander Sübe'edei. The three extant biographies all go back to a single service biography, probably dated to the early reign of Qubilai Sechen Qa'an. That of *YS* 122.3008–09 is too abbreviated to be useful in this connection, but the other two accounts, in Wang Yun's family biography and

---

Inner Asia up to the Kitan period, these vanguard fighters on probation were known as *war* (Atwood, 2012–13).

15 The latter version actually has *Anichu* 阿你出, but given the parallel as *Alichu* 阿里出, I have assumed that *ni* 你 must be an error for *er* 尔.

16 My reconstruction has benefitted from that in Buell 1992, although I differ with him on a number of points, particularly with regard to the chronology of the battle on the Chem River.

YS 121 must be read together to get as full as possible an understanding of the original whole text.

TABLE 3.1 *Additional details on the flight of the Merkid ruler Ghodu from the Chem to the Ölberli*

Wang Yun	YS 121.2975–76
	The Merkid tribe was strong and powerful and would not submit.
In *bing/zi* [1216], the emperor [Chinggis Khan] assembled the generals at Tule River and said, "The Merkid tribe still has not submitted. Who will conquer them for Us?" His Honor then acceded to the decree,	In *bing/zi* [1216], the emperor [Chinggis Khan] assembled the generals at the Black Forest on the Tu'ula River and asked, "Who is able to conquer the Merkid for me?" Sübe'edei asked to go; the emperor was impressed and agreed.
He selected a subordinate general Archuq[a] to command one hundred men as a reserve cavalry, and gave him a strategy.	Archuq was then selected as a subordinate general to command one hundred men and go as vanguard, and observe their situation, while Sübe'edei would advance behind him. Sübe'edei warned Archuq, "When you stop for the night you must advance carrying children's toys, and then depart leaving them behind, so as to make it look like you had carried your family along and fled."
Those people made no preparation.	The Merkid saw this and indeed thought he had fled, and therefore were not prepared.
The main army arrived, ranks were drawn up on the Chem River, and after one battle they scattered and their men were thus forced to surrender	In *yi/mao* [1219], the main army arrived at Chem River and engaged the Merkid. In a single battle two of their generals were conquered and all their men were forced to surrender.

Wang Yun	YS 121.2975–76
In *xin/si* [1221], he pursued the Merkid chieftain Ghodu and battling the Qipchaqs at Üyük 玉峪[b] defeated them.	Their tribal ruler Ghodu fled to the Qipchaqs. Sübe'edei pursued him and battling the Qipchaqs at Üyük 玉峪 defeated them.

a This Archuq is a garbled reference to the Uyghur king Barchuq-Art Tegin who commanded the vanguard.

b I reconstruct *Yuyu* 玉峪 as Turkic Üyük "hill" (*Drevnetiurkskii slovar'*, s.v. *Üjük*, 623). The Chinese transcription means "jade ravine," but the *shan* 山 "mountain" radical in the second character I take to be a mnemonic device keyed to the meaning of the original word. This type of device was systematized in the *SHM* as transcribed in Chinese, where *wu* 屼 "mountain, bare hill" with the same mountain radical was used in place of the usual *wu* 兀 "black" when transcribing oronyms. This mnemonic device indicates that the original Turkic was the name of a mountain or hill and confirms my linkage of it with *üyük* "hill."

Reference to Qipchaqs dwelling at Üyük between the Yayïq 押亦 and the Etil 也的里 rivers (the present-day Zhayïq/Ural and Volga rivers) is found in the biography of Toqtoq[17] written by Yan Fu 閻復. It reads:

> The Great Founder [Chinggis Khan] conquered the Merkid and their ruler Ghodu fled to the Qipchaqs. A messenger was sent to deliver a message to [the Qipchaq ruler] Yïnas,[18] saying: "Why do you hide the moose we marked with our arrow? Immediately give it back, lest the disaster reach you as well." Yïnas replied to the messengers saying, "The sparrow that flees the falcon hides in the underbrush as if it can save its life; could I then be less than some plant?"[19] (Yan Fu, 295.265; also cited in Su Tianjue/Yao, 3.47–48 and *YS* 128.3131).

17 This must be the correct restoration of Chinese transcription of the name of the Qipchaq general Tutuha 土土哈. His name is attested in Rashīd al-Dīn/Boyle, 286, 320, as Toqtaq. The *a* in the second syllable alternates in Mongolian only with *o*, never *u*, and *o* is allowed in the second syllable only when it is in the first syllable as well. The transcription of Turco-Mongolian *o* with Chinese *u* appears in transcriptions of other Qipchaq-Qangli Turkic names such as Boqum as *Buhumu* 不忽木; see Rásonyi and Baski, 159, s.v. Boqïm.

18 *Yinasi* 亦納思: I take this to be a dialect version of the name attested in Tatar as *Yanash*; see Rásonyi and Baski, 331, s.v. Yanaš.

19 On the metaphor of the falcon protecting the little bird, which occurs many times in Turco-Mongolian sources, see Kara, 1995.

More importantly for our purposes than this picturesque story is an additional story of this campaign which definitively establishes that Jochi was not only present, but functioning as commander of this expedition against the Merkid. In both his Persian paraphrase of the *VR* and his collective biography of the Merkid tribe, Rashīd al-Dīn twice recounts a story of Jochi campaigning against the Merkids which also must be placed here:

Rashid ad-Din/Khetagurov, 116; Rashiduddin/Thackston, 53

In the final battle, *Qūltūqān Markān*, Toqto'a Beki's youngest son, who was an excellent archer, fled to the Qipchaq. Jochi Khan dispatched a troop in pursuit of him, and he was captured. Having heard of his prowess at archery, he set up a target and ordered him to shoot. He shot and then [with a second arrow] split the notch of the first arrow. Jochi Khan was delighted and sent an envoy to Chinggiz Khan to ask that his life be spared. Chinggiz Khan did not approve and said, "There is no tribe worse than the Merkid. We have fought so many battles with them and suffered untold trouble and difficulties on account of them. Why should he be left alive to cause trouble again? I have stored up all these realms, armies, and peoples for you: what need is there of him? For an enemy of the state there is no place better than the grave." Therefore Jochi Khan had him executed, and his family was wiped out.

Rashid ad-Din/Smirnova, 178; Rashiduddin/Thackston, 227

They defeated the Merkid and killed them all so thoroughly that no one remained except for one of the younger sons named *Markān*. He was a really expert archer. They picked him up and took him to Jochi Khan. On account of his expertise at archery, Jochi Khan sent a messenger to Chinggiz Khan asking that his life be spared. Because he had suffered so much from the Merkid, Chinggiz Khan thought he should not be allowed to initiate sedition again and sent a reply to Jochi Khan saying, "I have stored up so many realms for you. What good will he do you?" Therefore he too was killed, and of that clan no trace remained.

A Merkid who had fled to the Qipchaq—there can be no other historical setting in which this event can be placed other than the Chem River battle and its aftermath. But in this account, Jochi appears not just as present, but functioning as the commander, entitled to make decisions of life and death, subject only to his father's approval. It is also worth noting that this account also clearly pictures Jochi as Chinggis Khan's heir apparent, who is expected to inherit the empire after his father's death. The Sübe'edei biographies, in line with the "standard narrative" had evidently eliminated Jochi's role, but this pericope was evidently recounted outside the "standard narrative" and allows us to restore the role of Jochi. This role is confirmed by the accounts of the Quylï River battle which follow soon after.

The Quylï River Battle

In addition to eliminating the role of Jochi, Sübe'edei's biographies are also marred by significant errors in the absolute dates. Even more importantly, however, the account confuses the denouement of the Chem River battle with Chinggis Khan's great western campaign and his dispatch of Jebe, Sübe'edei, and Toquchar to chase down the fugitive Khorazm-Shah, Sultan 'Alā' al-Dīn Muḥammad. Immediately after the portion I cited, the Sübe'edei biographies then record the Khorazm campaign and the dispatch of Jebe and Sübe'edei. Following that, the biographies include a notice about the following battle:

Wang Yun	*YS* 121.2976
When they reached Quylï 灰里 River, the battle was not successful. His Honor camped the army to the east of the river, and warned his followers to each light three fires to magnify the army's force. Their ruler fled in the night.	When they reached Quylï 灰里 River, Jebe's[20] battle was not successful. Sübe'edei camped the army to the east of the river, and warned his followers to each light three fires to magnify the army's force. Their ruler fled in the night.

The implication is that this Quylï River battle was part of the main Mongol campaign against Khorazm and took place during the pursuit of the fugitive Sultan. In fact, as Boyle (Juvaini/Boyle, 370n, 373n) and Buell already recognized (1992, 14–16), this battle at Quylï must be identified with an earlier battle between the Mongol and Khorazmian forces. This earlier battle is repeatedly

20 As I will explain, this reference to Jebe is certainly in error, and appears to be a replacement of "Jochi."

mentioned in Perso-Arabic sources as pre-dating the main Mongol campaign against Khorazm.

By separating the Quylï River battle from the Chem River battle, the Sübe'edei biographies became involved in further narrative and chronological errors. The narrative error was to associate Jebe with this campaign; in historical reality, while Jochi and Sübe'edei were pursuing the fugitive Merkid in western Kazakhstan, Jebe was pursuing the fugitive Naiman prince Küchülüg far off in Badakhshan (*VR* §47; Juvaini/Boyle, 67–68). The chronological error was to place the battle of Quylï in the year 1222, which was the usual date in Qubilai-era Mongolian sources for the dispatch of Sübe'edei and Jebe against the absconded Sultan Muḥammad. Putting the Quylï battle in 1222, rather than the correct 1219 (see below), led to a large chronological gap, to fill which the biographers apparently moved the dates of the Chem River and Üyük battles forward to 1219 and 1221, respectively.

The Quylï River battle is described in all the major histories of the Khorazmian (Mongolian, Qurumsi) dynasty, where it is treated as one of the two causes of war between the Khorazmian and Mongol empires, along with the massacre of the merchants and envoys by the governor of Otrār.[21] It is also touched on in the biography of the Kitan commander Liuge and his son Seche Ba'atur who as a hostage in Chinggis Khan's court participated alongside the Uyghurs in the vanguard (*YS* 149.3514).

Taking the shared elements found in at least three of the Perso-Arabic accounts,[22] the Khorazmian version of this battle may be described as follows: the Sultan initiated a large expedition from his border[23] into the far north.[24] There, unexpectedly, his scouts ran into a smaller Mongol force,[25] returning

---

21 See Ibn al-Athīr (Richards, 206–07), Nasawī §4 (Houdas, 16–19; Buniiatov, 47–50), Juvaini/Boyle, 69–70, 369–73, and Jūzjānī/Raverty, 268–270, 1096–97.

22 Ibn al-Athīr's account is the clear outlier, being the only one to see this expedition as intended to engage the main Mongol force under Chinggis Khan, in having the battle last four days, rather than one day, and in having the Khorazmians first plunder the Mongol base camp (*a'uruq*) and only then engage the Mongol men who were returning successfully from an expedition against Küchülüg.

23 From Jand in Juvaini/Boyle, 370.

24 Against Küchülüg in Nasawī §4 (Houdas, 16; Buniiatov, 47–48); against Toqto'a and his Mongol pursuers in Juvaini/Boyle, 370; against Qadïr Khan (possibly the Khorazm-Shāh's Qanglï father-in-law) in Jūzjānī/Raverty, 267–68; against Chinggis Khan in Ibn al-Athīr (Richards, 206), although Ibn al-Athīr also says that Chingiz Khan was unaware of this battle (Richards, 207).

25 Twenty *tümens* of Mongols vs. sixty *tümens* of Khorazmians in Nasawī §4 (Houdas, 16; Buniiatov, 47–48).

under the command of Chinggis Khan's son Jochi, laden with booty from a victorious pursuit of some long-standing enemies (either Küchülüg or the Merkid under Toqto'a).[26] The Mongols sent envoys to declare that they had no command from Chinggis Khan to fight the Sultan and that they wished to part without battle, but the Sultan forced them to fight. Despite being but a small detachment, the Mongol forces fought with extraordinary tenacity, and each side's right wing pushed back the others' left wing. The battle lasted[27] until nightfall, when the Mongols lit fires to cover their retreat and disappeared under the cover of darkness. The Sultan thus returned home deeply worried about this formidable new foe appearing to his east.

Since Boyle's treatment of the battle in the notes to his translation of Juwaynī's *History of the World Conqueror*, this battle has been recognized to be as that described independently in the biography of Sübe'edei cited above as well as in the biography of Liuge and his son Seche. The account in the biography of Liuge is placed in the mouth of Chinggis as he praises the service of Liuge's son in Chinggis Khan's *keshig*: "Seche has now already become a Mongol when he followed us in conquering the West. When the *Huihui* 回回 [Tajiks or Westerners] surrounded the Crown Prince at *Hemicheng* 合迷城, Seche led a thousand men to rescue him and was wounded himself by a spear. Again while observing the battle at Buqar and Semizkent cities, he was wounded by a stray arrow" (*YS* 149.3514). The account of the battle, in which part of the Mongol force came into danger, but was rescued, is consistent with that in the Muslim sources. This account also corroborates the unanimous testimony of the Muslim sources that a son of Chinggis Khan was present in the battle, and shows that this prince was commanding the wing that fell into difficulty.[28] The Islamic sources explicitly identify the son as Jochi. In both East Asian sources, the campaign against the Merkid flows into the later campaign against Khorazm and the West with no clear distinction, but the Perso-Arabic sources clearly distinguish the later campaign from the earlier skirmish.

The location of the battle is given as Ïrghïz by Nasawī (Houdas, 17; Buniiatov, 48), Yighūr in a land of the midnight sun by Jūzjānī (Raverty, 267), by Juwaynī in either the Qara-Qum desert northeast of the sea of Aral, or in the Qanglï lands

26 Küchülüg in Ibn al-Athīr (Richards, 207), and Nasawī §4 (Houdas, 16–18; Buniiatov, 47–49); Toqto'a in Juvaini/Boyle, 370.

27 For one day in Nasawī §4 (Houdas, 19; Buniiatov, 49), Juvaini/Boyle, 373, and Jūzjānī/Raverty, 269–70; for four days in Ibn al-Athīr (Richards, 207).

28 As Boyle notes, the Sultan in Juwaynī's account was similarly commanding the wing that fell into difficulty and had to be rescued by his son Jalāl al-Dīn.

between Quylï[29] and Qaymïch rivers (Juvaini/Boyle, 370), and four months' journey beyond the Sultan's frontier by Ibn al-Athīr (Richards, 206). Juwaynī's location of the Qara-Qum as north of the Aral and Nasawī's of the Ïrghïz River are consistent with each other, both being in west-central Kazakhstan; Jūzjānī's *Yighūr*, which Raverty says is variable in the various MSS, must be a corruption of Nasawī's Ïrghïz. Such a location confirms that the long-standing enemy the Mongols had been pursuing must have been the Merkid, not Küchülüg, since only the Merkids fled to western Kazakhstan; Küchülüg was pursued to Sarïgh-Qol in the Pamirs (*VR* §47; Juvaini/Boyle, 67–68). Juwaynī's two rivers of QYLY (Quylï) and QYMJ (Qaymïch) were identified by Boyle (Juvaini/Boyle, 370 n. 30) with the *Huili* 灰里 of Sübe'edei's biographies and the *Hemicheng* 合迷城 of the Seche's story; in the latter case Juwaynī's hydronym Qaymïch was corrupted by confusion with the more familiar city name of *Hami* 哈密 (Qamul or Qamïl, present-day Qumul). But Ibn al-Athīr's four-month journey, and Jūzjānī's description of the never-setting sun, complete with a *fatwa* from the legal authorities in Bukhara that prayers therefore need not be said, evidently derives from confusion with other narratives of voyages to the "Land of Darkness" above the Arctic Circle.

The Seche Ba'atur account is very helpful in establishing the chronological limits of the whole expedition. Since Seche was given as hostage to Chinggis Khan in *yi/hai* (1215), and then participated successively in the Chem River expedition and the sieges of Bukhara and Samarqand (spring, 1220) before being returned to take his father's place in *geng/chen* (1220), the Chem and Quylï River battles must have taken place between 1215 and 1220.[30] The Perso-Arabic sources assign various dates, explicit and implicit, to this battle. Explicit dates are A.H. 612 (May, 1215 to April 1216 A.D.) in Nasawī (Houdas, 16; Buniiatov, 47) or A.H. 615 (roughly A.D. 1218) in Jūzjānī (Raverty, 267, 1096). Juwaynī implicitly places it in A.H. 615 (Boyle, 369), while Ibn al-Athīr implicitly places it latest of all: A.H. 616 or roughly A.D. 1219 (Richards, 204–06). Of the potential dates, Ibn al-Athīr's date should be the correct one. All accounts are unanimous that this battle and the massacre at Otrār were two separate hostile actions, both of which took the Mongols by surprise. This could only have been the case, however, if they happened roughly simultaneously, as news of one incident would certainly have made the Mongols much more alert in the run-up to the other. Thus one should assume that both were conducted at roughly the same

29 Boyle's reading of Juwaynī's QYLY is Qaili, but given the identification with *Hūilï* 灰里 which he himself proposed (see below), Quylï is the preferable reading.

30 This dating is thus incompatible with the year date of 1209–10 proposed in Buell (1992, 9–16), although I agree with much of the rest of his reconstruction.

time, within a few months, given the slowness of news over the vast distances involved. As dated in *YS* 1.20, the massacre at Otrār was reported to Chinggis Khan in *yi/mao* 乙卯, VI (July–August, 1219); the battle with the Khorazmian forces could only be around that time or up to a few months before.

The chronology of this campaign may thus be tentatively reconstructed as follows:

(1) The initial *qurilta* (assembly) at the Black Forest on the Tu'ula River is dated to 1216 in the Sübe'edei biography and 1217 in *VR* §44. Given the frequent inaccuracy of the biography's dates, the *VR* would seem more trustworthy on this point. A date of 1217 would place the beginning of this campaign around the same time as that of Boroghul to the north and the appointment of Muqali as *Guyang* 國王 to conquer North China (following the dates in the *Dongping wang shijia* 東平王世家, the 1317 biography of Muqali's family by Yuan Yongzhen 元永貞, as cited in Su Tianjue/Yao, 1.4 and *YS* 1.19, rather than the 1218 date of *VR* §46).

(2) It appears from the statement about the iron-shod carts, which must have been large tent-carts pulled by oxen, and the statement by Ibn al-Athīr that the Sultan first attacked the Mongol *a'uruq* or mobile base camp, that this advance was by no means a lightning raid, but actually an advance at an ox cart's pace through the length of Kazakhstan. Thus arrival and return in the same year is unlikely. The biography's chronology places the Chem River battle three years after *qurilta*, the Üyük battle two years after that, and the Quylï River battle a year after that. Assuming these dates reflect some sense of the relative elapsed time, and fixing the *qurilta* in the late spring or early summer of 1217[31] and the Quylï battle around late spring to early summer, 1219, one could place the Chem River battle late in the campaign season of 1217–18, the Üyük battle early in the next campaign season of 1218–1219. But it is hard to see why a summer would be allowed to elapse between the attack on the Merkid and their Qipchaq supporters. It seems more likely that the three battles spanned the 1218–1219 campaign season, with the Chem River battle in fall 1218, and the Üyük battle in winter, 1218–19 or early spring 1219.

(3) Ibn al-Athīr states that the Sultan was able to attack the *a'uruq* of the Mongol army around the Ïrghïz before the battle force returned. If this is correct, it could indicate that the *a'uruq* with the women and children had been stationed on that river during the Chem River and Üyük

31 Campaigns were often planned on the 5th day of the fifth moon, which would have been June 10 in that year; see Zhao Gong/Wang, 8b/446.

> battles. This would put the Mughalzhar (Mugojar) hills and anywhere from 200 to 400 kilometers between the Mongol *a'uruq* and the battle site on the Chem River, thus allowing the Mongol battle forces' approach not to be revealed by the slow moving carts.

In conclusion, the Perso-Arabic sources, along with stray pieces of biographical information, show that the expedition against the Merkid, which the "standard narrative" came to treat as Sübe'edei's first great western triumph was, in the original version, commanded by Jochi at a time when Chinggis Khan was treating him as his recognized heir apparent. Its success legitimated the Jochid family's claim to hold the Qipchaq steppe as his territorial appanage.

The Siege of Ürgench

The conquest of Khorazm (Mongolian, Qurumsi) that followed Jochi's destruction of the Merkid in western Kazakhstan and Jebe destruction of Küchülüg Khan in the Pamirs was the foundation of Mongol rule in the West. The participation of the various sons in the campaigns was thus a kind of charter event establishing claims to primacy among the various branches of the family after Chinggis Khan's death. In these campaigns, Jochi was at first given the primary role. While his father undertook the sieges of Samarqand and Bukhara, his younger brothers Chaghadai and Ögedei were left to merely complete the siege of Otrār which Chinggis Khan had started. Jochi, however, was given an independent command sacking the cities along the Syr-Darya before taking up (as I will show) command of the conquest of the enemy's homeland in the Khorazmian oasis and its original capital of Ürgench. Treated briefly in the East Asian accounts, the siege is described in much greater detail in the Perso-Arabic sources. These include, in order of composition, Ibn al-Athīr (Richards, 227–28), Nasawī §41 (Houdas, 153–56; Buniiatov, 131–33), Jūzjānī (Raverty, 280–81, 1097–1101), and Juwaynī (Boyle, 123–28). Rashīd al-Dīn (Rashid ad-Din/Smirnova, 214–17; Rashiduddin/Thackston, 253–55) follows Juwaynī's account,[32] but adds material from both the Mongolian *Veritable Record* and

32 It is notable however that while Juwaynī says only that each Mongol soldier killed 24 Khorazmian men, he refused to give the number of Mongol soldiers, since it would imply an unbelievable number of slain (Juvaini/Boyle, 128). Rashīd al-Dīn, however, in his version of this passage adds that there were over 50,000 Mongol soldiers (Rashid ad-Din/Smirnova, 217; Rashiduddin/Thackston, 255), thus allowing the total number of slain to be

from a Mongol source post-dating 1251 that highlights an otherwise unknown intervention of Tolui in the siege, as well as a few other small notices.

The *VR* says that Chinggis Khan dispatched his sons to conduct the siege in autumn of the Snake Year (*xin/si* 辛巳), that is late July to early October, 1221. The year is obviously wrong, but the season fits the usual Mongol practice of war; if we make it autumn of the Dragon Year, then the dispatch would have been sometime in August to October, 1220. All accounts indicate that the siege was preceded by a long period of preparation. Nasawī dates the beginning of the actual siege as Dhū'l-Qa'da, A.H. 617 (January, 1221), and the city's fall in Ṣafar, 618 (April, 1221), which is consistent with Jūzjānī's statement that the siege lasted four months. Rashīd al-Dīn, in text derived from his post-1251 source, says the siege lasted seven months until Tolui's arrival when it was completed in seven days (Smirnova, 216; Thackston, 254–55)—the schematic nature of the dating indicates that the dates are not to be taken as exact.

The course of the siege as described in Ibn al-Athīr, Nasawī, and Juwaynī is quite similar. After the Khorazm-Shah's queen-mother Terken Khatun left during the initial Mongol advance, the city was once again briefly occupied by Muḥammad's son Jalāl al-Dīn and his brothers. After they too left to avoid the oncoming Mongol conquest,[33] there was a leadership vacuum until Khumar Tegin, a kinsman of Terken Khatun, was elected leader. After initial skirmishes with advance parties of the Mongol armies, the main bodies of the Mongol armies began to arrive in waves. Rather than immediately begin offensive activities, they began building siege weapons, using logs of mulberry wood in place of stones for projectiles. When the defenders rejected the last Mongol appeal for a peaceful surrender, the siege began in earnest, and was long and extremely bloody on both sides, but particularly for the Mongol side. Naptha was used extensively, and the city almost entirely burned down during lengthy house-to-house fighting. Ibn al-Athīr says that the Mongol army broke the dikes of the Amu Darya, flooding the city (Richards, 228). Once the last remnants of the city were taken, the inhabitants were marched into the plains and the artisans separated from the ordinary population. The artisans were exiled, while the remaining civilians were either enslaved (the women and children) or massacred (adult men). Jūzjānī, however, claims that the women were massacred as well.

---

calculated (24 × 50,000 = 1,200,000). Rashīd al-Dīn's addition strongly implies that he had access not just to Juwaynī's account, but also to Juwaynī's source as well.

33 On the situation in Ürgench before the arrival of the Mongols, see Nasawī §§18, 25–26, and 29 (Houdas, 66–67, 94–96, and 103–04; Buniiatov, 78–79, 95–97, 101), and Juvaini/Boyle, 465–66, 399–403.

The Mongols appear to have wished to take the city without destroying it, and were very frustrated with the stubbornness of the defense. Chinggis Khan allegedly wished to summon to himself the well-known Sufi shaykh, Najm al-Dīn Kubrā, born in the nearby town of Khīva and then resident in Ürgench, although this may have been a myth. However, the shaykh refused to leave, and died in the siege (Rashid ad-Din/Smirnova, 217; Rashiduddin/Thackston, 255; Le Strange, 251).

But in contrast to this relative unanimity on the conduct of the battle, the histories preserve numerous contradictory versions of the Mongol command during it. The oldest, that of Nasawī, writing during the reign of "Qa'an," that is Ögedei (Houdas, 153; Buniiatov, 131), is that the Mongols arrived in four bodies, first under Baichu-Beg, then another under Ögedei, then a third under Chaghadai, before finally Jochi (Dushī-Khān) arrived. In this account, from his arrival on, Jochi was in command and referred to the city as having been given to him. Jūzjānī's account, while brief, is consistent with this in having the siege only commence when Tūshī (Jochi) arrived at the city.

The "standard narrative," however, preserved two different versions which had in common exalting Ögedei's role and diminishing or even eliminating that of Jochi. As a result of a source-critical analysis, which will be presented in detail in my critical edition and study of the *Shengwu qinzheng lu*, I believe that the *SHM*, Juwaynī, and the *Veritable Record* all made use of two separate Mongolian sources, but in different proportions. For its account of the siege of Khorazm, the *VR* made use of one of the sources, the "S Source," in which Ögedei, Chaghadai, and Jochi were all present at the siege, but Chinggis Khan expressly put the armies under the command of Ögedei. Juwaynī, for his account, however, drawing on a Mongol source elsewhere also used by the *VR* tradent, one I call the "C Source," says that Ögedei and Chaghadai were present, but adds that Chinggis Khan "commanded Tushi also to send levies from Jand as a reinforcement" and thus implies that Jochi (Tushi) was not personally present.

Finally, the earlier, unaugmented text of Rashīd al-Dīn[34] preserves a fourth version in which all three sons were present, but making no progress for seven months, until Chinggis Khan in anger sent his youngest son Tolui, who first

34 This "unaugmented text" predominates in what Uno Nobuhiro (2011) has designated as the "first edition" MSS. As I have proposed elsewhere (Atwood, 2015), I do not think any purely "first edition" MS of Rashīd al-Dīn has actually been discussed or used by scholarship as of yet—whether any has actually been preserved is thus an urgent question of textual scholarship on Rashīd al-Dīn. All the "first edition" texts that he discusses in fact show plus pericopes or augmentations that indicate collation with MSS of the augmented

skillfully reconciled the brothers, and then conquered the city in seven days.[35] Already in the early unaugumented text, it appears that Rashīd al-Dīn tried to harmonize this account with the idea that it was Ögedei who was supposed to command the assault. Later, in his final, augmented text, Rashīd al-Dīn rewrote the story.[36] In these later drafts only Jochi and Chaghadai were initially at the seven-month siege, and Chinggis Khan dispatched Ögedei to reconcile them and take the city in seven days.[37] This latest version is the only one not to have Ögedei at the siege from the beginning and is obviously a product of Rashīd al-Dīn's attempt at harmonization between the "standard narrative" and a separate Tolui-centric narrative which he had incorporated into the earlier unaugmented MS of his history.

In an evaluation of these accounts, only that of Nasawī seems derived from non-Mongol sources. The words of Jochi (Dushī-Khān) to the leaders of Ürgench before the siege, and his interview with the cadi 'Alī al-Dīn al-Khayyāṭi, are quoted verbatim—the most likely source for the first would be the written text of his summons to surrender and for the last would be memoirs of the cadi in question, from whom the story was culled. These sources are thus all independent of the later succession issues among the Mongols. Thus, that Jochi was personally present and commanded the Mongol forces appears to be confirmed.

---

text. In other words, they are recensional texts or hybrids formed by collating a first edition MS with an augmented text MS.

35 This earlier text is followed by Rashīd al-Dīn/Karīmī, 373, and translated into English in Rashiduddin/Thackston, 254–55. Karīmī's edition for this section is based on a MS of the works of Ḥāfiẓ-i Abrū, i.e. *Majmu'a-yi Ḥafiẓ-i Abru* (Topkapı Sarayı Müzesi Kütüphanesi, MS. Bağdâd köşkü, 282). Uno Nobuhiro assigns this MS's text of Rashīd al-Dīn to family B3, which also includes the London British Library MS Or. Add. 7628, and the St. Petersburg Russian National Library MS PNS46 (also known as the Saltykov-Shchedrin Library MS). See Uno, 2011, 50–51, 47. This same family is designated no. 3 in Akasaka, 2005, 9.

36 The "augmented text" (Uno, 2011) is found in pure form in the Tashkent MS (Abu Rayhon Beruni Institute of Oriental Studies, MS. 1620) and the Istanbul MS (Topkapı Sarayı Müzesi Kütüphanesi, MS, Revân köşkü, 1518). These two MSS belong to Uno's A family and Akasaka's No. 1 family, and were used as the base text for the Russian translation (Uno, 2011, 50–52, 46–47; Akasaka, 2005: 9). They contain a great number of plus pericopes or augmentations not found, or at least not found in the same fullness, in the "unaugmented text." As I have noted previously, however, the extant MSS with an unaugmented text have in fact all been collated against one or another "augmented text" MS and hence inconsistently preserve a small number of plus pericopes.

37 See Rashid ad-Din/Smirnova, 216, based on the Tashkent MS, folios 81v–82r, and the Istanbul MS, folios 217–218. This is also the text followed in Rashīd al-Dīn/Rawshan and Mūsawī, 515, based on the Istanbul MS.

But this simple version appears to have been overshadowed by three controversies: first that of the siege of Ürgench itself, which appears to have been controversial because of its length, the high casualties among the Mongol attackers, and the total destruction of a city the Mongols hoped to preserve. Secondly, the assignment of the city to the Jochid family was disputed by the Chaghatayids. Thirdly, the siege of Ürgench was the last time the three brothers were together and their father still alive; if one of those brothers had been appointed by their father to command at that siege, then that brother had a strong presumption to rule after Chinggis Khan's death. The "S Source" version, in which Ögedei was appointed by Chinggis Khan to command the other brothers, would justify his later claim to be Chinggis Khan's heir apparent. The version in the "C Source," in which Jochi does not personally participate would weaken the Jochids' claim to Khorazm, while the version with Tolui as commander would blame the other three sons for the failure of the siege earlier, and justify the succession to power of his son Möngke in 1251.

Conclusion

The siege of Urgench was the last occasion in which Jochi appeared as clearly the leader of Chinggis Khan's sons. After this event, the "standard narrative" has him leave for the Qara-Qum desert north of the Aral Sea. There, pro-Jochid sources record that he continued to subdue the Qipchaq people (Jūzjānī/Raverty, 1101, 1283; Allsen, 1983, 12–13), while the "standard narrative" either ignores his activities (*VR* §51.3) or focuses merely on his hunting (Juvaini/Boyle, 139–40). This fact, and the persistent tradition according to which the sons of Chinggis Khan quarreled during this campaign, suggests that while Jochi commanded the siege, the outcome of the siege was that he lost his position as clearly favored heir apparent. The resulting conflict with his father was the subject of many contradictory stories and legends (Rashīd al-Dīn/Boyle, 118–19; Jūzjānī/Raverty, 1101–04, 1283–84).

The elimination of Jochi's role in the Chem River campaign and the siege of Ürgench only occurred posthumously. The "standard narrative" which codified this new version was primarily a Toluid creation, post-dating the 1251 coup. This reality is worth stressing, as the sources and historians have always pictured Chaghadai and his descendants as the chief antagonists of the Jochids, and the Toluids as their allies (Jackson, 1978, 196–97). Indeed, the Toluid family made numerous concessions to Jochi's son Batu in order to win support for Tolui's son Möngke Qa'an to seize the throne in 1252 (Jackson, 1978, 207–08, 219–20). In his open statements to William of Rubruck, Möngke Qa'an generously acknowledged the support, cooperation, and authority of Batu (Jackson and Morgan, 180, 238, 256). Yet the behavior of the Toluid historians bespoke another attitude entirely. Whether it was in retailing stories of Jochi's illegitimacy (all the while patting themselves on the back for not crediting them), picturing him solely as a hunter,[38] or writing him out of the early western expansion, the Toluid historians who crafted the "standard narrative" pictured Jochi in terms that were hardly flattering. Needing the Jochids' support too desperately to openly challenge him, the Toluid historians used their mastery of the written sources[39] to implant in the record facts that would work against the permanent recognition of the concessions made to Jochi in 1251–52.

Appendix

TABLE 3.2 *Comparative Table of the* Veritable Record of Chinggis Khan *§§37–51*

Sections	Text of *Shengwu qinzheng lu*		Text of Rashīd al-Dīn		
	Wang Guowei	Jia Jingyan	Persian text (Rawshan and Mūsawī)	Russian translation (Kh=Khetagurov; S=Smirnova; V=Verkhovskii)	English translation of Thackston (B=Boyle)
§37	73a–75b/ 151–156	151a–158b	423–26, 135, 573	S: 152–54, cf. Kh: 144, S: 254	205–06, cf. 73, 289–90
§38	75b–76a/ 156–157	158b–160b	440–441	S: 163	213
§39	76a–82a/ 157–169	160b–179b	441–48, 763, 785–86	S: 163–70, cf. V: 94, 108	213–220; cf. 374, 384 (=B: 145–46, 164–65)
§40	82a–86b/ 169–178	179b–193a	449–54	S: 170–75	220–24

38 Compare Jūzjānī/Raverty, 1096, which describes Jochi as "exceedingly energetic, intrepid, manly, and warlike" and Juvaini/Boyle, 40, which defined Jochi's special sphere as "hunting and the chase" while giving Tolui "the command and organization of troops and the equipment of armies."

39 On the absence of historiography in the early Jochid ulus see Halperin 2000.

TABLE 3.2 *Comparative Table of the* Veritable Record of Chinggis Khan *§§37–51* (cont.)

Sections	Text of *Shengwu qinzheng lu*		Text of Rashīd al-Dīn		
	Wang Guowei	Jia Jingyan	Persian text (Rawshan and Mūsawī)	Russian translation (Kh=Khetagurov; S=Smirnova; V=Verkhovskii)	English translation of Thackston (B=Boyle)
§41	86b–88a/ 178–181	193a–195b	454–55	S: 175–76	224–26
—[a]	88b/182	195b–196a	omitted	Omitted	Omitted
§42	88b–89a/ 182–182	196b–197b	455–56	S: 176–77	226
§43	omitted	omitted	456	S: 177	226
§44	89a–89b/ 183–184	197b–199a	456–57	S: 177–78	226–27
§45	89b–90a/ 184–185	199a–199b	458, 105, 106	S: 178, cf. Kh: 122, 123	227, cf. 58, 59
§46	90a–91a/ 185–187	200a–202b	459–60	S: 178–79	227–28
§47	91a/187	202b–203a	460	S: 179	228
§48	91a–92b/ 187–190	203a–206a	cf. 143–44, 575	cf. Kh: 151, S: 256	cf. 77–78, 291
§49	92b/190	206a–206b	cf. 575–576	cf. S: 256	cf. 291
§50	92b/190	206b	cf. 576	cf. S: 256	cf. 291
§51	92b–95a/ 190–195	206b–214b	496, 519–20; cf. 576–77, 733, 763–64, 786–787	S: 203, 219; cf. S: 256–57, cf. V: 78, 94–95, 109	245; cf. 291; cf. 359, 374, 385 (=B: 117–18, 146–47, 165)

a This is interpolated matter which I eliminated from the text.

CHAPTER 4

Iran's Mongol Experience

David Morgan

"There is no doubt that the destruction which happened on the emergence of the Mongol state and the general massacre that occurred at that time will not be repaired in a thousand years, even if no other calamity happens; and the world will not return to the condition in which it was before that event."[1] So wrote the Persian historian Hamd Allah Mustawfi Qazvini, around 1340—just a few years after the collapse of the Mongol dynasty which had ruled Iran since the time of Hülegü, grandson of Chinggis (Genghis) Khan, in the 1250s. It accurately characterizes what has been, ever since, the prevailing view of "the Mongol impact on Persia"—which, incidentally, was what I wanted to call my PhD thesis.

It is hardly surprising that that negative view should have prevailed. True, it is the impression that one would have from reading accounts by the Mongols' enemies. But the main sources are from the pens of historians who lived inside the Mongol Empire, and who in most cases were bureaucrats who were working for the Mongols: and their message is hardly different. A parallel case would be the appalling massacre perpetrated by the Crusaders when they took Jerusalem in 1099. The accounts of that massacre on which we mainly rely are those deriving from the Crusader sources, so why should one not believe them? They cannot be written off as hostile propaganda. Yet it is now fairly clear that, although many were indeed killed, as was inevitable when a city was taken by storm, the wholesale extermination of the Jews, Muslims and native Christians of Jerusalem which continues to be so much bewailed did not in fact happen. Is it possible that something similar was true of the Mongol conquest of Persia and of vast tracts of the rest of Asia?

In recent years, there has been a marked tendency to argue precisely that. A fairly extreme example is a recent biography of the Mongol Empire's founder, Jack Weatherford's *Genghis Khan and the Making of the Modern World*, published in 2004.[2] According to Weatherford, the Mongols were no worse than

1 G. Le Strange, trans. Hamd Allah Mustawfi Qazvini, *The Geographical Part of the Nuzhat al-Qulub*. (Frankfurt am Main: Johann Wolfgange Goethe University), 1993 rpt., p. 27.

2 Published by Crown Publishers in New York.

 | DOI 10.1163/9789004343405_006

any of their contemporaries: indeed, they compare rather favourably with them. He concedes that probably considerable numbers of people were killed during the Mongol campaigns, but argues that at least the Mongols did not torture them to death, unlike the practice of some of the supposedly "civilised" armies of the day—a point which is indeed, in general, fair enough. And it is certainly the case that some of what we are told by historians contemporary with the events can be best understood more as literary topoi than as accounts to be accepted at face value. One of these is the frequently repeated assertion that such and such a city was "razed to the ground" by the Mongols. A moment's reflection will make us appreciate that razing a city to the ground, once what will burn has been burnt, is not as easy as all that, if one lacks the resources of modern destructive technology. Also, it takes time, and the Mongols were often in a hurry. My favourite counter-example is Bukhara, now in Uzbekistan. If the Mongols did indeed raze Bukhara to the ground, they were remarkably unobservant, since they apparently failed to notice, in the center of the city, a 12th-century minaret, 150 feet tall, which is still there, as are a number of other pre-Mongol stone and brick buildings.

Nor can the numbers of those who, according to our sources, were killed, be taken at anything approaching face value. One of our historians, Juzjani, was living in the eastern Persian province of Khurasan at the time of Chinggis Khan's invasion, between 1219 and 1223. According to him, when the city of Herat was taken, 2,400,000 people were killed. One may legitimately ask who was counting. But more than that, we know how large Herat was at the time, because the existing walls of the old city have been shown to follow the lines of the pre-Mongol walls. Even granting that the population was no doubt swollen by refugees who had fled to imagined safety from the countryside, Juzjani's figure remains wholly incredible.[3]

I have argued that these vast figures parallel the figures that the same historians give for the size of the Mongol invading armies. Chinggis Khan's army, so Juzjani tells us, was 800,000 strong. Most scholars would put the size of Mongolia's population at the time at around one million. Even granting that Chinggis could mobilise a much higher proportion of his subjects than any sedentary state could manage—all Mongol males were expected, and trained, to serve as soldiers when required—and that the Mongols are likely to have rolled up considerable numbers of the Turkic population of Central Asia into their ranks as they headed westwards, 800,000 is a great many soldiers. More

3 Major H.G. Raverty, trans. *Tabakat-i-Nasiri.* (New Delhi: Oriental Books Reprint Corp, 2 vols., 1970), vol. 2. p. 1038; Minhaj al-Din Juzjani, *Tabaqat-I Nasiri, ed.* 'A. Habibi. (Kabul: Anjuman-I Tarikhi Afghanistan, 1964–1965), vol. 2, p. 121.

telling, perhaps, is a logistical point. Chinggis Khan's army was, siege engineers apart, an entirely cavalry force. Each cavalryman travelled on campaign with a string of perhaps five horses—and, according to at least one well-informed source, thirty head of sheep and goats on the hoof. Hence, the army would have been campaigning with some 4 million horses and 24 million sheep and goats. Khurasan was a large province, but one may wonder how such enormous numbers of animals could have been fed.

My view, then, is that these figures, both for those killed and for the size of the Mongol armies, should not be treated as though they were statistics. But that does not mean that they should simply be discounted. Their significance, in my opinion, is psychological. What they show is evidence of shock. For those who were alive at the time, and who managed to survive, nothing in their experience could equal the impact of the Mongol invasion. In a celebrated passage, the great Arab chronicler Ibn al-Athir observed that "If anyone were to say that since God (glory and power be His) created Adam until this present time mankind has not had a comparable affliction, he would be speaking the truth. History books do not contain anything similar or anything that comes close to it... Perhaps humanity will not see such a calamity, apart from Gog and Magog, until the world comes to an end and this life ceases to be."[4]

Lest we should be tempted to resort to that favourite old dictum, "medieval chroniclers always exaggerate," we might note that the very similar historians who recorded the Seljuk invasion of Iran in the eleventh century do not quote figures for armies or numbers killed which are remotely comparable with those we have for the Mongol period. Iran has had to suffer successive invasions from the east; and the Mongols were not the last: perhaps not even the worst—the later conqueror Tamerlane has a lot to answer for. But it seems to me that we can explain the difference between the evidence for the Seljuks and that for the Mongols in terms not just of how the chroniclers saw things, but of the fact that the two invasions were very different. The Seljuks were not by any means the first Central Asian Turks to settle in the Muslim Middle East; but they were certainly the first who arrived en masse, still organised tribally. In what respect did they differ from the Mongols? Their numbers were undoubtedly much smaller; but more importantly, they had lived for a century on the borders of the Islamic world, and they had already been converted to Islam. So they knew what they were getting in to. The Mongols did not. They came too fast: too fast to understand the nature of the society they were attacking; too fast to appreciate, for the moment, what the point of cities and settled agriculture was. You

4 D.S. Richards, trans. *The Chronicle of Ibn al-Athir for the Crusading Period* (Aldershot: Ashgate, 2008), vol. 3, p. 202.

did not need agricultural land to feed flocks and herds, nor cities to live in. And we should remember that Chinggis Khan's invasion was a punitive expedition. The dominant ruler in Persia, the Khwarazm-Shah, had permitted one of his frontier governors to plunder a peaceful caravan from Mongolia and kill the merchants; and he had executed the principal Mongol ambassador who had been sent to protest.

It will be evident, then, that I see no grounds for accepting the revisionist view of the first Mongol invasion of Iran. Whatever reservations one may have about the details, there seems to me to be no reason to think that it was significantly less brutal than has traditionally been supposed. To say that is one thing. But to say that Iran's Mongol experience, taken as a whole, was entirely negative, which has also been the tradition, is to say something quite different; and that view I do not consider to be defensible.

It has often been observed that Iranians have a tendency to blame outside forces, foreign exploiters, for all the troubles which have beset their country down the ages: not that this is by any means a tendency unique to them. A recent conspicuous example was the attempt of the government of the Islamic Republic of Iran to attribute the protests which followed the dubious re-election of President Ahmadinejad in 2009 to meddling by the British (not, interestingly and unusually, to meddling by the Americans). Implausible, to say the least, though this was, there can be no denying that in the past the British have indeed meddled extensively in Iran's internal affairs; so they are always available when a scapegoat is required. But Iranians, and others in the region, have long if sometimes selective memories, and the Mongols have not been forgotten. Osama bin Laden likened the American attack on Baghdad in the first Gulf War to Hülegü's sack of the city in 1258; and it has been pointed out that, interestingly, he did not consider it necessary to explain to his audience who Hülegü was. The equation of the Americans with the Mongols could evidently be expected to find immediate resonance. A few years ago, I gave a lecture in London in which I made some of the points I include here. Afterwards I was surrounded by a group of affronted Iranians, much distressed at being told that, in my opinion, it would not do to say that the province of Khurasan had been so devastated by the Mongols that, to this day, it has never recovered. This point, incidentally, seems to be confirmed by an impressive book on the later Timurids, the descendants of Tamerlane in the fifteenth century, Maria Subtelny's *Timurids in Transition* (2007).[5] From Professor Subtelny's

5 The full title is *Timurids in Transition: Politics and Acculturation in Medieval Iran*, and the publisher was Brill in Leiden.

research it is clear, based on impeccable documentary evidence, that Khurasan was at that time an exceedingly flourishing agricultural area; and this was two and a half centuries after the Mongols had allegedly devastated it beyond possible repair.

One needs, then, to distinguish between the immediate catastrophic impact of the Mongols, and the nature of their subsequent rule in Iran. The Mongol assault came in two successive waves. Thus far I have been mainly discussing Chinggis Khan's invasion. In the aftermath of that, Mongol rule of a sort was established in parts of Iran, especially in the north of the country, but there was no really stable Mongol regime. In the 1250s it was decided that Iran and what we now call Iraq, and perhaps an indeterminate tract of territory beyond that, should be definitively incorporated into the Mongol Empire. The Great Khan at the time, Möngke, sent his brother Hülegü to accomplish this, as he simultaneously despatched his other brother Qubilai to complete the conquest of China. It should be recalled that at this stage, the Mongols were of the view that the world and the Mongol Empire were, by the decree of the Eternal Blue Heaven, coterminous, at least potentially. In the 1250s, so far as the Mongols were concerned, there was still a long way to go.

There is a good deal of debate about what Hülegü was supposed to do when he got to Iran. It is clear that he was to remove the menace presented by the Nizari Isma'ili sect of Islam, alias the Assassins, whose main strongholds were in the northern Iranian mountains; and that he was to bring the Abbasid Caliph in Baghdad to submission by whatever means were necessary. But was he then to head back to Mongolia, or were his instructions to stay in Iran and found a subordinate kingdom for himself, as he in fact did? The evidence is, to say the least, ambiguous. But either way, his invasion was necessarily a very different affair from that of his grandfather more than thirty years earlier. His army moved very slowly from Mongolia, through Central Asia and into Iran; and it was much less destructive than its predecessor. The Mongols had learnt a good deal since the 1220s about how sedentary society worked; and this time they were coming to stay. Hülegü could have no interest in the unnecessary destruction of his own potential property. He did, indeed, sack Baghdad and execute the last Abbasid caliph; but that is to be explained more as the elimination of a perceived alternative focus of loyalty and power than as savagery for its own sake. It was a political act.

Nevertheless, the prevailing view of the nature of Hülegü's regime, and that of his immediate successors until 1295, has been distinctly negative: a situation which remained more or less unchallenged until the publication, in 2003, of George Lane's *Early Mongol Rule in Thirteenth-Century Iran: a Persian*

Renaissance, a book based on his thesis at the School of Oriental and African Studies at London University.[6] Lane argues that the early Mongol rulers of Iran, the Ilkhans, were in fact remarkably enlightened monarchs who have been sadly misunderstood. My own view is that he has a case that needs to be answered, even if he tends to overstate it. One of his strengths is that he has carefully examined the sources for some of Iran's provinces—most historians have concerned themselves mainly with the centre—and he has found there a good deal of evidence to support rendering a favourable verdict on the benevolence of Mongol rule.

Why has this not been apparent before? I think the major reason is that historians have been inclined to rely, perhaps excessively, on one source, the *Jami' al-tawarikh*, the "Collection of Histories", of Rashid al-Din, written in the early fourteenth century. For the last twenty years of his life (he was executed in 1318), Rashid al-Din was joint chief minister of the Ilkhanate, the Mongol kingdom which Hülegü had founded. He was also its major historian: indeed, the major historian of the Mongol Empire as a whole. There are those who consider him to be the greatest of all Persian historians. Commissioned by his master, the Ilkhan Ghazan, who reigned from 1295 to 1304, he wrote, or caused to be written—I have some doubts about the extent of his actual involvement in the writing itself—a history of the Mongols, from their supposed beginnings up to his own time. He later, at the instance of Ghazan's brother and successor Öljeitü, added histories of the peoples with whom the Mongols had come into contact—the Turks, the Jews, the Chinese, the Indians, even the Franks, the people of western Europe. This has, in the opinion of one of his leading students, entitled him to be called "the first world historian".

His work is undeniably exceedingly well-informed: it has been shown that much of his material derives from collaboration with Bolad Chingsang, a Mongol who was expert in the history and traditions of his own people, and who spent many years as the official representative in Iran of the Great Khan in China. For Iran itself, he was well positioned to obtain full and accurate information, by virtue of his extremely powerful official position. The book is very persuasive; and it is, for the most part, fairly easy to understand, being written in a straightforward and unadorned Persian style which was remarkably atypical (the two other major historians writing as servants of the Mongols in Iran, Juvayni and Vassaf, write in a much more elaborate style which was much admired and emulated, but which is much harder work to read). It is not difficult to account for the dominance which Rashid al-Din's view of Mongol rule has always exercised.

6 Published by Routledge in London in 2003.

But that dominance has resulted not just from the quality of his work, but also from the fact that historians have been all too ready to ignore the context in which he wrote. In 1295, Ghazan declared his conversion to Islam, and he inaugurated a series of administrative reforms which were designed to rectify the abuses that had grown up during the previous seventy years or so. Rashid al-Din has preserved for us the texts of Ghazan's reforming edicts; and as chief minister he was undoubtedly deeply involved in the reform programme.

When writing his history of Mongol rule in Iran, then, Rashid al-Din had an agenda. If we take our history from him at face value, what we have is the brutal imposition of alien and infidel rule on Muslim Iran. From the time of Hülegü to the accession of Ghazan, Mongol government, if we follow Rashid al-Din, amounted to little more than exploitation of the Persian subjects for the benefit of their non-Muslim Mongol masters. Then the sun rises. Iran is restored to the Dar al-Islam, the Abode of Islam, as a result of the conversion of Ghazan, followed by the Mongols of Iran as a whole; and all the troubles that had resulted from infidel rule are put right by that enlightened monarch, ably assisted by his principal Persian minister, who happens to be writing the official history of these events. Hence it was clearly in Rashid al-Din's interest to paint the period before Ghazan in the darkest possible colours. That does not mean that we are obliged necessarily to believe him.

Now, I am not proposing that the Mongols were thoroughly nice people, kind to children and animals, etc.—though something on those lines is probably what George Lane and some other scholars would wish us to believe. What I am suggesting is that, however awful the original Mongol assault may have been, that is not all there is to be said about the Mongols. And that is the conclusion one would arrive at in the light of what has been the most remarkable body of scholarship in the field in recent years, the work of Professor Thomas Allsen.

In numerous articles and three seminal books, of which the most important is his *Culture and Conquest in Mongol Eurasia* of 2001,[7] Allsen has transformed the way in which we see the impact of the Mongols—not in the military, but in the cultural sphere. He is able to do this, in the first instance, because of his linguistic expertise. One of the main difficulties which faces anyone who tries to study Mongol imperial history is the number of languages in which the primary sources are written. This is hardly surprising, when one considers that the Mongols conquered territory that stretched uninterruptedly from Korea to Hungary. Three languages dominate. First, Mongolian: but for this period it is useful mostly for one, though a crucial, early source: the enigmatic document

7 Published by Cambridge University Press.

known as the *Secret History of the Mongols*. The other two are the languages that really count above all: Persian and Chinese.

People have often spoken of something they call the "Pax Mongolica". They suppose that because most of Asia was ruled by members of a single family, general peace prevailed throughout the length and breadth of their dominions. That is, except for some comparatively brief periods, a fantasy—though it is certainly the case that for much of the time, internecine warfare between different branches of the Mongol royal house was not allowed to interfere with transcontinental trade, whose maintenance was in everyone's interest. The Mongols in their early period of expansion may not have appreciated fully all the virtues of "civilisation", but they certainly knew, even then, that trade was beneficial to them and that it should be encouraged.

Be that as it may, the major lesson one draws from the work of Allsen is that the Mongols were engaged not merely in military conquest and long-distance trade, but also in cultural transmission. They not only encouraged and patronised it: they were actively involved. This touched many fields: historiography, as in the example already quoted of collaboration between Rashid al-Din and Bolad Chingsang ("Chingsang" being a Persianised or Mongolised version of the Chinese term for "minister"); geography and cartography; agriculture; cuisine; medicine; astronomy; printing. Much of this exchange took place between the Mongol kingdoms of Persia and China, which were ruled by the same branch of the royal family. The process was more China to Persia than the other way round, but ideas did flow in both directions.

Allsen does not discuss the most conspicuous example of this kind of cultural transmission: that is, art. For a considerable time, at least since the 1930s, historians of art, and especially Islamic art, have realised that the Mongol period was one of extraordinary fertility. This is the time when Persian miniature or book painting really came into its own; and one does not need to know a great deal about Chinese art to recognize the extraordinary proliferation of Chinese motifs in Persian painting of the period. And under Mongol rule, the rule of a people who preferred to live in tents, great buildings were erected: most notably, among those that survive, the magnificent mausoleum of the Ilkhan Öljeitü at Sultaniyya in northwest Iran, the double-skinned dome of which, according to scholars who are far from being crackpots, may have influenced the design of Brunelleschi's dome for Florence cathedral, a century later.

One remarkable piece of evidence for the vitality of intellectual life in Mongol Iran has only recently come to light. This is a vast manuscript called the *Safina-yi Tabriz*, literally "The Ship of Tabriz"—*safina* was used as a term for a collection of works on different subjects. This is an anthology of 209 works, some of them previously unknown, which were copied out for his own use by a

Persian man of letters, Abu'l Majd Tabrizi, between 1321 and 1335; that is, during the reign of Abu Sa'id, the last ruler of the line of Hülegü.[8] About two thirds of the works are in Persian, the remainder in Arabic. It was acquired by the library of the Iranian Majlis, the parliament, and a magnificent facsimile edition was published by the Iran University Press in 2003—a perhaps salutary reminder that there are things going on in contemporary Iran which have nothing to do with nuclear power or presidential elections. A volume of papers about it followed in 2007. The range of subjects covered—bear with me—is: "Prophetic traditions, ethics and mysticism, jurisprudence, scholastic theology, exegetical literature, history, verse encomiums, lexicography, grammar, literary criticism, philosophy, literary texts containing epic and didactic poetry, surveys of religions and sects, astronomy and astrology, geomancy, mineralogy, mathematics, medicine, epistles and testaments, administrative texts, collections of poetry, collections of quatrains, Persian and bilingual dictionaries, music, cosmography and geography, and several collections of individual poets."[9] Study of the *Safina* is in its infancy; but it is at least clear that, on this showing, "civilisation" was very much alive and well in the principal city of Mongol Iran in the first part of the fourteenth century.

I should emphasise again that, if there are positive aspects to Mongol rule, that does not negate the massacre and destruction that accompanied their first appearance in the Persian world. Even if Mongol rule in Iran was a good deal more enlightened and benevolent than used to be supposed, the massacres in Herat, Nishapur and the other great cities of eastern Persia still happened. What I am arguing for is not total revisionism, but balance and differentiation.

Let us now look at some broader considerations. Can one suggest that the Mongols in any way contributed to the long-term development of Iran: in particular, to the formation of its identity? Were the Mongols relevant to the notion of *iraniyyat*, "Iranian-ness"? This might at first sight seem a surprising notion: how could a group of alien conquerors who ruled for a century make a significant difference? After all, Iran has been in some sense an identifiable entity for two and a half millennia, since the time of Cyrus the Great—a point the last Shah made much of: possibly not, in the end, to his own advantage. The present Persian language is a lineal descendant of the Persian of Achaemenian times.

8 See A.A. Seyed-Gohrab and S. McGlinn, eds. *The Treasury of Tabriz: The Great Il-Khanid Compendium* (West Lafayette: Purdue University Press, 2007) and Abu'l Majd Muhammad ibn Mas'ud Tabrizi, *Safineh-ye Tabriz* (Tehran, 2003).

9 See footnote 8.

Looking at more recent history, there can be no denying that the Safavid dynasty, which ruled Iran between 1501 and 1722, played a crucial role, in two senses: in terms of political geography and religion. The present borders of Iran, though they were somewhat reduced in the nineteenth century, especially in the Caucasus, are essentially those inherited from the first Safavid Shah, Isma'il. The state he took over in 1501 consisted of what is now western Iran, eastern Turkey and parts of Iraq. In 1510 he won a battle against the Uzbeks of Central Asia, which added what is now eastern Iran, the province of Khurasan, to his kingdom; and in 1514 he lost a battle against the Ottoman Turks, as a result of which he also lost eastern Anatolia, and something like the present Iran-Turkey border came into existence. Those two battles determined the geographical shape of Iran up to the present day. On the religious front, Shah Isma'il inaugurated the process—in its initial stages it was a forcible one—by which Iran became an overwhelmingly Shi'i country, as of course it remains today. It is important to remember that Iran was a majority Sunni country before 1501.

What have the Mongols to offer, to compare with Cyrus and Isma'il? Here I follow to some extent some interesting ideas put forward by Professor Bert Fragner.[10] He goes so far as to suggest that, in a sense, modern Iran was a legacy of the Mongols. First, nomenclature: the Mongols called their kingdom "Iran", the ancient name of the country. That name had hardly been used since the Arab conquest of the seventh century: when the Mongols arrived, no state called "Iran" had existed for six centuries. Then, language. The Persian language, in its written form, had been submerged beneath Arabic (though no doubt it continued to be spoken). To quote one example: the most important Arabic historical source for the early Islamic period is the work of al-Tabari, a Persian from the northern Iranian province of Tabaristan who, however, wrote in Arabic. Eventually a written "New Persian" emerged, grammatically like pre-Islamic Persian (and nothing like Arabic), but using a slightly adapted form of the Arabic script, and incorporating a vast quantity of Arabic loan words. This took time. It was the Mongol period that saw the final triumph of written New Persian over Arabic—not least because for the Mongols, Arabic had no special status, since they were not, till near the end of the thirteenth century, adherents of Islam. Then, geography and political boundaries: the shape of Mongol Iran was much the same as that later established by the Safavids. Lastly, the population and ethnic composition of the country. The Mongol period saw a

10 Bert Fragner, "Iran under Ilkhanid rule in a world history perspective" in Denise Aigle, ed. *L'Iran face à la domination mongole* (Louvain: Institut français de recherce en iran, 1997), pp. 121–131.

large influx of Turks from Central Asia—probably much larger than the influx that had occurred earlier under the Seljuks. They remained, and remain; and as one result, the nomadic tribal population of Iran retained an importance that was much greater than in most other areas of the Middle East. Incidentally, the number of ethnic Mongols who came to Iran in this period was probably quite small. The likelihood is that most of at least the rank and file of the Mongol armies were in fact Turks. It is noticeable that the Mongols were never evicted from Iran, as they were from China in and after 1368. They were simply absorbed into the existing population—presumably, to a large extent, into the existing Turkish population.

Why did the Mongol regime in Iran come to an end? There are at least two views about this. One, represented most conspicuously by Professor Charles Melville of Cambridge, is that the collapse of Ilkhanid rule in 1335 and after was the culmination of a long process of decline:[11] an example, in fact, of what, in an article on "The decline and fall of the Mongol Empire", published in 2009, I called Gibbon's Law: "Empires may not fall until they have previously undergone a process of decline."[12] I do not see things this way. It seems to me that we have ample evidence that the reign of the last Ilkhan, Abu Sa'id (1316–35) was one of great prosperity (for example, the quality of the coinage was extraordinarily high, not only by Mongol-period standards but also by those of the whole of the Islamic era till that date), and that its political instability was no worse than in other, earlier reigns. The great North African traveller Ibn Battuta, who went absolutely everywhere in the Islamic world of his day, or so he says, gives an account of Abu Sa'id's Iran which, while showing that he was very well aware of the factional struggles that were going on, nevertheless confirms the view I have suggested.

What Abu Sa'id signally failed to do was to provide a male heir. The factions were already there, and in the absence of an unquestioned heir of the house of Hülegü, the throne was there to be taken. Had Abu Sa'id left a son, there is every reason to suppose that the Mongol regime would have continued after 1335. The arguments and negotiations about the succession that took place at that time are vividly described, with a degree of detail previously quite unknown, in a letter written by the chief minister Ghiyath al-Din Rashidi (the son of Rashid al-Din) which is preserved in the *Safina-yi Tabriz*. As it was, the

11 Charles Melville, *The Fall of Amir Chupan and the Decline of the Ilkhanate, 1327–1337: A Decade of Discord in Mongol Iran* (Bloomington: Indiana University Research Institute on Inner Asian Studies, 1999).

12 David Morgan, "The decline and fall of the Mongol Empire," *Journal of the Royal Asiatic Society*, 3rd. series, 19:4 (October, 2009), pp. 427–437.

kingdom was divided between different groups, some Mongol, some Persian, until, near the end of the fourteenth century, the situation was resolved, not at all to Iran's advantage, by the arrival from Central Asia of Tamerlane, a conqueror whose wanton cruelty and destructiveness leaves Chinggis Khan entirely in the shade. A number of histories written in Iran after 1335 tell us how splendid things were during Abu Sa'id's time. Human beings do seem to have an ineradicable tendency to imagine that there were Golden Ages in the past. But that was the very recent past; and at least by comparison with the chaos that followed Abu Sa'id's death, the rule of the Mongols must have seemed a period to look back on with nostalgia and appreciation.[13]

13 I offer this essay on the character of the western part of the Mongol Empire as a tribute to Morris Rossabi whose work, more than that of any living scholar, has shed remarkable light on the history of the eastern part of that empire.

CHAPTER 5

Qipchak Networks of Power in Mongol China

Michael C. Brose

Introduction to the Qipchaks

The people known to the Mongols as the Kibca'ut, the Qipchaks, were a confederation of Turkic tribes who inhabited a large area of the Russian steppe, in present-day southern Ukraine and the Russian Federation around the Volga River and to the west of Central Asia that is more commonly known as the Qipchak steppe.[1] They are perhaps better known to Western readers as Comans, who allied with Ukrainian Russian princes in the 1220s to fight the expansion of the Mongol confederation to the west.[2] The Comans were the largest and

1 When I first entered doctoral studies and expressed an interest in working on Yuan Dynasty social history, my advisor urged me to read two books as a good introduction to this most complex of imperial periods, *China Among Equals*, edited by Morris Rossabi, and his biography of Qubilai. This was good advice because these two books taught me a lot about how to research and write about history, and provided a standard of scholarship that I have tried to meet, however partially, in my own work. His detailed and lively biography of Qubilai brought this most important figure to life in a way that few biographies had done, and provided me with a superb and quick introduction into the Mongol world and their domination of China. It was also one of the most accessible monographs I had ever read, not least because there was something for everyone from the graduate student and advanced scholar looking for the most obscure details to the general reader getting their first taste of the history of the Mongols. His edited volume on China's foreign relations provided a role model of a different kind, one that made it acceptable to question the standard Sino-centric trope and showed the value of studying the other members of that world where China really was one state and society "among equals." This was great reading for a first-year doctoral student! Morris's subsequent work on Yuan and Ming, and also in contemporary Mongolian history and society, continues to be a model of scholarship for me and my own students, notable as usual for his deep analytical insights spun out in persuasive, accessible prose, and always favoring an approach that looks, if even slightly, outside the box. I hope that my contribution honoring Morris's career and groundbreaking scholarship can, in some small way, live up to the standards and approaches he provided in those first works I read as a student and that continue to shape his work.

2 See Paul D. Buell, *Historical Dictionary of the Mongol World Empire* (Lanham, MD & Oxford: The Scarecrow Press, 2003):, p. 180, and Douglas S. Benson, *The Mongol Campaigns in Asia* (Chicago, 1991).

 | DOI 10.1163/9789004343405_007

most powerful tribal contingent of the greater Qipchak confederation who dominated the broad swath of territory between the Atil and Dinester rivers.[3] But Qipchak tribes also played important roles in the eastern half of the new Mongol Empire, especially in service to Möngke and Qubilai. This paper examines one Qipchak clan who were at the center of that service and who created a powerful social and political network in Mongol China that reached to the very highest levels of political power for a time. As the paper illustrates, these Qipchaks relied on the substantial social capital they accrued as payment for their military service to extend their influence in the Mongol civil bureaucracy in China. The paper also demonstrates the utility of social network analysis as an analytic approach to illustrate and understand how the Qipchaks in this family grew beyond military actors into the powerful individuals and family they became.

Qipchak History

The ethnic origin of the Qipchak tribes is complex, but most scholars agree that they are Turkic tribes with some Turkicized Mongol elements.[4] The Qipchaks first came to the notice of Muslim writers starting in the eighth century, and to Russian and Chinese chroniclers in the early twelfth century. The first appearance of the term Qipchak as an ethnonym is found in a runic stone inscription that was set down by the Uyghur Qaghan Eletmish Bilge Qaghan (747–759). A ninth-century Islamic writer, Ibn Xurdadbih, recorded them in a list of northern Turkic peoples, next to the Kirgiz. In western sources (Rus, German, Latin, Armenian) the Qipchaks were known as Polovčin. Much about the specific tribal composition of the Qipchaks is still unclear, but they lived in a very loose tribal confederation in a large swath of land that was known by Islamic writers as the Dašt-i Qipchak (the "Qipchak Steppe"). One of the questions that has

3 See, for example, Ahmet Gökbel, "Kipchaks and Kumans," in *The Turks*, ed. Hasan Celâl Güzel, C. Cem Oğuz, and Osman Karatay (Ankara: Yenı Türkıye, 2002), vol. 1, pp. 643–659), and István Vásáry, *Cumans and Tatars: Oriental Military in the Pre-Ottoman Balkans, 1185–1365* (Cambridge: Cambridge University Press, 2005), "Introduction."

4 This discussion on the ethnic makeup and earliest sources of the Qipchaks relies on Peter B. Golden, "Nomads and Their Sedentary Neighbors in Pre-Činggisid Eurasia," *Archivum Eurasiae Medii Aevi* 7 (1987–1991): 41–82; Peter B. Golden, *An Introduction to the History of the Turkic Peoples* (Wiesbaden: Otto Harrassowitz, 1992), esp. ch. 8; Moshe Gammer, "Russia and the Eurasian Steppe Nomads: An Overview," in Reuven Amitai and Michal Biran, eds., *Mongols, Turks, and Others: Eurasian Nomads and the Sedentary World* (Leiden & Boston: Brill, 2005), pp. 483–502; and Thomas T. Allsen, "The Mongols and North Caucasia," *Archivum Eurasiae Medii Aevi* 7 (1987–91): 5–39.

driven the scholarship on the Qipchaks is why they never formed their own state. It appears that they preferred to remain as a loose confederation who got involved with other regional states and warlords from Hungary, Byzantium, Rus', Georgia to Khwarazm, usually in their capacity as hired military elites.[5] In fact, the sub-confederation of Qipchaks who eventually ended up in China, the Baya'ut, first became known to Chinggis because they provided military muscle to the Khwarazm state when the Khwarazm Shah incurred the Mongols' wrath for abusing their envoys. In fact, even before that time they had integrated so thoroughly into Khwarazm society that a Qipchak woman of the Baya'ut clan, Terken Khatun, was married to the Khwarazmshah Tekish (1172–1200). It was their son, the Shah Muhammad, whose ill treatment of Mongol envoys spelled the eventual destruction of his state by the Mongols. Qipchak tribesmen had also sheltered another steppe tribe, the Merkit, when they were being hunted by Chinggis, around 1218.[6]

When Chinggis sent his two generals Subudei and Jebe into the Caucasus and Pontic steppe region to confront the Russian principalities and to reconnoiter potential allies in 1221, they separated the Qipchaks from their Alan allies by appealing to the shared nomadic culture of the Mongols and Qipchaks. It was at that time that Chinggis also finally conquered the Merkid tribes. The leader of the Baya'ut Qipchaks, Inos (who, according to the Chinese sources, held the title of King, *guowang*), offered to submit to Chinggis, apparently around 1222 (Qipchaks from the Baya'ut and other tribes, however, took a different course and remained allied with the Russian princes and fought the Mongols at the Kalka River in 1223).[7]

5 In fact, the stateless status of the Qipchaks is the focus of Peter B. Golden's article "The Qıpčaqs of Medieval Eurasia: An Example of Stateless Adaptation in the Steppes," in G. Seaman and D. Marks, ed., *Rulers from the Steppe: State Formation on the Eurasian Periphery* (Los Angeles: Ethnographics Press, 1991), pp. 132–157.

6 See Golden, "Nomads and their Sedentary Neighbors," pp. 66–68 for discussion of Qipchak involvement in Khwarazm. It is important to note, however, as Golden emphasizes, that it was not the involvement of the Qipchaks in Khwarazm politics that led to that state's demise; Khwarazm fell to the Mongols because of internal structural weaknesses that had nothing to do with the Qipchaks.

7 There is some confusion in the Chinese sources concerning the actual date when the Qipchaks submitted to Chinggis, and whether it was Inos or his son, Qursman, who submitted. Resolving this question is beyond the scope of this paper. See Charles J. Halperin, "The Kipchak Connection: the Ilkhans, the Mamluks and Ayn Jalut," *Bulletin of the School of Oriental and African Studies* 63.2 (2000): 229–245, for discussion of the various groups of Qipchaks who were involved with states from medieval Kievan Rus to the Delhi Sultanate to Khwarazmshah to China, and generally remained highly visible political actors throughout the thirteenth century across much of Eurasia!

The Chinese sources pick up the same Baya'ut Qipchaks several decades later when their leader Banduchaq submitted to Möngke, who employed them in his military campaigns into the far southwest against the Dali State, a campaign that was led by Möngke's younger brother, Prince Qubilai, and that was really aimed against the Southern Song. The focus in this paper is on those Baya'ut Qipchaks, who eventually became important military and political actors in Mongol China as a result of their submission to Möngke. They are superb examples of the ways in which some Central Asian nomadic clans maintained their sense of clan identity for many generations in entirely new social, geographic and economic settings. As we shall see by the case study presented here, the strong sense of Qipchak identity survived because of their deployment of their martial abilities that made them invaluable additions to the Mongol military machine in the campaigns prosecuted by both Möngke and Qubilai, and as part of the imperial bodyguard. Their unique capabilities can be handily summed up, as one scholar has done, by describing them as border commanders par excellence.[8]

One of the more interesting and unresolved questions about the early Qipchaks, why they did not develop their own conquest state in the steppe, may be answered in part by their long and successful history of deployment as core military units by other states such as Khwarazm. In many of those cases the Qipchaks were entrusted with command of strategic border zones. We should also not lose sight of the fact that the norm for nomadic steppe tribes was not to form their own state.[9] We might better understand the Qipchaks in their service roles for the Mongols and how those affected their eventual integration into China if we view them as a type of "borderland" people rather than, or as much as a confederation of tribes united around the concept of establishing their own state. Especially in their early history across the Pontic steppe, the Qipchaks are notable for their involvement as hired military elites in service to the political elite of other states. That precedent served them well when they encountered the Mongols because their submission and immediate use in military campaigns was entirely in keeping with how they had traditionally acted and had been viewed by others. And as we know, Chinggis and his successor khans were all too happy to induct exactly this kind of tribe into the

8 Liu Yingsheng illustrates this quality in his article, "War and Peace Between the Yuan Dynasty and the Chaghadaid Khanate (1312–1323)," in Reuven Amitai and Michal Biran, eds., *Mongols, Turks, and Others: Eurasian Nomads and the Sedentary World* (Leiden & Boston: Brill, 2005), pp. 339–358.

9 Peter Golden argues this convincingly in his 1991 article, "The Qıpčaqs of Medieval Eurasia," cited above.

confederation, both because they could be counted on for their loyalty and because the Mongols were always in need of more troops to subsidize their own rather slim numbers.

The Baya'ut Qipchaks who ended up living in China as members of the conquering elite narrated and performed their identity through specific political, social and cultural methods and discourses that were established by the Mongols in their new, hybrid administration of China, but were also time-honored forms of identity performance in the Chinese imperial world that the Mongols and their subjects inhabited. The most powerful device that the Qipchaks wielded to preserve and cultivate their status as elites in China was their sense of being a distinct tribe or lineage defined by their martial skills. We can assess the effectiveness of these Qipchaks' identity strategies by examining how the members of that group interacted with each other and with other powerful actors that included Mongols, *Semuren* and even Chinese personnel in Yuan China. This paper focuses on these identity strategies, described here as networks, that came with their settlement into China. Thus we will describe only briefly the actions of certain well-known members of this Qipchak clan or family, as background to our inquiry.[10] Figure 1 provides a diagram of this Baya'ut Qipchak clan. Please refer to this diagram for reference to specific members of this clan discussed throughout this paper. For a point of reference, this Qipchak clan became known by their most famous ancestor/member, Tuq Tuq'a. References to the clan in Chinese local records in south China all refer to members of this clan by his name.

Immediately after their submission, the Qipchaks were distributed as booty across the growing Mongol Empire. They were especially sought out by Möngke for his campaign down through Sichuan and into the Dali area to establish a basis for attacking Southern Song from the west. Then-prince Qubilai led 100 Qipchak tribesmen in that campaign, and Banduchaq and his son, Tuq Tuq'a, both received special honors for their actions. It was probably also during that campaign that Qubilai became aware of the military prowess of the

10 There are several studies that discuss the histories of specific members of this Qipchak clan as political actors in Mongol China. See, for example, Zhang Peizhi 张沛之，元代土土哈家族探研, "Yuandai Tutuha jiazu tanyan" cited above; Ma Juan 马娟，元代钦察人燕铁木儿事迹考伦, "Yuandai Chincha Yan Tiemuer shiji kaolun," *Yuanshi Luncong* 10 (2003): 98–106; and John W. Dardess, *Conquerors and Confucians: Aspects of Political Change in Late Yüan China* (New York: Columbia University Press, 1973. There is even new archaeological evidence that confirms Yuan accounts of the Qipchak El Temur's actions at the northern capital, Shangdu, discussed below. See Ye Xinmin 叶新民, *Yuan Shangdu Yanjiu* 元上都研究 (Hohot: Neimenggu Daxue chubanshe, 1998), pp. 192–205.

Qipchaks, whom he later inducted into his very selective imperial bodyguard unit that was stationed at his new capital city, Dadu.[11] The Qipchak members of the Imperial Guard were also granted landed estates ("appanages") in the area just south of Dadu for their support. This was a common way to reward tribes that were known for their military expertise and had contributed to the Mongol conquests. Of course, by that time, members of this same Qipchak clan had already distinguished themselves in action against Qubilai's rival for power, Qaidu.

Military Networks

The Qipchak personnel were involved as military actors in two separate but related succession disputes for the Yuan throne, first in 1307, and then again in 1328. In the first case, the dispute arose between two contenders for the Yuan throne upon the death of the reigning Qaghan and Yuan emperor Temür, Qubilai's grandson. At the time of Temür's death, he had sent out into the northern steppe a military force to suppress an alliance of Mongol princes who disputed the leadership positions of descendants of Tolui as qaghans ruling over the entire Mongol imperium. The Central Asian alliance was spearheaded by Qaidu, a grandson of Ogodei, who took up the position of qaghan when his father, Chinggis, died in 1227 (r. 1229–41). The dispute between the Mongols in the steppe and those in China arose over two related issues, a dispute over who would replace the qaghan Möngke as leader of the Mongol confederation when he died in 1259 while on campaign in China, and a disagreement over whether to maintain the traditional nomadic life and customs or to integrate into China. The first dispute, over the legitimate claimant to the title of qaghan, broke out between Möngke's younger brothers Qubilai and Arigh Böke. That dispute simmered throughout Qubilai's reign, and by the time he died in 1294 Arigh Böke had been replaced by Qaidu, a grandson of Ogodei.

Tuq Tuq'a (1237–97) was a vigorous and effective military leader on behalf of his Mongol masters. His most important assignment was to suppress the simmering rebellion against Qubilai's power that had first erupted between him and his brother Arigh Böke when Qubilai claimed the title of qaghan of the united Mongol confederation in 1260, and that was continued by his cousin Qaidu, grandson of Ogodei, after Arigh Böke's death in 1266. This was a long and complex civil war and eventually resulted in Qubilai's ceding power over

11 The Qipchaks were organized into left and right imperial bodyguard units (*zuo* and *you Chinchawei*) at the Yuan capital in 1286. They were maintained and directed by the Yuan Grand Military Commission (*da dudufu*). See Toghto, *Yuanshi* 99 "Suwei" 宿衛, p. 2529.

Central Asia to his nomadic cousins, and the details need not detain us here.[12] But Qubilai did not give up easily, and Tuq Tuq'a led Qipchak tribesmen north on several different occasions between 1278 and 1296, often in joint campaigns with the great Mongol general Bayan. The numbers of Qipchak horsemen that Tuq Tuq'a led in these campaigns was impressive; the sources report him leading over a thousand of his fellow Qipchak mounted tribesmen in several campaigns during that time. And he was effective, at least in the short term. For example, he helped rescue Qubilai's son Nomoqan after he was captured by Qaidu's generals in 1278. He recaptured the Mongol imperial tent that Qaidu's forces had taken, and he managed to secure the release of hundreds of fellow Qipchak tribesmen who had initially been recruited by the other side. Tuq Tuq'a military actions on behalf of Qubilai occurred in two distinct periods, first in the 1270s, then again in the mid-1280s. After Qubilai's death Tuq Tuq'a was yet again called up to defend Yuan China's northern borderlands against Qaidu's forces.[13]

Tuq Tuq'a was most handsomely rewarded after each of these campaigns. As an example of Qubilai's largess, after the 1278 campaign Qubilai showered him with such things as 100 taels of silver, gold and silver wine goblets, gold coins and a set of imperially-commissioned robes called *jisün* that were worn by the Mongols on important state occasions.[14] More important for the long-term fortune of his clan, Qubilai granted estate lands and resident populations in southern China to Tuq Tuq'a and his Qipchak clan. These grants were different from the old landed estates (appanages, C. *fendi*) that earlier Mongol qaghans gave to members of the Mongol imperial clan and other loyal retainers across north China. For one thing, the grantees of estates in south China did not have exclusive and virtually autonomous rule over the populations in these areas. Their reward seems to have been rather to an annual income and tax advantages provided by the Yuan court.[15]

---

12 This civil war and its outcome are discussed by Michal Biran, *Qaidu and the Rise of the Independent Mongol State in Central Asia* (Surrey: Curzon, 1997), and she offers a different interpretation for the causes of this conflict.

13 Detailed information about Tuq Tuq'a's various military campaigns is contained in his biography compiled by Su Tianjue 蘇天爵, comp., Yao Jingan 姚景安 corrector, "Shumi Jurong Wuyiwang" 樞密句容武毅王, in *Yuanchao Mingcheng Shilue* 3, 47–51 (Beijing: Zhonghua shuju, 1996).

14 A complete list of the honors bestowed on Tuq Tuq'a for his actions in various campaigns are included in his official biography in Toghto, *Yuanshi* 128, pp. 3131–35. His son Chong'ur's biography follows in the same section, pp. 3135–38. For a description of the ceremonial *jisün* robes, see Thomas T. Allsen, *Commodity and Exchange in the Mongol Empire* (Cambridge: Cambridge University Press, 1997): pp. 19–22.

15 See Dardess's discussion of these fiefs, *Conquerors and Confucians*, p. 180, nn. 50–51.

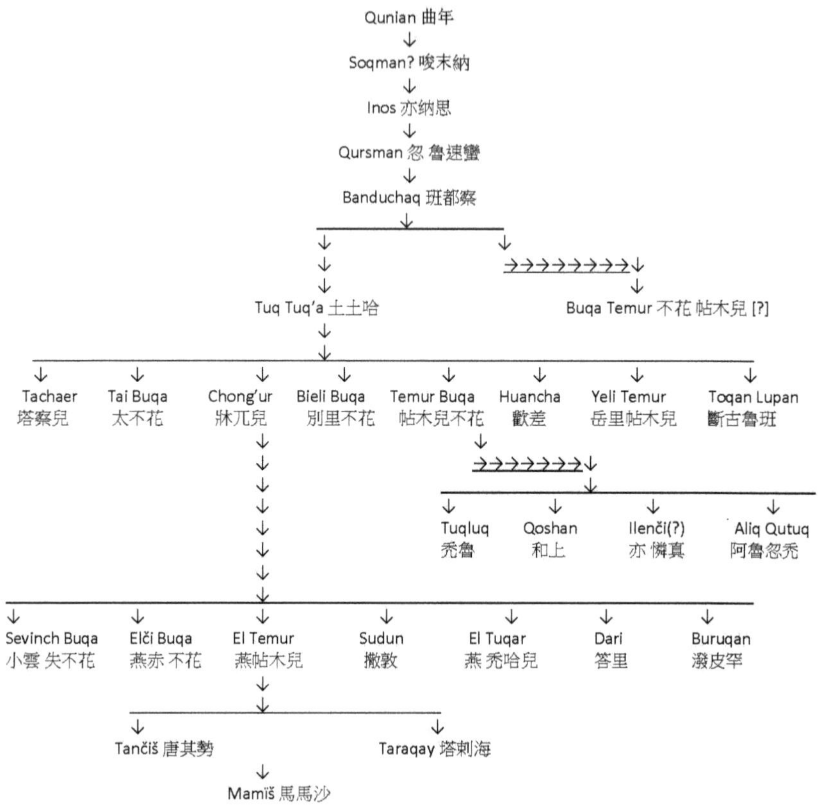

FIGURE 5.1 *Baya'ut Qipchaks in China.*[16]

Qubilai initially granted Tuq Tuq'a the income of 1,700 households in three separate locations in southern China, Jiankang (renamed Jiqing, present-day Nanjing), Luzhou (modern Hefei) and Raozhou (modern Boyang). These were to be registered as "Qipchaks" (*Qarachi*) in the population registers. Tuq Tuq'a was also allowed to bring in some 10,000 of his own troops to settle in those places. It is to this distribution of southern Chinese land and residents to Tuq

16 Renderings of the family tree of this extended Qipchak clan can be found in Louis Hambis, *Le Chapitre CVIII du Yuan Che* (Leiden: E.J. Brill, 1954): =, pp. 163–169; the "Table of Families and Clans in the Yuan" ("Yuanshi shizubiao") in the six volumes of corrections and additions to the monographs and tables in the twenty-five dynastic histories, *Ershiwushi bubian* (Shanghai: Kaiming Shudian, 1955), pp. 8368–70; and Zhang Peizhi 张沛之, 元代土哈家族探研, "Yuandai Tutuha jiazu tanyan," cited above.

Tuq'a that we now turn, since it was after these Qipchaks had settled into China that Tuq Tuq'a's descendants began to branch out from their military roles to begin to work in and influence the Yuan civilian bureaucracy. We turn to examine the Qipchaks in Jiqing Circuit.

Jiqing Circuit

The gifts of land and access to the production of resident populations that Tuq Tuq'a and his fellow Qipchaks were given in southern China by Qubilai were different from the old-style appanage landed estates that earlier Mongol qans had provided to members of their own extended tribes and to other loyal tribesmen across north China. For one thing, these were not autonomous estates that were really outside of the reach of the central state. Qubilai understood that the old appanage system was a huge drain on the state, and in his determination to create a self-sustaining state organized along Chinese bureaucratic principles, he needed to stop that practice, especially to insure that the newly conquered lands of Southern Song were not treated the same.

Jiankang, renamed Jiqing Circuit after Qubilai had conquered southern Song, was not just any old place to settle the Qipchaks. Situated on the south bank of the Yangzi River with its administrative seat at old Jiankang City, now Jiqing City, was a place full of historic and cultural significance for the Chinese. Jiankang served as a political capital for several southern Chinese dynasties (and as recently as the Jurchen Jin period), and was also an ancient cultural center. The local records record stiff resistance against the invading Mongol troops by Song troops at Jiankang and across its hinterland. This was because Jiankang was strategically important because of its situation on the Yangzi River and its control of important agricultural, commercial and transit areas. Holding old Jiankang and its hinterland would have been an important part of larger Mongol efforts to control the Southern Song state, and what better group to locate there than the Qipchaks, who already were well experienced in controlling borderland areas for other earlier clients and masters!. Figures 2 and 3 provide population data for Jiqing Circuit that illustrate the spread of population by category in the major sites in this Circuit, and the spread of Qipchak personnel in those sites.

Several interesting facts emerge from this data. First, we note that there were two clearly distinct groups of Qipchaks who lived across Jiqing Circuit. Tuq Tuq'a's clan is distinguished in all of the local population registers from other Qipchaks, who are identified by the term *qarachi* that was applied to Qipchak

Place	total	Nanren	Military	Qipchak	Beiren	Semuren
Jiqing 1290	94992	79191	26027	0	15810	2919
Jiangning (xian)	113525	99535	3930	4137	0	0
Shangyuan (xian)	146385	141310	530	3940	5055	85
Jurong (xian)	214790	173825	105	4800	245	50
Liyang (pref)	317410	316825	265	3215	585	95
Lishui (pref)	316425	289275	35	6445	205	30

FIGURE 5.2 *Jiqing population figures, 1303 CE.*

Qipchak Population in Jiqing Circuit:

Place	Qipchaks ("Qarachi")	Tuq Tuqa's Qipchak Clan
Jiangning xian	4137	0
Shangyuan xian	4000 (788 households)	0
Jurong xian	3300 (737 households)	4900 (1093 households)
Lishui prefecture	4725 (1050 households)	1075 (239 households)
Liyang prefecture	0	2893 (643 households)

FIGURE 5.3 *Qipchak households in Jiqing Circuit by location.*

tribesmen generally. Literally meaning "black mare's milk," the Qipchaks early on became known by this epithet because they sent this fermented milk product to the Mongols as a form of tribute. Western travelers such as Marco Polo and William of Rubruck knew it as *caracosmos*.[17] Second, it is interesting to note that the Qipchaks were distinguished from the *Semuren* population. In fact, the Jiqing gazetteer included all Qipchaks under the larger category of *Nanren*, those people in the Mongol fourfold classification scheme who lived in southern China and were brought into the Mongol Empire only after the conquest of the southern Song state.[18] The gazetteer is silent regarding the rationale for categorizing Qipchaks as part of the population of Southern

17 Emil Bretschneider, *Medieval Researches from Eastern Asiatic Sources* (London: Kegan Paul, Trench, Trübner & Co., 1910), vol. 2, pp. 68–73.

18 I have separated out Qipchak population figures from both *Nanren* and *Semuren* in my table, which reflects the gazetteer's presentation of population in tabular format.

China, but this may reflect the Qipchaks' somewhat liminal status in Jiqing as residents who arrived at their positions by fiat from the court, rather than from personal decision to settle there. Finally, the data show that a good many Qipchaks settled down across Jiqing Circuit. It was doubtless from their ranks that sprang those who were part of this Baya'ut Qipchak clan who went on to careers in the military and civil bureaucracies for decades after they initially settled in Jiqing. We briefly examine some of the more notable Qipchak men and women who acted in the military and civilian sectors of Yuan state and society, because the networks of power in which they moved and operated had important long-term consequences for the new Mongol Chinese state.

Of course, the imperial grant of estates in southern China also came with honorary titles, and several generations of this Qipchak clan benefitted from these. Tuq Tuq'a's grandfather, Qursman, and his father, Banduchaq, were both awarded posthumous imperial titles as a result of Tuq Tuq'a's merit; both enjoyed the title "Prince of Jurong Prefecture," and Tuq Tuq'a's father was given the additional title of "Prince of Liyang" (溧陽王), another important prefecture in southern Jiqing Circuit. This is reflected in the population statistics that show some 643 households of Tuq Tuq'a's immediate clan residing at Liyang. Altogether five generations in Tuq Tuq'a's clan held these same titles with their perquisites (see list, below. See Figure 4 for a list of the imperial titles held by members of this Qipchak clan). There were other imperial honorary titles linked to other places in Mongol China that several members of Tuq Tuq'a's clan enjoyed not described here. We limit our discussion here to the imperial titles in Jiqing Circuit as an example of the kinds of benefits that accrued to this clan over time and across several generations as a result of the martial skills that they loyally wielded in service to Qubilai and his Yuan descendants.

Reflecting the importance that the Qipchak tribesmen had come to play in Qubilai's military, he created a special Qipchak Guard (*Qincha wei* 欽察衛) and Tuq Tuqa was put in charge.[19] Subordinate positions in the Qipchak Guard were specifically allotted to members of his own clan. All seven of his sons followed in his footsteps, serving as military personnel and being rewarded with very high positions such as commander of Qipchak troop units at regional and

However, in the narrative explanation that precedes the population tables in the gazetteers, Qipchaks are listed as a sub-category of *Nanren*.

19 David M. Farquhar, *The Government of China Under Mongolian Rule* (Stuttgart: Franz Steiner Verlag, 1990), pp. 272–73 describes this bureau and its rapid growth and subsequent division into Right and Left Guard units in 1322 to accommodate the 35 chiliarchies of troops that the bureau regulated by that time.

Qipchak Imperial Fief Holdings in Jiqing Circuit

Qurusman, Prince of Jurong 句容郡王 (posthumous)
↓
Balduchaq, Prince of Jurong 句容郡王, Prince of Liyang 溧陽王
↓
Tuq Tuq'a, Prince of Jurong 句容郡王
↓
Chong'ur, Prince of Jurong 句容郡王
↓
Dari, Prince of Jurong 句容郡王

FIGURE 5.4 *Jiqing Circuit honorary titles.*

national levels. His second son, Chong'ur (1260–1322) was the most successful, rising to the position of Director of the Bureau of Military Affairs at the Yuan court. Tuq Tuqa's grandsons and nephews also had successful military careers, but we see a shift in that generation as many of those men were distinguished as much for their civil careers as for their identities as military personnel.[20] And it is with that generation, Tuq Tuq'a's grandsons, that we see this more general shift in career patterns into the civilian bureaucracy.

Political Networks

The most famous of Tuq Tuq'a's family to serve in the civil bureaucracy was undoubtedly his grandson El Temür (fl. 1320s–30s, d. 1333). El Temür cut his teeth as a military man, leading Qipchak troops in the same campaigns against Qaidu that propelled his grandfather to fame. After Qubilai died, El Temür and his father, Chongwu'er got involved in the strategies of competing Mongol factions to replace him, and they played important roles in the eventual enthronement

20 This does not mean that subsequent generations of Qipchaks did not serve in military roles. In fact, the Qipchak Guard units continued to exist down to the end of the dynasty, and several of Tuq Tuq'a's descendants were appointed leadership positions in that unit, including the last man listed on the family tree in Fig. 1, Mamïš (fl. 1350s), who filled his great-great grandfather Tuq Tuq'a's old office of Commander of the Qipchak Guard.

of the next Yuan emperor, Qaishan in 1308. For their roles they were all rewarded with important government positions and extravagant financial rewards. Qaishan, unfortunately, only ruled for two years, and the throne was carried by his brother and descendants until 1328 when many of these same Qipchaks led a faction of activist administrators to revive Qaishan's line on the Yuan throne.[21]

The eventual enthronement of Qaishan's son, Tugh Temür, as Yuan emperor in 1328 was essentially a coup d'état against the reigning emperor, a cousin to Qaishan. This was just one example of the inherent instability in the succession issue that plagued the Mongols in China, and those disputes put a severe strain on the power and potency of the Yuan court. The disputes also involved an increasing division among the non-Chinese *Semuren* group of stakeholders. These Qipchaks were thus part of a larger socio-political trend that shaped the last decades of the Yuan state, and their actions were by no means unique or isolated. The history of the Yuan court after Qubilai's long reign can be understood as the seesawing back and forth of power of these two political factions. The inherent instability that the factional struggles caused the Yuan court and its world can be said to have been one of the causes for the rather rapid decline in Mongol power in China, which really ended many years before the next dynasty, the Ming, was officially proclaimed in 1368.

El Temür did not act alone in his bid to see that his side in the succession dispute won power; he relied on a strong network of other non-Chinese leaders, mostly from other Turkic tribes like himself (see Fig. 5). In fact, one of the principal sources of friction at the Mongol Yuan court at the time was the power of Turkic tribesmen versus Chinese and non-Chinese who were more dedicated to establishing a Confucian-based civil society along the lines of traditional Chinese dynasties.

Understanding who El Temür's political allies were and how he created that network to bring about the kind of political change he desired brings to light another important network that members of this Qipchak clan forged, that of marriage alliances. The most famous example of an important marriage alliance is, again, seen in El Temür; his daughter became the wife of the last Yuan emperor, Toghon Temür (r. 1333–68)! A visual rendering of this network of marriage alliances reveals a much larger network, however, that involved the marriage of several generations of Qipchaks from this clan to Mongol women, both from the Chinggisid royal tribe and other tribes (see Fig. 6). In fact, this network diagram reveals some interesting patterns that shed light on the strategies of this clan to use marriage as a mechanism to situate themselves into

21 See Dardess, *Conquerors and Confucians* for the roles that these Qipchaks played in those events. This discussion draws on Dardess's account.

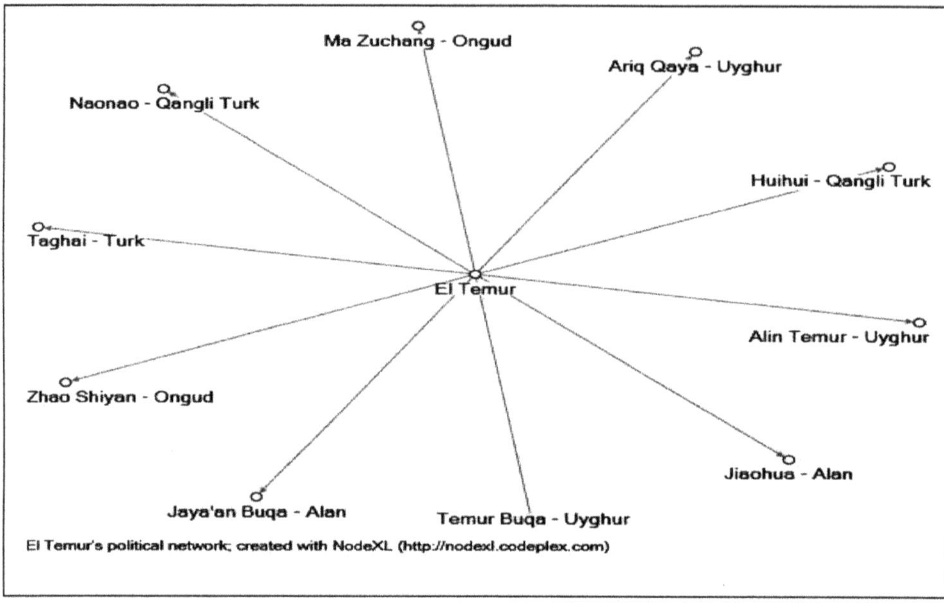

FIGURE 5.5 *El Temür's political network.*

networks of power. First, Banduchaq, the first Qipchak of this clan to actually live in China, was in fact married to at least two women from other Central Asian tribes (*Semuren*). His son, Tuq Tuq'a, invested heavily in marriage alliances exclusively with Mongol women, including one from Chinggis's imperial tribe. The sources do not record any Qipchak women among his marriage partners. As we have seen above, Tuq Tuq'a made his name as a military commander in the field working to suppress the emperor Qubilai's opponents, and undoubtedly more than one of his Mongol wives came to him as gifts from the emperor. The sources only provide information on the marriages of two of Tuq Tuq'a's sons. His son Temür Buqa married a Uyghur woman from the southern Tarim Basin city of Khotan, and we know something about her because she was accorded her own stele inscription, written by the very well-known *Semuren* writer Ma Zuchang (1279–1338).[22] Her father, one Ali Beg, was in charge of Zhedong Branch Province and Assistant Military Commander of the military bureau in that same province. The family also may have been Muslims since the Khotan Uyghurs converted to Islam well before the Mongol conquest,

22 Ma Zuchang, "Gu zhenjie zeng Rongguo furen Safalishe beaming" 故貞節贈 容國夫人薩法禮氏碑銘, in Ma Shitian Wenji 馬石田文集 14.11a–13a; rptr. *Yuanren Wenji zhenben congkan* (Taibei: Xinwenfeng chubanshe, 1985), vol. 6, pp. 672–73.

but the sources are silent on this. Temür Buqa's career was not at the national level, but he was appointed to the important position of Overseer (darughuachi) of Qipchak households in Jiqing and Lurao Circuits.

Chong'ur engaged in far more strategic marriage alliances, including to two women of the Chinggisid imperial Mongol tribe and to two Tatar women. We do not know anything more about his wives than their names and tribal or ethnic identities, but he was clearly mindful of positioning himself within the ruling Mongol tribe, as well as maintaining his ties to other important *Semuren*.

Finally, rounding out our information on marriages that members of this Qipchak clan engaged in that served to build or extend their networks of power, the primary sources provide some interesting information on the

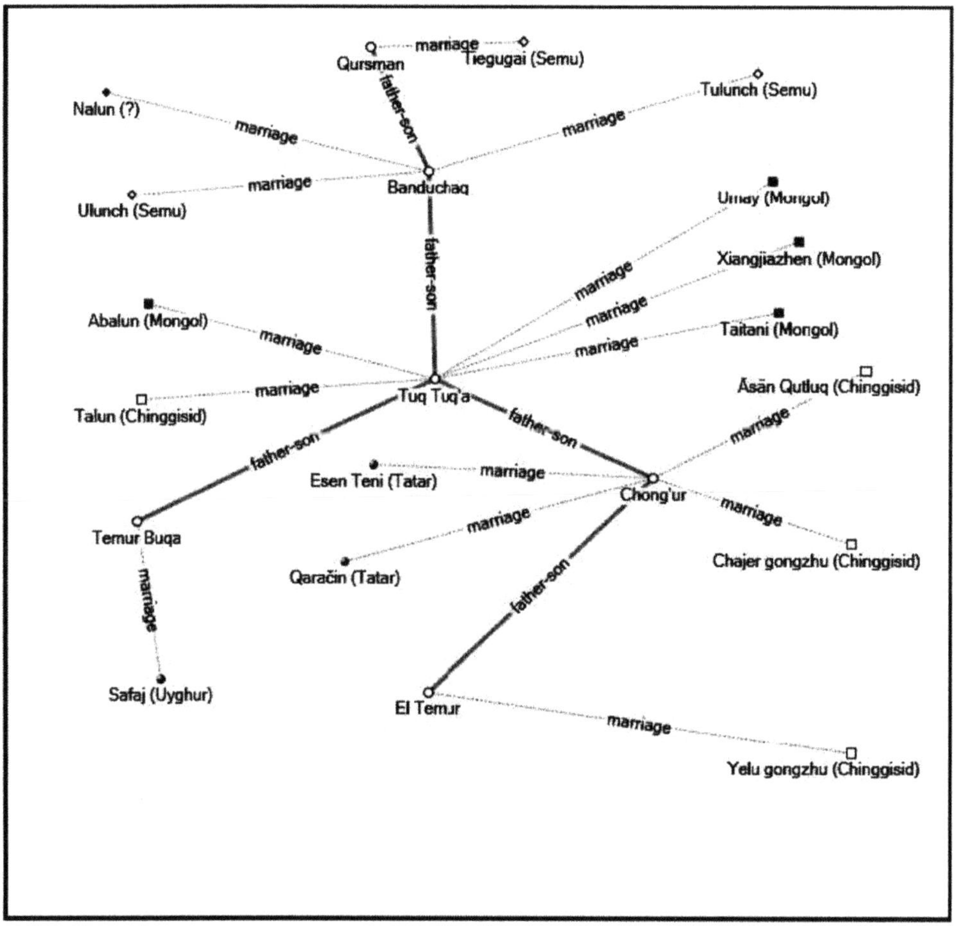

FIGURE 5.6 *Qipchak clan marriages.*

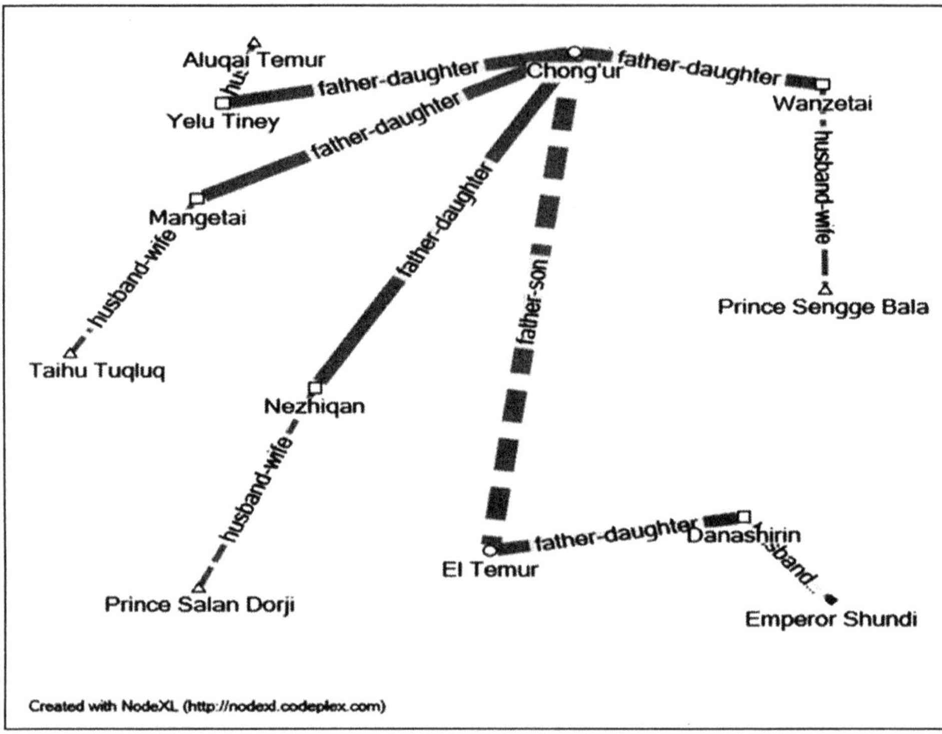

FIGURE 5.7 *Qipchak daughters.*

daughters of two Qipchak men, Chong'ur and his son, El Temür (see Fig. 7).[23] We have the most information on the men that Chong'ur's four daughters married; all four married men of the Chinggisid imperial tribe. We know something about two of these men. Prince Salan Dorji (fl. 1330s), who was married to Chong'ur's daughter Nezhiqan, was given two separate honorary titles as Prince.[24] Another daughter, Yelu Tiney, was married to another prince of the royal blood, one Aruqi Temür, who was involved in a dispute with a prince from a different line of the imperial Mongol tribe.[25] And most important, El Temür's daughter Danashirin was married to the last Yuan emperor.

23 Zhang Peizhi, "Yuandai Tutuha jiazu tanyan," provides a nice tabulation of these people.
24 His titles are listed in the tables of Imperial Princes (主王表), *Yuanshi* 108, pp. 2735–50.
25 This man was listed among the "Rebellious Officials" (叛臣) in *Yuanshi* 206, pp. 4596–98.

Conclusion

The Baya'ut Qipchaks were but one of many tribes from the steppe who were recruited into the growing Mongol confederation to subsidize the relatively small numbers of Mongol personnel as they campaigned to expand their hold over more and more states and peoples. Their experience as hired military forces for other earlier states such as Khwarazm, especially in manning critical borderland areas, was an important asset to the Mongols as they pushed their control into the southwest with the conquest of the Dali state, in later campaigns against Southern Song China, and, for Qubilai, more urgently as the loyal vanguard in his service in the long civil war in the steppe. Their signal importance to the Mongols as a military force can be seen in Qubilai's designation of the Qipchak tribes into a special Imperial Guard unit with one of their own, Tuq Tuq'a, as commander.

Tuq Tuq'a's Qipchak clan took a path in many ways similar to other tribes who were inducted into the Mongol Empire, using their skills and assets to insinuate themselves firmly into the ranks of the Mongol conquering elite. Like other tribes and groups who came into China with the Mongols, later generations also identified with an apical ancestor, in this case Tuq Tuq'a. But these Qipchaks also occupied a particularly liminal space in Mongol China that most other tribes and non-Chinese did not experience; they occupied an entirely separate category, set apart from the standard social classes in the records. That liminal identity is only apparent in the Yuan-era local records for Jiqing Circuit, the place in southern China where this clan and many fellow Qipchaks eventually settled. While Jiqing became home to many prominent immigrants during the Yuan period, in all cases apart from the Qipchaks those people were identified as belonging to one of the stable social categories devised and implemented by the Mongols to categorize all social groups in China at the time. For example, prominent Uyghur individuals and their families who settled into areas within Jiqing Circuit were all categorized as *Semuren*. Many prominent northern Chinese people who migrated south in the wake of the conquest of Southern Song were categorized as "northerners." The Qipchaks who settled into areas across this circuit were, however, always classified into one of two groups, either as members of Tuq Tuq'a's own clan or as generic Qipchaks.[26]

---

26 Actually, a third category of households, titled "the former slaves of Tuq Tuq'a and Yesudar," is also listed in one place in Jiqing Circuit. These, like the Qipchaks, were also considered "nanren" in the local record.

This curious identification of the Qipchak tribesmen as native southerners is difficult to reconcile with their actions and identities as military men, some of whom eventually migrated into careers as important members of the civil bureaucracy. It may reflect their unique status as imperial fief holders in Jiqing. Alternatively, it may reflect the confusion on the part of the compilers of the local-level Jiqing gazetteer over just how to include this rather large group of non-Chinese personnel who were so clearly aligned with the highest levels of the Mongol imperial tribe. Perhaps this special treatment of the Qipchak tribesmen in these local records reflects the relative independence of these tribesmen throughout the Yuan dynasty, at least as compared to other non-Chinese personnel who settled in China. That independence may perhaps be seen in the fact that, unlike most other Central Asians, none of these men ever adopted a Chinese-style surname. Just as important, the men of Tuq Tuq'a's extended clan also made sure to maintain their identity as an elite military unit down through the end of the dynasty. Even though several men made names for themselves as powerful political figures in the civilian bureaucracy, at least one man in every generation of this clan inherited the position that was created for Tuq Tuq'a by the emperor Qubilai, that of Commander of the Qipchak Imperial Guard. That this important and powerful military clan received huge property and financial perks across one of the more strategically and culturally important parts of newly conquered southern China, Jiqing, meant that they never really "settled" into Jiqing society like other Chinese and non-Chinese immigrants. For example, unlike the many prominent Uyghurs who came to call parts of Jiqing home and who became famous for their expertise as Neo-Confucian scholars and statesmen, no Qipchak man ever made a name for himself in that way. What the sources do leave us with is a sense of solidarity among the members of Tuq Tuq'a's clan as members of a unique group bound by their kin association with their well-known "ancestor" Tuq Tuq'a and their identification with the Qipchak Imperial Guard. They are an important part of the story of Yuan state and society, whose unique structure and history are reflected in the history of this group of nomadic tribesmen who settled into China.

The Qipchaks also played significant roles in nearly all parts of the Mongol Empire. In the Golden Horde of Russia, they were part of the military forces, and in the Ilkhanate of West Asia, a few are mentioned in the Ilkhan's detachments. The Mamluks of Egypt, one of the most powerful of the Mongols' enemies, also had large contingents of Qipchak soldiers in their army. The stories of these other Qipchaks constitute another study in the history of the Mongol Empire.

CHAPTER 6

"How the Mongols Mattered: A Perspective from Law"

Bettine Birge

In the title of a 2003 essay, John Dardess asks "Did the Mongols Matter"? And in the body of the essay, he answers a resounding "yes," discussing such aspects as: the consolidation of territory, which became what we think of as "China" proper; the authority and agenda of the central government; and the development of a national Confucian intelligentsia, presaging intellectuals in modern China.[1] Nevertheless, the extent of Mongol influence on China continues to be downplayed and unappreciated. In the arena of law, much of the literature emphasizes the continuity of the Chinese legal tradition, its precepts codified in the great Tang code, which formed the basis for all subsequent law codes in China. Significantly, the Yuan rulers never adopted a formal law code, and the historical record shows that law in the Yuan was quite fluid, with frequent reversals of policy. What has been overlooked is the extent to which new laws in the Yuan, unprecedented in Chinese history, were carried over into later dynasties. In this short essay, I will give an overview of three aspects of Chinese law where the Mongols left a significant legacy; namely: penal law, inheritance law, and marriage law. Each one of these represents an aspect of law that most of the current literature regards as fundamentally Chinese, it having persisted since early times. In fact, in each case Mongol influences rendered the law qualitatively different from that which was in place before the Mongol–Yuan dynasty. It is too simplistic to describe the influence as simple borrowing. Rather, changes in the law were the product of negotiation and innovation over many decades. The Yuan administrators, when faced with the challenges of governing a multi-ethnic empire, devised new and hybrid forms of law that sought to reconcile Chinese Confucian sensibilities with those of steppe peoples and other constituents of their empire. These often built on similar solutions found by their Liao and Jin predecessors, but the Mongols were remarkably successful in overcoming the obstacles that plagued their predecessors and finding

1 "Did the Mongols Matter? Territory, Power, and the Intelligentsia in China from the Northern Song to the Early Ming," in *The Song–Yuan–Ming Transition in Chinese History*, ed. Paul Smith and Richard von Glahn (Harvard University Press, 2003), pp. 111–134.

 | DOI 10.1163/9789004343405_008

forms of law that could operate across ethnic and cultural divides. These in turn left a lasting mark on Chinese legal prescriptions.

1 Penal Law

In the general area of penal law, the Tang code embodied basic principles that were not unlike those of the modern West. According to these fundamental principles of law, crimes like homicide and theft were treated as offenses against the collective social and political order, and the state was therefore solely responsible for prosecuting them and punishing the offender. The state was understood as a disinterested third party, which could discern an objective truth through investigation and trial, and could restore social order by imposing physical punishments on the offender. The law focused on penalizing an offense against the rules of the community, rather than on compensating the victim.

By contrast, penal law among many Inner Asian peoples was based on the principle of redemption. In cases of homicide or theft, the offender had to pay compensation to the victim or the victim's family to make up for the loss they had suffered. This could include livestock or valuables but also a daughter or other family member sent to be a slave in the victim's household. The practice had a long history in steppe societies. It derived from the custom of private revenge, which operated among Inner Asian lineages where centralized states might be weak or non-existent. Later, state actors took over the function of deciding amounts and types of compensation and enforcing the payments, thus transforming it away from a system of private vendetta and preventing unending cycles of feuding and retribution between clans.[2]

Both the Khitan and the Jurchen incorporated the steppe custom of redemption into their penal systems. In cases of homicide or theft, the offender had to make restitution to the victim, usually with livestock. According to early laws of the Khitan Liao dynasty (907–1125), if a Khitan man killed someone in a brawl, he had to pay a fine of oxen and horses that went to the victim's family. Similarly, the dynastic history of the Jurchen Jin records that the founding

2 See discussion in Françoise Aubin, "Some Characteristics of Penal Legislation among the Mongols (13th–21st Centuries)," in *Central Asian Law: A Historical Overview: A Festschrift for the Ninetieth Birthday of Hebert Franke*, ed. Wallace Johnson and Irina Popova (Lawrence, Kansas: Society for Asian Legal History, 2004), pp. 131–132. A similar system existed in some early European societies, as in the payment of *Wergeld* in early Germanic law. The practice is found in modern Pakistan, Afghanistan and other countries.

ancestor of the ruling house brought an end to clan feuds by instituting state-enforced rules of compensation. If a man killed another, he had to give "one person from his family, ten pairs of horses, ten cows and six ounces of gold" to the victim's relatives. Later Jurchen customary law reduced the compensation for murder to thirty horses.[3]

As these non-Chinese dynasties expanded their conquests, they had to confront the dilemma of governing a multi-ethnic population with different legal traditions. The Khitan Liao established a dual system of law and government, whereby one set of rules applied to those labeled "Khitan" (*qidan* 契丹) or "various tribes" (*zhuyi* 諸夷), and another to those labeled "Chinese," (*hanren* 漢人). The Liao founder Abaoji (r. 907–926) in 921 ordered that Khitan and other steppe peoples come under Khitan customary law, as codified by his ministers, while people understood to be of Chinese ethnic origin came under the provisions of the Tang code.[4] Punishments in the Tang code were in some cases harsher than those of steppe customary law. For instance, if a Chinese killed someone in a brawl, the punishment was death by strangulation as stipulated in the Tang code.[5] But if a Khitan committed the same crime, the punishment was a fine of oxen and horses.[6] This difference generated serious tensions among the population, and Khitan rulers made several attempts to unify the law and apply the same law to all people under their jurisdiction. For instance, Empress Chengtian (regent 982–1009) tried to apply the Tang code to Chinese and non-Chinese Khitan alike. Each attempt, however, generated a backlash from Khitan subjects, who refused to be subject to Chinese law, and in 1044 the Liao reverted to special commissioners in each of their capitals to

---

3 Herbert Franke, "Chinese Law in a Multinational Society: The Case of the Liao," *Asia Major* 3rd Series 5:2 (1992), p. 115; *Jinshi* 金史 (Beijing: Zhonghua shuju, 1975 rpt.) 1:2; Herbert Franke, "Jurchen Customary Law and the Chinese Law of the Chin Dynasty," in *State and Law in East Asia: Festschrift Karl Bünger*, ed. Dieter Eikemeier and Herbert Franke (Wiesbaden: Otto Harrassowitz, 1981), p. 218.

4 *Liaoshi* 遼史 (Beijng: Zhonghua shuju, 1974) 61:937. For a discussion of the fluidity of ethnic identity and the difficulties of defining who was Chinese, see Bettine Birge, "Law of the Liao, Chin, and Yuan and Its Impact on the Chinese Legal Tradition," in *New Perspectives on Chinese History, Legal History: The Formation and Transformation of Traditional Chinese Legal Culture*, ed. Liu Liyan (Taipei: Academia Sinica-Lianjing, 2008), pp. 444–7.

5 *Tanglü shuyi* 唐律疏議 (Beijing: Zhonghua shuju, 1983) (Article 306) 21:387.

6 *Dongdu shilüe* 東都事略, by Wang Cheng 王稱 (Taibei: Wenhai chubanshe, 1967) 123:1899; and *Xuzizhi tongjian changbian* 續資治通鑒長編, by Li Tao 李燾 (Beijing: Zhonghua shuju, 1980) 72:1646; Franke, "Chinese Law in a Multinational Society: The Case of the Liao," p. 115.

handle crimes involving Khitans.[7] Chinese were never subject to a system of redemption, and the Liao government maintained separate laws and special courts for different ethnic groups to the end of the dynasty. Ultimately they were unable to unify the law across ethnic and cultural boundaries.

The Jurchen confronted similar problems. Surviving records show that Jurchen law was unstable and arbitrary in the early years of their dynasty. Judges might apply Liao, Song, or Jurchen customary law. Over time, however, they made strenuous efforts to codify their law, on the model of the Tang code. These efforts culminated in the Taihe code, promulgated in 1202. Only fragments of the Taihe code survive, but from these we can surmise that about half of the articles overlapped with the Tang code. Others often included harsher punishments than in the Tang. In the case of killing someone in a brawl, the Taihe code prescribed strangulation, as did the Tang code.[8] In other areas, such as Inheritance and Marriage law, the Taihe code explicitly applied different laws to Chinese, Jurchens, and others, to which I'll return below.

Mongol customary law from early times also included the practice of redemption, or compensation paid by the perpetrator to the victim of a crime.[9] Nevertheless, unlike the Liao and Jin, the Mongols were able to incorporate the concept into a system of traditional Chinese law and apply it to all peoples. For the Liao in particular, the provision of compensation created a barrier between laws for Chinese and non-Chinese and generated accusations of unfairness, but for the Mongols, it became a means to unify the law for all ethnic groups.

The Mongols introduced the idea of compensation in cases of homicide through an institution they called *shaomaiyin* 燒埋銀, "silver for funeral and burial expenses," or *shaomaiqian* 燒埋錢, "money for funeral and burial expenses."[10] *Shaomaiyin* was a payment made by the perpetrator of a homicide to the bereaved family members of the deceased. Khubilai first established the

---

7 Franke, "Chinese Law in a Multinational Society: The Case of the Liao," pp. 115–17; *Liaoshi* 19:230, 112:1502; Birge, "Law of the Liao, Chin, and Yuan," pp. 451–2.

8 Ye Qianzhao 葉潛昭, *Jinlü zhi yanjiu* 金律之研究 (Taibei: Shangwu chuban she, 1972), pp. 142–3.

9 See Paul Ratchnevsky, "Die Mongolische Rechtsinstitution der Busse in der Chinesischen Gesetzgebung der Yüan-Zeit," in *Studia Sino-Altaica: Festschrift für Erich Haenisch zum* 80. *Geburtstag*, ed. Herbert Franke (Wiesbaden: Franz Steiner Verlag, 1961); and Françoise Aubin, "Les sanctions et les peines chez les Mongols," *Transactions of the Jean Bodin Society for Comparative Institutional History*, LVIII, *Punishment, Non European Worlds* (Brussels: De Boeck University, 1991).

10 I follow the conclusion of Françoise Aubin in translating these terms. As Aubin persuasively argues, we can conclude that *shao* (to burn) refers to the burning of paper objects and paper money at funerals for the comfort of the deceased in the afterlife, not to

practice in 1265, but he combined it with traditional Chinese punishments found in the Tang code and applied it to all ethnic groups. Thus the law stated that one who killed another would be punished by death, and in addition his relatives would have to pay the high price of 50 ounces of silver as *shaomaiyin* to the bereaved.[11] Mongols, Chinese, and other peoples all had to pay *shaomaiyin* in homicide cases. They paid the same amounts, even when the prescriptions of the Tang code were not applied to Mongols. For instance, if a Mongol killed a Chinese in a brawl, he was sent away to do military service rather than being executed, but he still had to pay *shaomaiyin* to the bereaved's family.[12] The payment of *shaomaiyin* nicely correlated with Confucian prescriptions for proper funeral rites to honor the deceased. It therefore could operate as a bridge between Mongol customary law and traditional Chinese sensibilities surrounding death ritual.

The way that *shaomaiyin* operated during the Yuan reflects the original steppe concept that the compensation served to restore a sense of moral balance between non-state actors. If the killer escaped punishment through one of the frequent amnesties during the Yuan, the *shaomaiyin* was doubled. If the deceased himself was a criminal subject to the death penalty, the *shaomaiyin* was waived; when both parties were executed, no moral imbalance remained to be remedied. Over the succeeding decades, a body of case law determined the operation of *shaomaiyin* in a wide range of circumstances; all applied to both Mongols and Chinese, as well as other groups. These demonstrate the characteristic of private retribution for a victim with the purpose of maintaining a moral equilibrium between private parties, in contrast to the principle behind the Tang code of punishing an offender against society and thus restoring a universal moral order. For instance, if no bereaved family members

---

cremation, which was practiced only by a minority; see Aubin, "Some Characteristics of Penal Legislation among the Mongols," pp. 133–134.

11 The payment could also be ten *ding* of paper money. *Da Yuan shengzheng guochao dianzhang* 大元聖政國朝典章 [called *Yuan dianzhang*] (Photo reprint of 1322 Yuan edition: Taibei: Gugong bowu guan, 1976) [hereafter cited as YDZ], 43:6a. The basic law is also found in the Treatise on Punishments (Xingfa zhi) of the Yuan dynastic history; *Yuanshi* 元史 by Song Lian 宋濂 et al. (Beijing: Zhonghua shuju, 1976; rpt. 1992) [hereafter cited as YS], 105:2675. As Aubin points out, the bereaved, or "master of sorrow" (*kuzhu* 苦主), referred to the person in charge of the funeral. She also notes that the sum of 50 liang of silver was quite considerable; Aubin, "Some Characteristics of Penal Legislation among the Mongols," p. 134. For the basic law, see also Paul Heng-chao Ch'en, *Chinese Legal Tradition under the Mongols* (Princeton: Princeton University Press, 1979), p. 53.

12 YS 105:2675; Paul Ratchnevsky, trans., *Un Code des Yuan*, 4 vols. (Paris: Collège de France, Institut des Hautes Etudes Chinoises, 1972–1985) IV, p. 259 (Article 831).

could be found, the *shaomaiyin* did not have to be paid. If the killer had already died, *shaomaiyin* still had to be paid by the perpetrator's family. And if the killing was accidental and not punished by death, the perpetrator still had to pay *shaomaiyin* to the deceased's family. Even if the corpse was never found, the convicted killer was responsible for paying the *shaomaiyin*. If the killer was indigent and could not pay directly, he (or she) had to work for the victim's family or surrender a family member (usually a daughter) to be their slave. In 1305, Khubilai's grandson Emperor Chengzong (r. 1294–1307) decreed that if the killer could not be made to pay the *shaomaiyin* or its equivalent, the state should pay.[13] In all cases, *shaomaiyin* was paid to the victim's relatives, never to the state.

The Mongols applied the same principle of private compensation to cases of injury not leading to death. This took the form of a payment called *yangjizhizi* 養濟之資, or "fees to nourish and succor," implying money for food and medicine to help the victim recover. As in the case of homicide, these payments were combined with Chinese-style physical punishments of the perpetrator. If one person hit another with an instrument and inflicted injuries that rendered the victim disabled or seriously ill, the offender was punished by 77 blows of the heavy stick. In addition he had to pay ten *ding* worth of Zhongtong paper currency to the injured person, to provide "fees to nourish and succor" (*yangjizhizi*).[14] The payment varied, according to the severity of the injuries and the relation between the parties, from twenty *ding* worth of paper currency down to 500 *guan* (strings of cash). The physical punishments also varied from 77 to 107 blows. These Chinese-style punishments of graded beatings inflicted on the perpetrator were more lenient than those prescribed by the Tang and Song codes. The Tang code specified three years of penal servitude for inflicting injuries resulting in disability, compared with only 77 blows and the payment of compensation, as described above. The Ming and Qing codes added on 100 blows with the heavy stick to the three years of penal servitude.[15] In these cases, the Yuan compensation payments might be seen to be partially replacing the Chinese-style punishments of the perpetrator.

---

13 YDZ 43:6a–11b; and YS 105:2675.

14 YS 105:2673. Ratchnevsky, *Un code des Yüan*, IV, pp. 243–248 (Articles 788–798). See also discussion in Aubin, "Some Characteristics of Penal Legislation," p. 136; and Paul Ch'en, *Chinese Legal Tradition*, p. 54.

15 *Tanglü shuyi* 21:386 (Art. 305); Ming code Art. 325; Jiang Yonglin trans., *The Great Ming Code/ Da Ming lü* (Seattle: University of Washington Press, 2005), p. 178. See also Paul Ch'en, *Chinese Legal Tradition*, p. 54.

The steppe concept of compensation paid to the victim was completely absent from the Tang code and other Chinese law codes before the Yuan. Nevertheless, both the Ming and the Qing adopted the practice and incorporated it into their legal systems. The institution of *shaomaiyin* was reconstituted in the Ming under names such as *maizangyin* 埋葬銀 "silver for burial expenses," or *maizangyin* 埋瘞銀 "silver for internment expenses." As in the Yuan, this was money paid to the family members of the victim of a homicide to compensate them for their loss and ensure proper funeral and burial rites. The Ming system of compensation operated somewhat differently than in the Yuan, but it still maintained the nature of redressing a wrong committed against a private party. In particular, the *maizangyin* payments were only levied when the perpetrator of a homicide did not receive the death sentence. The Ming code describes a dizzying array of variations on homicide. Nevertheless, only in cases of unintended homicide, when the punishment was something other than execution, did the killer have to pay the burial expenses. In this way, the compensation payments operated as a punishment given in place of execution of the killer; and the Ming procedure in many respects matched the original steppe concept of resolving a private vendetta more closely than in the Yuan.

The amount of the *maizangyin* payments that were levied in Ming law were in most cases 10 ounces of silver, considerably less than the 50 ounces levied in the Yuan. As with offenses punishable by execution in its various forms, the possible circumstances under which one might inflict death accidentally are spelled out in excruciating detail. If one person accidentally killed another by driving their carriages or horses too fast, the punishment was 100 strokes of the heavy stick if committed in the countryside and 100 strokes plus life exile to 3,000 *li* if committed in an urban area. In both cases, the offender had to pay 10 ounces of silver for "burial expenses" to the bereaved family.[16] Similarly, 10 ounces for burial expenses was levied when a hunter accidentally killed someone in a trap or with a preset spring bow in the woods, and in addition the offender would be punished with a beating of 100 strokes and penal servitude for three years.[17] If one person caused another's death by an act of coercion, or if an official caused someone's death by inflicting a beating improperly (for

16 Ming code Article 319; Jiang, *The Great Ming Code*, p. 175; *Da Ming lü jijie fuli* 大明律集解附例 (Wanli ed. Reprint, Taipei: Taiwan xuesheng shuju, 1970) 4:1523–4. (Article numbers are taken from Jiang, *The Great Ming Code*, and appear in the on-line reprint of the Wanli code at: http://lsc.chineselegalculture.org/eC/DMLJJFL_1610/. They are not found in the print edition.).

17 Ming code Article 321; *Da Minglü jijie fuli*, 4:1529; Jiang, *The Great Ming Code*, p. 176.

instance on the back instead of the buttocks), the penalty for either of these offenses was 100 strokes plus the payment of 10 ounces of silver for the burial expenses.[18]

The idea of restoring a moral balance between private parties similar to that in the Yuan is contained in the Ming provision that if, thanks to an amnesty, a killer escaped the death penalty, he had to pay 20 ounces of silver to the family of the deceased, in other words, twice the usual amount of 10 ounces.[19] The seemingly harsh law of the Ming, with its many crimes punishable by severe beatings or execution, was considerably tempered by the fact that in many cases the sentences of criminals were commuted to monetary payments. But if a sentence for killing someone was commuted to a payment, the money went to the family of the victim as compensation. Thus if one person killed another by negligence or accidentally in play, the punishment was strangulation, the same as for killing someone in an affray, but the offender could redeem his sentence with a payment, and this payment went to the family of the victim to "arrange for the burial." A substatute in the code specified that the redemption for strangulation could be paid in copper cash instead of silver, and it specified the amount.[20] This was similar to the Yuan, which allowed payment in paper currency instead of silver.

As in the Yuan, Ming law also provided for medical expenses to be paid to a victim in cases of injury. If one person injured another accidentally through negligence or in play, the harsh beatings could be commuted to a payment, but the money went to the victim for "medical expenses" (*yiyao zhi zi* 醫藥之資).[21] If someone injured and incapacitated another person with some object or by depriving them of food or clothing, the offender would be punished with 100 strokes of the heavy stick and life exile to a distance of 3,000 *li*. In addition, they would have to give half of their property to the victim, for their "support" (*yangshan* 養贍).[22]

Qing law also adopted the practice of compensation; and as in the Yuan and Ming, it functioned as a way to restore moral equilibrium through private restitution. Like the Ming code, the Qing code prescribed restitution payments

18 Ming code Articles 322 and 437; *Da Minglü jijie fuli*, 4:1530–31, 5:2019–20; Jiang, *The Great Ming Code*, pp. 176, 237.

19 But if the offender was desperately poor, the amount was halved (back to 10 ounces). This provision is found in the substatutes (*tiaoli* 條例) appended to the Great Ming Code during the Wanli period; *Da Minglü jijie fuli*, 4:1512–13 (Article 315, *tiaoli* 1).

20 *Da Minglü jijie fuli*, 4:1513 (Article 315, *tiaoli* 2).

21 *Da Minglü jijie fuli*, 4:1507–8 (Art. 315); Jiang, *The Great Ming Code*, p. 174.

22 *Da Minglü jijie fuli*, 4:1504 (Art. 314); Jiang, *The Great Ming Code*, p. 173.

only in cases where the killer was not executed. The Qing code closely resembled the Ming code in many of its articles, and many of the Ming statutes specifying compensation are found verbatim in the Qing code. If one person killed another by driving carriages and horses too fast, or if a hunter killed someone in a trap or with an unattended springbow, the punishments were the same as in the Ming code (100 strokes accompanied by life exile to 3,000 *li* or three years penal servitude respectively), and the wrongdoer had to pay 10 ounces of silver to the family of the deceased "for burial expenses."[23] If death resulted from an "act of coercion" or by an official administering punishments incorrectly, the Qing code again prescribed the same sanction of 100 strokes of the heavy stick and the payment of 10 ounces of "silver for burial expenses" (埋葬銀).[24] The wording of each of these statutes was identical in the Ming and Qing codes, though in the latter case, the Qing code adds the clarification that the payment is to be made to the "family of the deceased" and that the person who administered the improper beating was to be punished one degree less than the official and did not have to pay the burial expenses. In other words, the compensation was assessed only once for the crime. As in the Ming code, if someone caused another to be incapacitated by an object or by depriving them of food or clothing, they would be punished with 100 strokes of the heavy stick and life exile to 3,000 *li*, and in addition would have to give half of their property to the victim, for their "support" (*yangshan* 養贍).[25]

Just like the Ming code, the Qing code stated that if an amnesty allowed the killer to escape execution, he had to pay 20 ounces of silver to the family of the deceased, double the usual amount.[26] If one person killed or injured another but had his sentence commuted to a monetary payment, this payment would go to the family of the victim for "burial or medical expenses" (營葬及醫藥之資).[27] In his famous commentary on the Qing code, the legal scholar Xue Yunsheng 薛允升 (1820–1901) noted that these payments began in the Yuan as *shaomaiyin* and were adopted into the Qing code from that of the Ming.[28] He thus acknowledged the Mongol–Yuan origins of the practice.

23 *Duli Cunyi* 讀例存疑, comp. Xue Yunsheng 薛允升, 5 vols. (1907; rpt. Taibei: Chinese Materials and Research Aids Service Center, 1970) [hereafter cited as DLCY]; 4:868, 869 (Articles 296, 298); William Jones trans., *The Great Qing Code* (Oxford: Clarendon Press, 1994) pp. 281–2.

24 DLCY 4:870, 5:1276 (Art. 299, 413); Jones, *Great Qing Code*, pp. 282, 395.

25 DLCY 4:845 (Art. 291); Jones, *Great Qing Code*, pp. 276–7.

26 DLCY 4:849 (Art. 292, substatute 01). The substatute also repeats the Ming substatute that if the killer was extremely poor, the payment was halved.

27 DLCY 4:849 (Art. 292); Jones, *Great Qing Code*, pp. 278–9.

28 DLCY 4:850.

Both the Ming and Qing codes included a prohibition against accepting private settlements in cases of homicide.[29] Compensation payments went to private parties, but they were still controlled by the state. There was no return to a system of private agreements.

On the whole, the Qing code followed the Ming in prescribing compensation payments, but the Qing code includes additional prescriptions and circumstances for the payment of compensation that were not found in the Ming. Many of these involve cases where the convicted offender was allowed to redeem his or her sentence with a monetary payment. In all the cases the payment went to the victim's family. If an incompetent physician accidently killed a patient, he would be allowed to redeem his death sentence with a payment that went to the victim's family.[30] In the case of killing with carriages and horses, the Qing code adds a provision not recorded in the Ming code, that if an official hurrying on official business killed someone, he could have his sentence commuted with the payment going to the victim's family.[31] If one person killed another accidentally by shooting an arrow into a residential area, or by tossing stones or bricks, they were punished with 100 strokes and exile to 3000 *li*, as in the Ming code. But the Qing code adds that they must pay 10 ounces of "silver for burial expenses" (*maizangyin* 埋葬銀), a provision not found in the Ming.[32] A large body of case law in the Qing addressed the issue of compensation payments, including the amount of these payments and under what circumstances they applied or could be waived. Superior judges sometimes censured lower courts for not adequately addressing the issue of compensation.[33] It is not clear if this additional attention in Qing law to the practice of compensation seen in the historical record is merely a function of the more detailed sources we have for the Qing or if the Qing did indeed apply compensation more widely than did the Ming. It is possible that the Manchu rulers were familiar with it from their own steppe heritage and applied it more liberally than in the Ming, but such a conclusion will have to await further research.

---

29 *Da Minglü jijie fuli*, Art. 323; Jiang, *The Great Ming Code*, p. 177; DLCY 4:884 (Article 300); Jones, *Great Qing Code*, 283.

30 DLCY 4:869 (Article 297); Jones, *Great Qing Code*, 281.

31 DLCY 4:868 (Article 296); Jones, *Great Qing Code*, 281.

32 DLCY 4:867 (Article 295); Jones, *Great Qing Code*, 280–1.

33 See examples in Derk Bodde and Clarence Morris, *Law in Imperial China, Exemplified by 190 Ch'ing Dynasty Cases* (Harvard University Press, 1967), pp. 338–341. The judgments in these cases reiterate that the payment of compensation applied only when the punishment was other than execution.

2 Inheritance Law

The principle of compensation or private redemption introduced by the Mongols and incorporated into Chinese imperial law parallels similar influences that the Mongols had on inheritance law. The Tang code outlawed the division of family property as long as the parents were alive, and the establishment of separate household registration of parents and children. The punishment was three years of penal servitude.[34] The Mongols, however, had a very different tradition of inheritance. In a Mongol family, a grown son upon his marriage would move out of his parents' home and with his new wife establish a separate household. At this time, the son would receive a portion of his father's assets, usually in the form of animals. Only the youngest son would stay in the household of his parents, and he could expect to inherit the remainder of his father's property and all of his mother's assets.[35] The Jurchen Jin followed similar customs. The Taihe code of the Jin prescribed different inheritance laws for the Chinese and for Jurchen and other steppe peoples. Jurchens and other non-Chinese were allowed to register separate households while the parents were alive, but Chinese were not.[36] Inheritance law was an area where unified laws eluded the Jurchen Jin dynasty.

In contrast to the Jurchen, the Mongols unified inheritance law for all peoples. In the seventh month of 1271, the newly constituted Secretariat for State Affairs (*Shangshusheng* 尚書省) issued a ruling that legalized, for all peoples, family division and separate registration of households while the parents were still alive.[37] The Secretariat for State Affairs was only in existence during limited periods of Yuan rule and was generally staffed by Mongols and Inner Asians; thus it is no coincidence that the ruling came from their office. The Censorate, a branch of government usually staffed by native Chinese, objected to the ruling, which violated the provisions of the Tang code and went against Confucian precepts of filial piety. But the Censorate was overruled. The Ming and Qing adopted this provision and allowed pre-mortem family division if the parents agreed, and that remained the law into the twentieth century. Already in the Yuan, the change in the law may have reflected social and economic

---

34 *Tanglü shuyi* 12:236 (Article 155).

35 See my discussion in Bettine Birge, *Women, Property and Confucian Reaction in Sung and Yüan China (960–1369)* (Cambridge: Cambridge University Press, 2002), chap. 4; and Jennifer Holmgren, "Observations on Marriage and Inheritance Practices in Early Mongol and Yüan Society," *Journal of Asian History*, 20:2 (1986).

36 YDZ 17:12a.

37 YDZ 17:12a.

developments in society. From Song times on, increasing commercialization and mobility made it harder for families to stay together until the death of the parents.

The Mongol reconceptualization of inheritance law also affected the transmission of property, especially to daughters. The Mongols instituted new inheritance laws that made it harder for daughters to receive property, either as dowry or in family division. These new laws reflected Mongol practices of taxation and military service that were quite different from Chinese administrative practices in the Song and before. Song taxation, following the Tang and earlier dynasties, was based primarily on quotas of grain and cloth levied on parcels of land, each registered in the name of a particular household.[38] When a family divided, each plot of land was reregistered under the name of the new household head. In the same way, when a daughter inherited land as part of her dowry, a common occurrence in Song China, this land was registered in the name of the household into which she married (though it was marked as dowry property and still under control of the daughter and her husband). If a couple had no sons, upon their death their household was considered "extinct" and any property could be inherited by their daughters, after funeral expenses were paid. Over the course of the Song dynasty, a series of changes in the law resulted in stronger rights of daughters to their parents' property in extinct households at the expense of agnatic relatives or a posthumously adopted heir who could rescue a household from extinction. As long as land remained on the tax registers, Song law freely allowed land to pass to daughters who took it into a new household at marriage, and it did not prioritize keeping households from going extinct.[39] Military service in the Song was not tied to land holding; rather, career soldiers paid by the government staffed the Song armies.

The Mongol rulers of the Yuan, following steppe traditions, conceived of taxation and military service quite differently than Chinese governments in the Song and earlier had done. Mongol taxation from early in the formation of their state was based on people and households rather than parcels of land, as appropriate to a non-farming, nomadic population. Somewhat later in the dynasty a land-based tax was introduced, but goods and services essential to the workings of government continued to be levied on households and people, rather than land. Most importantly, the Mongols sustained their fearsome

38 The Song levied commercial and other taxes as well, which became more important sources of revenue as the dynasty went on, but the basic tax was still a land-based tax assessed on farmers.

39 For a detailed study of this rather complicated inheritance regime and its effects on daughters, see Birge, *Women, Property and Confucian Reaction*, chap. 2.

armies through a system of hereditary soldier households, which each had to supply and equip one able-bodied male for military service at all times. The Yuan implemented this policy in China, classifying households as either civilian or military. Military households comprised between a third and a seventh of all households in any one district.[40] In addition, the Mongol rulers established more than eighty hereditary occupational households among the civilian population who each owed products and services to the court. These included such diverse professions as goldsmiths, falconers, weavers, or wine makers, and a disparate and elaborate bureaucracy in the capital Dadu was developed to maintain them and requisition products and services from them.[41] In this way, tax revenues, essential services, and the Yuan military establishment were all dependent on the continuation of designated households. If a household went extinct, it would be lost to the registers, and the goods and services it provided would be lost to the government.

Song laws that allowed households with no sons to become extinct and daughters to inherit their property contravened Yuan priorities and threatened to undermine the foundations of the state. Accordingly, the Yuan instituted new inheritance laws, unprecedented in Chinese history, that deprived daughters of inheritance in extinct households unless they invited in an uxorilocal husband (i.e. a husband who resided with the wife's family) who could rescue the household from extinction and take on the military or other corvée duties owed to the state.[42] New laws also established that an agnatic nephew, who by previous Chinese law could inherit in an extinct household, could only receive property if he could take on the military or other service obligations of the household. The rulings applied specifically to both military and civilian households.[43] Taken together, these new inheritance laws reduced inheritance of daughters and prioritized keeping households intact. They also tied the transmission of property to a male line of succession to a much greater extent than had Tang and Song law. The latter coincided with Confucian ideals of patrilineality, which Confucian reformers in the Ming were to capitalize on.

---

40 On military households, see Chen Gaohua 陳高華, "Lun Yuandai de junhu" 論元代的軍戶, *Yuanshi luncong* 元史論叢 1 (1982), pp. 72–90; Hsiao Ch'i-ch'ing, *The Military Establishment of the Yüan Dynasty* (Cambridge, Mass.: Harvard U.P., 1978).

41 For a good overview, see Huang Qinglian 黃清連, *Yuandai huji zhidu yanjiu* 元代戶計制度研究 (Taibei: Guoli Taiwan daxue wenxue yuan, 1977).

42 YDZ 19: 8b–9a, 9a–b, 10b–11a.

43 YDZ 17:13a; *Tongzhi tiaoge jiaozhu* 通制條格校注, punct. and annot. by Fang Linggui 方齡貴 (Beijing: Zhonghua shuju, 2001) [hereafter cited as TZTG] (Article 26) 3:117.

Ming law incorporated the basic features of Yuan inheritance law and the steppe-influenced concepts behind it. The Ming continued to allow family division while the parents were alive, thus breaking with Tang and Song law and adopting Yuan practices. The Ming also continued the institution of hereditary soldier households, and, following the Yuan, they instituted policies that ensured a male heir and the continuance of these households generation after generation. Property in households without sons no longer went to daughters. Instead, the law required that lineage elders designate an agnatic male relative as heir who could take on the military and other service obligations of the household. Ming law further designated a line of succession starting with an agnatic nephew and extending out to more distant agnatic male relatives. Natal daughters were left out of this inheritance scheme and could only inherit under rare circumstances when no agnatic relatives could be found.[44] The Ming founder Zhu Yuanzhang criticized the Mongols and claimed that he was re-establishing laws to uphold Confucian values, but the influence of the Yuan and concepts derived from steppe practices are unmistakably evident in Ming law.

The Qing also carried on Yuan and Ming legal developments in inheritance law. Qing law allowed family division before the death of the parents, and it continued policies that favored the continuance of households through male heirs. Moreover, it facilitated posthumous agnatic adoption by allowing an heir to succeed to two family lines. In Ming law (and earlier Chinese law), an heir had to renounce any inheritance from his natal family and owed sacrifices and mourning obligations only to his adoptive parents.[45]

3 Marriage Law

Finally, a third broad area where Mongol rule left a distinct mark on Chinese law of later dynasties is marriage law. I have written extensively on this subject elsewhere, but a brief summary is warranted here.[46] Marriage law proved the

44 *Ming huidian* 明會典 (Wanli edn.; rpt. Beijing: Zhonghua shuju, 1989.), 19:130; and *Da Ming ling* 大明令, in Zhang Lu 張鹵, ed., *Huang Ming zhishu* 皇明制書, 6 vols. (rpt. Taibei: Chengwen chuban she, 1969) 1: 6b–7b (vol. 1, pp. 20–21). Edward Farmer, *Zhu Yuanzhang and Early Ming Legislation: the Reordering of Chinese Society Following the Era of Mongol Rule* (Leiden: E. J. Brill, 1995), pp. 159–160.

45 DLCY 2:248 (substatute 078–05).

46 The conclusions that follow are drawn from Bettine Birge, "Levirate Marriage and the Revival of Widow Chastity in Yüan China." *Asia Major* 8:2 (1995), pp. 107–146; Birge,

most intractable for the Liao and Jin in trying to reconcile the customary law of steppe peoples and the codified law of Chinese dynasties. In particular, the Khitans and the Jurchen, like steppe peoples across Inner Asia, practiced the levirate, whereby a widow could be forced to marry a younger male relative of her deceased husband. The Khitan never tried to apply the levirate to sedentary populations under their control, and the Taihe code of the Jin explicitly forbade Chinese and Bohai from practicing the levirate.[47] Initially, the Yuan emperors allowed the Taihe code of the Jin to remain in effect and applied different marriage laws to different ethnic groups. This proved unworkable over time, however, and Khubilai Khan repeatedly voiced his discontent with applying different laws to different peoples, however vaguely defined.[48]

Then at the end of 1271, just one month after he abrogated the Taihe code of the Jin, Khubilai declared levirate marriages legal for all peoples in the realm.[49] This generated much confusion and a flood of lawsuits, as widows and their families went to court to prevent forced levirate marriages, especially when these violated other aspects of Chinese marriage law, such as when the levir already had a wife, was underage, or when the marriage was over the objections of either the wife's or husband's parents. After an initial period of harsh enforcement of the levirate, the Yuan government began to issue various exceptions to the levirate, especially when it violated traditional Chinese law. In the process, they established a new provision that if a widow chose to remain chaste and not remarry at all, she could escape a levirate union. But if she backed out of her chastity vow, she could be forced to marry an eligible levir. This coincided with an exception to the levirate practiced by Mongols themselves. Elite Mongol women had always been able to resist levirate unions

---

Women, Property and Confucian Reaction, esp. chap. 4; and Bettine Birge, "Women and Confucianism from Song to Ming: the Institutionalization of Patrilineality," in *The Song-Yuan-Ming Transition in Chinese History*, ed. Paul Smith and Richard von Glahn (Cambridge, Mass.: Harvard U.P., 2003), pp. 230–240. See these works for full citations and documentation. I repeat only a few of the major sources in the summary here.

47 *Jinshi* 6:144. The Bohai were a sedentary peoples residing mainly in the border area of Korea and Manchuria.

48 Some of the difficulty faced by the state in trying to define a person's ethnic identity can be surmised from the sources, which reveal the fluidity of identity, as people in north China at this time adopted Mongol or Chinese names, borrowed customs from each other, or married across cultural and linguistic lines. For an example of this cultural borrowing and identity shifting, see Nancy Steinhardt, "Yuan Dynasty Tombs and Their Inscriptions: Changing Identities for the Chinese Afterlife," *Ars Orientalis* 37 (2007): 138–172.

49 YDZ 18:23a.

and stay as the head of their households if they refused to remarry at all. This tradition was now applied to the Chinese.

Over the course of two decades beginning in 1299, the Yuan instituted a series of laws that promoted widow chastity and severely restricted the right of widows to remarry. These laws stripped widows of personal autonomy and property rights that Chinese law of previous dynasties had granted them, and they introduced into Chinese law a new understanding of the rights of widows and their natal families. In 1299, the Ministry of Rites barred widows of officials serving in the far south from remarrying and forced them to return north to their in-laws with their dowry property. In 1303, the Ministry forbade widows from taking their dowry property home or into a remarriage. They had to leave it behind for the parents of their first husband. Rulings in 1304 offered rewards for widow chastity. Local officials were ordered to offer support to indigent chaste widows, and new rules granted special door insignia and exemption from corvée labor to households with chaste widows. The new provision also defined a "chaste widow" as someone widowed before the age of thirty who vowed to remain chaste and had attained at least the age of fifty. The most dramatic ruling came in 1309, under the steppe-raised Emperor Kaishan (Wuzong r. 1308–11). It ordered widows to stay in the home of their late husband and prevented them from returning to their natal family. It also gave a woman's in-laws the authority to contract a remarriage for her and keep any betrothal gifts received.[50]

Each of these rulings made Chinese law more consistent with Mongol marriage practices. Upon marriage, a Mongol wife transferred her person and property to the camp of her husband and would have little future contact with her natal family. If widowed, she would not anticipate returning to her natal home or remarrying outside of a levirate union. This contrasted sharply with previous Chinese law and practice. Widows and divorcées in the Song and earlier dynasties overwhelmingly returned to their natal families, often with children in tow, and from there usually contracted remarriages. Chinese law in all earlier Chinese dynasties gave widows strong legal rights to remarriage. Widows and divorced women could take all of their dowry property out of a marriage and into a remarriage, and they themselves or their natal parents had the right to contract a remarriage and keep any betrothal gifts paid by the new husband. The husbands' parents could not prevent a widow from remarrying and had no part in the negotiations. The new Yuan laws of the early fourteenth century exactly contradicted these practices and introduced a new marriage

50 For each of these rulings, see YDZ 18: 15b–16a, 21b–22a, 13a–b, 14a–b, 19a–b; and TZTG (Article 49) 3:148.

regime into Chinese law. These greatly reduced a woman's personal autonomy and financial independence found in traditional Chinese law.

At the same time, however, the new laws overlapped with concerns about widow chastity that were emerging among the Chinese elite. Fundamentalist Confucian reformers, called Neo-Confucians, in particular had from Song times on promoted widow chastity in harsh terms and advocated laws to support it. The Neo-Confucian pioneer Cheng Yi 程頤 (1033–1107) famously declared that it was better for a widow to starve to death than to remarry, and the pre-eminent Neo-Confucian philosopher Zhu Xi 朱熹 (1130–1200) included Cheng Yi's severe dictum in his foundational anthology *Reflections on Things at Hand*.[51] But Neo-Confucians of the Song found their efforts thwarted by long entrenched laws and practices. The expectation in the Song that a young widow would remarry was so pervasive that the pre-eminent Neo-Confucian philosopher Zhu Xi, while promoting widow chastity as an ideal, admitted that it might not be feasible to practice in all cases.[52] Nevertheless, some of Zhu Xi's followers took a harder stance. Most vocal was Zhu Xi's son-in-law Huang Gan 黃幹 (1152–1221), who strenuously tried to promote widow chastity through his legal judgments and lamented that the law did not support him in the endeavor. Huang Gan was unsuccessful during the Song, but followers of Huang Gan's brand of Neo-Confucianism, such as Xu Heng 許衡 (1209–1281), were active at the Mongol court.[53] The new laws nicely converged with the Neo-Confucian agenda of promoting widow chastity even as they introduced into Chinese law a new concept of marriage that, following Mongol custom, represented a fundamental change in how the law viewed the rights of widows and their natal families. The introduction of the levirate by the Mongols and the chaos and instability in marriage law that it created allowed for a rethinking of fundamental values and an opportunity for major changes in Chinese marriage law. The Yuan eventually outlawed the levirate for Chinese in 1330,

---

51 *Henan Chengshi yishu* 河南程氏遺書, in *Er Cheng quanshu* 二程全書 (Sibu beiyao ed.), 22B:3a; Wing-tsit Chan, trans., *Reflections on Things at Hand; The Neo-Confucian Anthology* (New York: Columbia University Press, 1967), p. 177.

52 *Zhuzi yulei* 朱子語類 (Beijing: Zhonghua shuju, 1986) 96:3928; Wing-tsit Chan, *Reflections on Things at Hand*, p. 179. See also discussion in Bettine Birge, "Chu Hsi and Women's Education." In *Neo-Confucian Education: the Formative Stage*, ed. Wm. T. de Bary and J. Chaffee (Berkeley: Univ. of California Press, 1989), pp. 339–41.

53 Wm. Theodore de Bary, *Neo-Confucian Orthodoxy and the Learning of the Mind and Heart* (New York: Columbia U.P., 1981), p. 55ff. For Huang Gan's influence, see also Wing-tsit Chan, "Chu Hsi and Yüan Neo-Confucianism," in *Yüan Thought: Chinese Thought and Religion under the Mongols*, ed. Hok-lam Chan and Wm. Theodore de Bary (New York: Columbia University Press, 1982), pp. 197–231.

but the new laws promoting widow chastity and attaching women more fully to their marital families remained. As in the case of penal law and inheritance law, the interlude of Mongol rule resulted in a new synthesis of Chinese and Mongol marriage law.

The most important of the new laws of the Yuan were all incorporated into Ming and Qing law, sometimes copied verbatim. These included the provision that a widow leave her dowry behind if she left her late husband's home, that households with chaste widows be given exemption from corvée labor and other rewards, and that a wife's in-laws could control her remarriage and keep any betrothal gifts.[54] The Ming and Qing governments steadily augmented the rewards given to households with chaste widows, and over the centuries after the Yuan, the cult of widow chastity grew and flourished in Chinese society, reaching an extreme degree by the end of the Qing.

In the course of their Eurasian conquests, the Mongols faced the challenge of ruling peoples of many cultural and ethnic backgrounds. In China, they instituted a number of administrative policies that reflected ideas imported from the steppe. In the arena of law, the Mongols reworked aspects of penal law, inheritance law, and marriage law based on concepts they brought with them from the steppe. In each case, new laws broke with previous Chinese legal traditions and were based on concepts not previously found in Chinese legal practice. The law codes of the Ming and Qing absorbed these new concepts and continued the new policies of the Yuan in these areas. The Ming and Qing rulers loudly proclaimed their allegiance to timeless Confucian values and their intention of establishing laws to uphold and reinforce these. But a number of their laws represented a change in legal values and social ethics from those of the Tang and Song. These laws bear the unmistakable influence of Mongol rule and a reconceptualization of the basis of law incorporated into the Chinese legal tradition during the Yuan dynasty.

54 *Da Ming ling* 1:7a (vol. 1, p. 21); *Ming huidian*, 19:130; 79: 457; DLCY 4: 295 (Substatute 105-01).

CHAPTER 7

Celebrating War with the Mongols

David M. Robinson

Introduction

War with the Mongols was a formative experience for the Ming dynasty (1368–1644).[1] From the 1360s to the 1380s, Zhu Yuanzhang 朱元璋, the founding ruler who is commonly known as the Hongwu 洪武 emperor (r. 1368–98), ordered military campaigns against Mongol leaders first in north China, then on the steppe, in the forested hills and plains of Liaodong 遼東, and in the semi-tropical region of Yunnan 雲南 to the southwest. His son, Zhu Di 朱棣, the Yongle 永樂 emperor (r. 1403–24), personally led his armies into the steppe five times, a signature feature of his reign. Such campaigns were an enormous burden on the fledgling Ming dynasty, requiring massive commitments of manpower, administrative energy, financial resources, and political capital. The results were mixed. The Ming court expelled or coopted Mongol forces in north China, Liaodong, Yunnan, and the southern edge of the steppe. During the 1360s and again in the 1380s, Ming imperial armies inflicted serious defeats on the remnants of the Yuan court deep in the steppe but failed to eliminate Mongol polities in either the eastern or western Mongolian steppe. The Yongle emperor and his court claimed victories but seldom achieved decisive triumphs.

Given their significance, the Ming dynasty's conflicts with the Mongols have been one of the most thoroughly studied facets of the Ming period, as scholars have analyzed their implications for foreign policy, trade, border defense, logistics, political legitimacy, and perceptions of the Other.[2] Rather than replicate

1 I would like to acknowledge my gratitude to Joseph Lam who generously shared his expertise of Ming court music with me. I would especially like to thank Stephen West and Huang Ch'i-chiang for their detailed comments on the translations found in this paper. I have gratefully adopted nearly all their suggestions. I am responsible for any remaining errors and infelicities.

2 A modest sampling of relevant scholarship with an emphasis on the Hongwu and Yongle reigns includes Dreyer, *Early Ming China*, pp. 71–76, 140–43, 173–82; Waldron, *The Great Wall of China*, pp. 55–86; Rossabi, "The Ming and Inner Asia," pp. 224–31.

 | DOI 10.1163/9789004343405_009

such work, this essay explores how the early Ming court represented its wars against the Mongols in prose, poetry, and music.

The Hongwu Emperor's Court

From the dynasty's earliest days, celebration of military victory through music and dance formed an integral element of court life; official guidelines detailed performances at state banquets.[3] Groups of musicians and dancers were arrayed to the right and left of the emperor's dais. Titles included the Dance of Pacifying the Realm 平定天下之舞, which symbolized the "suppression of rebellion through military merit," the Dance of Soothing Foreign People of the Four Quarters 撫安四夷之舞, which symbolized "inducing men from afar to submit through awe and virtue," and the Dance of the Eight Foreign Peoples Submitting Treasures 八蠻夷獻寶之舞.[4] Such performances were to remind audiences of military force's importance in establishing the dynasty, forging order from chaos, and winning recognition from surrounding neighbors. Yet judging by the titles, they did not explicitly or exclusively focus on victories over the Mongols.

More open references to war with the Mongols are found in the tunes (*qu* 曲) that accompanied state banquets. As one facet of a comprehensive court protocol related to ritual and music instituted in 1370, the throne ordered that nine tunes be performed at court audiences. Several of them invoke victory over the Mongols but with a clear emphasis on accepting surrendered Mongols into the new polity. The first of the nine is entitled "Rising in Linhao" 起臨濠, Linhao being the hometown of the Ming founder.

---

3 Standaert, "Ritual Dances and Their Visual Representations." For the importance of music at the Ming court as both an instrument of orthodoxy and a vehicle of expression, see Lam, *State Sacrifices and Music in Ming China*. On martial rituals, including military tunes and processions, during the Ming, see Ren, *Ming Qing junli yu junzhong yongyue yanjiu*, pp. 17–72.

4 "Da yan yi" 大宴儀, "Yan li" 宴禮, in Shen Shixing, compiler, *Da Ming hui dian*, 72.1a–3b, vol. 2, pp. 1151–52; Zhang Tingyu, compiler, *Ming shi* (henceforth cited as MS), *juan* 61, p. 1503 志第三十七樂一. These guidelines seem to have been first established in 1370. See *Ming Taizu shilu*, 56.8a–16b, pp. 1101–14 洪武三年九月乙卯. The Dance of Martial Virtue 武德之舞 figured in most major ritual offerings at court including sacrifices at the round-mount-altar compound (圜丘), at the imperial ancestral temple (太廟), and sacrifices to the sun (朝日).

Once in a thousand years, China gives birth to a sage ruler.	千載中華生聖主
The aura of kingship creates dragons and tigers.[5]	王氣成龍虎
He hefted his sword to rise up west of the Huai River.	提劍起淮西
His commanders were brave and his troops stalwart.	將勇師雄
In a hundred battles they brought to heel powerful caitiffs.	百戰收強虜
Spurring their steads through cold winters and hot summers, in their mounts, they endured the hardships of war.	驅馳鞍馬經寒暑
Commanders and soldiers shared the sweet and the bitter.	將士同甘苦
One after another, they settled the wind-blown dust [of war].	次第靜風塵
They eliminated the cruel and brought security to the people.	除暴安民
Their accomplishments are like those of Kings Tang and Wu.[6]	功業如湯武[7]

This song refers to the Mongols only in passing as the powerful caitiffs who are brought to heel by Zhu Yuanzhang's generals. The verb *shou* 收 can also mean to induce into surrender 首服/收伏. In such a reading, the power of the Ming armies is not diminished, but the relationship between the Mongols and the Ming throne becomes less adversarial. The emperor and his troops are a moral force that brings the Mongols within the fold of civilization.

The battle with the Mongols figures slightly more prominently in the second song, entitled "Inaugurating Peace" 開太平之曲名風雲會.[8]

5 Dragons and tigers are cliché phrases for two things: lord/minister and heroes/eminences; this creates the idea that true rulers and true heroes emerge together; what makes a ruler great is (in addition to the civil virtues) his ability to rise to military occasions. My thanks to Stephen West for pointing this out to me.

6 Known as sage rulers of antiquity, Tang founded the Shang dynasty and King Wu the Zhou dynasty with, it was widely held, the support of both Heaven and the people. See "Ge" 革, *Zhou yi* 周易, translated by James Legge. "Tang changed the appointment (of the line of Xi? to the throne), and Wu (that of the line of Shang), in accordance with (the will of) Heaven, and in response to (the wishes of) men. Great indeed is what takes place in a time of change." 湯武革命, 順乎天而應乎人, 革之時大矣哉!

7 *Ming Taizong shilu*, 56.11b, p. 1108, 洪武三年九月是月; "Di wu zou Ping you du" 第五奏平幽都, "Jiu zou yue ge" 九奏樂歌, "Chao hui yue" 朝會樂, Xu Yikui, *Da Ming ji li, juan* 53 *xia* 下, pp. 52–1; "Yue kao wu" 樂考五, Wang Qi, *Xu Wen xian tong kao, juan* 157, p. 9601; MS, "Yue san" 樂三, "Yue zhang er" 樂章二, *juan* 63, p. 1560.

8 See Wang Qi, "Yue ge xia" 樂歌下, "Yue kao liu" 樂考六, *Xu Wen xian tong kao, juan* 158, p. 9690.

The jade fort gives a bird's view of the river city,	玉壘瞰江城
winds and clouds coil about the emperor's camp.	風雲繞帝營
[They] navigate towering ships, dragons and tigers course freely.	駕樓船龍虎縱横
The ballista stones were thrown, Driving off the Six Armored units.[9]	飛砲發機驅六甲
They induced caitiff generals to surrender, and defeated northern horsemen troops.	降虜將勝胡兵
Chatting and laughing, they control the great whale.	談笑掣長鯨
The brave spirits of the Three Armies grow.	三軍勇氣增
With a single warrior's garb, the cosmos is brought to peace.	一戎衣宇宙清寧
From this time onward, Hua and Yi, all revert to a single unified whole.	從此華夷歸一統
They inaugurate the dynastic enterprise; Celebrate the ascendant peace.[10]	開帝業慶昇平

During the Ming period, the word caitiff (*lu* 虜) often denoted Mongols or Jurchens. However, some writers also used caitiff as a derogatory reference to enemies of the Ming (including the pre-dynastic "Ming-in-the-making" years). For instance, one of the Ming founder's leading ministers, Song Lian 宋濂 (1310–81), repeatedly described Chen Youliang 陳友諒 (1320/21–1363), a warlord and rival to Zhu Yuanzhang in the 1350s and 1360s, as "Chen the caitiff" 陳虜.[11] The reference to "northern horsemen troops" 胡兵, however, does refer to the Mongols.

The fifth song relates the capture of the Yuan capital at Daidu, today's Beijing, and addresses Zhu Yuanzhang's victory over the Mongols in clear terms.

9 *Liu jia* 六甲 can mean "Six Periods," a form of occult knowledge used to manipulate space and time, often in a military context, but here seems to refer in a more generic sense to units of armored cavalry troops.

10 *Ming Taizong shilu*, 56.11a, p. 1108 洪武三年九月是月; Xu Yikui, "Di wu zou Ping you du" 第五奏平幽都, "Jiu zou yue ge" 九奏樂歌, "Chao hui yue" 朝會樂, *Da Ming ji li, juan* 53 *xia* 下; "Yue kao wu" 樂考五, *Xu Wen xian tong kao, juan* 157, p. 9601; MS, "Yue san" 樂三, "Yue zhang er" 樂章二, *juan* 63, p. 1561.

11 Song Lian, "Ping Jianghan song" 平江漢頌, *Luan po qian ji* 鑾坡前集, *juan* 1, in *Song Liang wenji*, vol. 1, p. 325. In the same essay, Song uses caitiff as an adjective to denote "enemy," for instance "caitiff general" 虜將, "caitiff plot" 虜計, even "caitiff grain" 虜食. For Chen Youliang, see Romeyn Taylor's note in Goodrich and Fang, *Dictionary of Ming Biography*, pp. 185–88; Mote, *Imperial China*, pp. 530–32.

Heavenly Fortune compels change, the caitiff's fortune shifts.	天運推遷虜運移
The royal army campaigns northward, To secure the Yanjing Capital Region.	王師北討定燕畿
One hundred years of rites and music, [this is] the day of revival.	百年禮樂重興日
Winds and clouds rise within the four seas, celebrating their time of assembly.[12]	四海風雲慶會時
They root out violence and cruelty, [And] soothe the suffering people.	除暴虐撫瘡痍
South of the steppe once more witnesses the former grandeur.	漠南重覩舊威儀
The ruler, with his sage virtue, forgives the surrendering caitiffs.	君王聖德容降虜
Members of the fallen dynasty, in caps and gowns, are permitted to bow to the jade dais.[13]	三恪衣冠拜玉墀

The nine songs performed at court audiences narrate the major landmarks in Zhu Yuanzhang's rise to the throne. They culminate with unification under the Ming, universal recognition by neighboring peoples and polities, and a vision of enduring peace and harmony in the world extending infinitely into the future. As Clifford Geertz and others have observed, court ritual is often an attempt to both represent and summon into existence an idealized order.[14] To acknowledge ongoing conflict with the Mongols would have subverted such an idyllic image of Ming rulership. Zhu Yuanzhang, now the Hongwu emperor, and his senior ministers, however, suffered no illusions about the intense rivalry between the Ming and Chinggisid ruling houses.

In fact, from 1368 to 1372, the Hongwu emperor repeatedly sent his armies into war with the rump Chinggisid court, which had established itself first in the city of Yingchang (located on today's Lake Taal in Inner Mongolia) and

12 An assembly of wind and clouds refers to a meeting of ministers and their lord at a crucial moment. The implication here is that as a result of their successful meeting, the world has been ordered and all restored to their proper place in the moral and political order. My thanks to Stephen West for clarifying my understanding of the line.

13 *Ming Taizong shilu*, 56.11a, p. 1108 洪武三年九月是月; Xu Yikui, "Di wu zou Ping you du" 第五奏平幽都, "Jiu zou yue ge" 九奏樂歌, "Chao hui yue" 朝會樂, *Da Ming ji li, juan* 53 *xia* 下; "Yue kao wu" 樂考五, *Xu Wen xian tong kao, juan* 157, p. 9601; MS, "Yue san" 樂三, "Yue zhang er" 樂章二, *juan* 63, p. 1561.

14 Geertz, *Negara*, p. 13; Mote, "Yüan and Ming," p. 219; Robinson, "The Ming Court," p. 28.

then Qara-Qorum (near today's town of Kharkhorin in the northwestern corner of the Övörkhangai Province of Mongolia); he also dispatched envoys to the Chinggisid court's various affiliates in Liaodong, Yunnan, and Shaanxi. Having suffered several losses on the steppe and in Liaodong, for the next decade the Ming court halted major campaigns against the Mongols. Having consolidated domestic control and done much to fracture the internal cohesion of the Chinggisid court and its affiliates, in the 1380s, the Ming court renewed its military campaigns.

The fullest and most varied celebrations of war with the Mongols took the form of prose and poetry pieces composed by leading court ministers and occasionally the emperor himself. Such early Ming writers drew connections between victory over the Mongols and a wide variety of topics. In 1369, the Hongwu emperor waived taxes for several regions in north China, including Beiping, Henan, and Shanxi. In an imperial edict he explained the measure by recounting his rise from humble beginnings, his military triumphs over his rival warlords, and his consolidation of power in southern China.

> When We reflect that the Chinese should always be ruled by a Chinese sovereign, it is hard to believe that it has already been a hundred years since the occupation by the men of the northern horseriders. Because Heaven abhors the muddle-headed and dissipated, masses of heroes all arose simultaneously, and by this brought forth weapons and divisive contention and the people were cast into desperate straits. For this reason, We ordered the generals to campaign northward. When the army crossed the Yellow River, the people of Qi and Lu greeted them with joy and supplied grain to the troops undeterred by thousands of *li*. We recall that during the Yuan's last years, those people were exhausted from supplying provisions. When We recall that they have expressed their loyal obedience, how could We bear to burden them again? 重念中國本我華夏之君所主豈意胡人入據已及百年天厭昏淫羣雄並起以致兵戈分爭生民塗炭是用命 將北征兵渡大河齊魯之民歡然來迎饋糧給軍不辭千里朕思其民當元之末疲于供給今既效順何忍復勞[15]

Here, the Hongwu emperor casts the triumph over the northern horseriders, that is the Yuan dynasty, as a joint enterprise between his armies and the people of north China, who volunteered their enthusiastic support to the restoration

15 Anonymous, *Huang Ming ben ji*, in Deng Shilong, compiler, *Guo chao dian gu, juan* 2, vol. 1, pp. 38–39. A slightly fuller version of this edict is found in *Ming Taizu shilu*, 38.10a–b, pp. 773–4 洪武二年正月庚戌.

of Chinese rule after a century of foreign occupation. That such an appeal to nativism was explicitly tied to material benefits, here tax waivers, reminds us that the early Ming court knew that it had to win the support and obedience of its subjects.

Another way to secure support and legitimacy for the fledgling Ming dynasty was to remind contemporary audiences that it enjoyed Heaven's special favor. In June 1370, the people of Baoji County 寶鷄縣 in Shaanxi 陝西 submitted a stalk of "auspicious wheat" to the throne.[16] The senior court minister, Liu Ji 劉基 (1311–75), explained the wheat's significance in the context of extended drought, crop failure, and cannibalism that had followed widespread warfare in north China during the 1360s, often instigated by men who claimed to be fighting on the Yuan dynasty's behalf. As Liu Ji wrote in his preface to his "Ode to Auspicious Wheat," "during the fourth month of this year, the imperial armies reported victory at Lanzhou; the northern steppe was swept clean; and Guanlong was pacified. Heaven then bestowed sweet rains, which nurtured auspicious signs. Harmonious essence (*qi* 氣) brings propitiousness to completion. Isn't this evident?"[17]

Liu Ji's poem reads in part:

The empire slipped from the house of Yuan like a fleeing deer;	元失其鹿
All the world joined in its pursuit.[18]	天下共逐
Chaotic and confused, one followed after another.	擾擾紛紛
The strong fed on the flesh of the weak.	強食弱肉
Great Heaven rose in wrath,[19]	皇天震怒

16 For the motives behind and representation of submitting auspicious plants and animals to the throne, see Schneewind, *A Tale of Two Melons*.

17 今年夏四月王師奏捷于蘭州朔漠掃清關隴底定天乃大降甘雨滋為嘉瑞和氣致祥不亦昭哉. Liu Ji, "Rui mai song (bing xu)" 瑞麥頌並序, *Liu Bo wen ji, juan* 10, vol. 1, p. 216. Liu Ji then observed that it had long been held that the last years of the Shang dynasty had been marked by successive years of drought and crop failure, whereas once King Wu established the new Zhou dynasty, Heaven bestowed bountiful harvests. "Viewing it from today," he pointed out helpfully, "truly there is no mistake," that is, the Ming was the present-day equivalent of the Zhou, the late Yuan the equivalent of the late Shang, the Hongwu emperor the direct successor to King Wu, and Toghan-Temür the fabled failed ruler Jie.

18 The line comes from the biography of Han Xin 韓信 in Sima Qian 司馬遷's *Records of the Grand Historian* 史記, translation Burton Watson, p. 199. In the original, it is the Qin that has lost the empire.

19 These lines echo a passage in the *Book of History*. Legge translates it as follows: "Great Heaven was moved with indignation, and charged my deceased father Wen to display

and bestowed its great mandate on the true lord,[20]	誕命真主
He solemnly takes Heaven's authority,	肅將天威
to pacify the realm.	以靖區宇
The cavalry troops are numerous like the clouds;	騎士如雲
the fierce generals are valorous like dragons.	猛將如龍
Commands and instructions issued	發蹤指示
all come from the emperor's mind.	悉出帝衷
Once he pacified the southeast,	既平南東
He then settled the northwest.	遂定西北
The people will long dwell in peace;[21]	民居攸奠
The myriad things all propagate.	品物咸殖

The victory at Lanzhou (today's Lanzhou, Gansu Province) refers to the Ming dynasty's successful defense of the border city in January 1370 when the powerful Yuan commander Köke-Temür (d. 1375) laid siege to the city.[22] At this time, the Ming did not fully control either Lanzhou or the northwest region more generally. Ming armies had taken Lanzhou only six months earlier in May 1369,[23] and in October one of Köke-Temür's generals, He Zongzhe 賀宗哲, had sacked the city.[24] In response, the leading Ming commander in the region, Xu Da 徐達 (1332–85), had dispatched a contingent of 17,000 infantry and cavalry

its terrors" 皇天震怒，命我文考，肅將天威. See "Tai shi shang" 泰誓上, *Zhou shu* 周書, *Shang shu* 尚書, in Legge, *The Shoo King*, Bk. 1, Pt. i, 6, p. 285. Liu Ji changes "charged my deceased father Wen" to "[bestowed its] great mandate on the true lord." See below.

20 *Dan ming* 誕命 appears to be an abbreviation of *dan shou jue ming* 誕受厥命. Legge translates the passages as follows: "The favour and help of great Heaven lighted upon him, and he grandly received its appointment…" 皇天眷佑，誕受厥命.

21 The line seems to derive from a passage in the *Book of History* related to establishing new beginnings and eliminating conflicts between the ruler and his subjects. It reads, 盤庚既遷，奠厥攸居，乃正厥位，綏爰有眾. Legge translates it, "Pan-geng having completed the removal (to the new capital), and settled the places of residence, proceeded to adjust the several positions (of all classes at an assembly); and then he soothed and comforted the multitudes." See Legge, "Pangeng xia" 盤庚下, Shang shu 商書, *Shang shu*, in Legge, *Shoo king*, Bk. VII, Pt. iii, p. 242. I thank Huang Ch'i-chiang for bringing the allusion to my attention.

22 For Köke-Temür's career, see John Dardess, Goodrich and Fang, *Dictionary of Ming Biography*, pp. 724–28.

23 *Ming Taizong shilu*, 41.5a, p. 823 洪武二年四月丁丑.

24 *Ming Taizong shilu*, 45.1b, p. 878 洪武二年九月甲午. He Zonghe's connections to Köke-Temür date back to the 1350s, when He fought under Chaghan-Temür, Köke-Temür's adoptive father. See Song Lian, compiler, *Yuan shi, juan* 45, p. 948 本紀至正十九年八月辛酉; *juan* 141, p. 3387 察罕帖木兒傳.

troops to bolster Ming control. Before the relief force arrived, He Zongzhe retreated, at which point the Ming contingent withdrew. Exploiting the continuing vulnerability of Lanzhou, Köke-Temür began his attack on Lanzhou in January 1370. Köke-Temür's armies intercepted a Ming relief column from the main Ming base in Gongchang 鞏昌 and dragged several officers to the walls of Lanzhou with the hope of persuading the defenders to surrender. Köke-Temür withdrew before Xu Da's army arrived,[25] but his men pillaged widely in the area.[26] To consolidate Ming control, in March 1370 the emperor ordered the establishment of Lanzhou Garrison 蘭州衛.[27]

When four months later, in July, rewards and promotions were announced for outstanding military service in the Shaanxi theater, the emperor referred explicitly to the "Victory of Lanzhou."[28] When, in November 1370, the Hongwu emperor sent a letter to Ayushiridara (1338–78), the new Chinggisid *qaghan*, he mentioned Lanzhou in a long list of Köke-Temür's military failures. This was an attempt to persuade Ayushiridara that further resistance was futile.[29] Just weeks later, in an edict to his commanders, the Hongwu emperor again referred to Lanzhou, stressing its strategic importance in the northwest. He praised Lanzhou's defenders. Their victory, the emperor declared, "greatly stirred up military might; the strength of the Yuan army gave out" 大振軍威，元兵力屈.[30]

The "Victory at Lanzhou" can hardly count as a major military success. Lanzhou's defenders (one of whom had been drunk on duty and failed to respond to Köke-Temür's initial assault)[31] allowed the city to be surrounded, were unable to inflict substantial casualties, and failed to break the siege. Although the imminent arrival of Xu Da's relief force ended the siege, Köke-Temür's army escaped without injury. In fact, just days after Köke-Temür's withdrawal, the Hongwu emperor decided he needed a better plan to neutralize continued

---

25 *Ming Taizong shilu*, 47.8a, p. 943 洪武二年十二月庚寅. Ming sources variously refer to He Zonghe as Grand Councilor of the Right 右丞 (Wang Shizhen 王世貞, compiler, "Bei lu shi mo zhi" 北虜始末志, in *Yanzhou shi liao* 弇州史料, 9.2), "Grand Councilor of the former Yuan" 故元平章 (*Ming Taizong shilu*, 35.3a, p. 631 洪武元年九月壬申), and "Supreme Commander of the former Yuan" 故元總制 (*Ming Taizong shilu*, 44.1a, p. 858 洪武二年八月甲子).

26 *Ming Taizong shilu*, 48.5a, p. 955 洪武三年正月癸卯.

27 *Ming Taizong shilu*, 51.9b, p. 1008 洪武三月四月丁丑; Tan Qian, *Guo que, juan* 4, vol. 1, p. 413 洪武三月四月丁丑.

28 *Ming Taizong shilu*, 53.10a, p. 1051 洪武三年六月庚辰.

29 *Ming Taizong shilu*, 57.3a, p. 1119 洪武三年十月辛巳.

30 *Ming Taizong shilu*, 58.7a, p. 1135 洪武三年十一丙申.

31 *Ming Taizong shilu*, 53.6a, p. 1043 洪武三年六月丙子.

Yuan military pressure—a two-prong attack against the Yuan; one was directed against Köke-Temür in the northwest and the other against the *qaghan* on the steppe.[32]

Put simply, Ming control over western Shaanxi was so precarious at this point that simply not to lose was a victory worth celebrating. Liu Ji directly attributed to "the victory at Lanzhou" not only enhanced control over the frontier but signs of Heaven's favor such as sweet rain and auspicious stalks of wheat in a county that was more than 350 kilometers away. The emperor may have dismissed Baoji County's offering as of little help to the area's starving people,[33] but he did use the events of Lanzhou as evidence of Ming military prowess and terminal Yuan decline.

If Lanzhou was a small moment in the early Ming court's war with the Chinggisids, the occupation of Yunnan was a milestone. Yunnan's ruler in the late fourteenth century was a descendant of Qubilai named Vajravarmi (also known as the Prince of Liang 梁王), who oversaw a loose confederation of small polities comprised mainly of Tibeto-Burmese-speaking peoples in Yunnan.[34] Vajravarmi remained allied to the Yuan dynasty after Toghan-Temür's flight from Daidu, continuing to mark time by the Yuan calendar, using Yuan reign periods rather those of the Ming court in everything from government orders to inscriptions in Buddhist halls. The Yunnan court periodically traded envoys with the Chinggisids on the steppe. After repeated, failed political overtures, in fall 1381, the Ming sent an army of more than 300,000 men against Vajravarmi, who was said to have been able to put a reputed 100,000 troops into the field. In the end, Ming forces prevailed. Early in 1382, Vajravarmi abandoned his seat, burned his garments of nobility, and committed suicide (with more than two hundred other members of his court) rather than surrender.[35]

The significance of the Ming victory over Vajravarmi and the conquest of Yunnan are often underappreciated. In the broader context of Eurasia, Yunnan sits at the intersection of East Asian, South Asian, and Southeast Asia cultural traditions. It had figured prominently in Silk Road trade. In geopolitical terms, the Mongols had shown Yunnan's importance to the Central Plains' security.[36]

---

32 *Ming Taizong shilu*, 48.1a, p. 947 洪武三年正月癸巳.

33 *Ming Taizong shilu*, 52.11a–b, pp. 1031–32 洪武三年五月丁巳; Tan Qian, *Guo que, juan* 4, vol. p. 417 洪武三年五月丁巳.

34 Vajravarmi is also known as Basalawarmi (Chin. Bazalawaermi 把匝剌瓦爾密). He appears in some Qing period sources as Batu 巴圖 (Mong. Batü).

35 Langlois, "The Hung-wu Reign," pp. 144–46.

36 Ueda Makoto, *Umi to teikoku*, pp. 123–26.

Thus, perhaps it is not surprising that Ming officials wove the emperor's latest success into the broader tapestry of dynastic triumphs against the Mongols. In his preface to a series of twelve military tunes dedicated to the rise of the Great Ming, the official Wang Shen 王紳 (1360–1400) observes that when the Ming founder vanquished the Mongol rulers of the Yuan dynasty in order to "cleanse the humiliation of recent generations" 以雪近代之恥, his accomplishments were in no way inferior to the storied sovereigns of high antiquity Tang and Wu.[37] The last of Wang Shen's twelve military tunes celebrated the Ming dynasty's victory over Varjarvarmi. Given that the original nine military tunes had been created in 1370, Wang Shen's work represented a new piece, albeit one explicitly in the mold of the original nine tunes. He entitled it "Pruning the Buds" 斮苞枿.

A giant tree once infested with insects,	巨木既蠹
Can be shaken and toppled at the root.	根本繇傾
When buds grow in profusion,	爰有萼枿
It can still avail itself of the last breath of life.	猶假息以生
The emperor said, "Take heart. Indulge Us.	皇曰肆哉
Do not resent Our armies.	毋讟我兵
[But rather] cause them to return of their own accord;	俾其自歸
Hopefully they will not harm Our people."	庶不戕我氓
[His Highness] repeatedly dispatched envoys with orders,	屢遣使命
Instructing [Vajravarmi] to [act in] perfect good faith.	諭以至誠
Foolish, they did not use the power of goodness,[38]	蠢茲弗靈
But indulged their benightedness.	恣其頑冥
The emperor rose majestic in his wrath;	皇赫斯怒
He marshaled his hosts for campaign.[39]	爰整旅以行
One million [warriors as brave as] bears and grizzlies;	熊羆百萬
[Fierce] like lightning, like thunder.	如雷如霆

---

37 Wang Shen, "Ni Da Ming rao ge gu chui qu shi er shou bing xu" 擬大明鐃歌鼓吹曲十二首 並序, in He Qiaoyuan, compiler, *Huang Ming wen zheng*, 6.1a (*Siku Quanshu cunmu congshu, ji* 328, p. 157).

38 This reading follows Legge. The expression "fu ling" 弗靈 is a derived from a line in the *Book of History*, 苗民弗用靈，制以刑, where 弗 means 匪 and 靈 means 命. Legge translates the line as "Among the people of the Miao, they did not use the power of goodness but the restraint of punishments." See Legge, "The Prince of Lu upon Punishments" 呂刑, Book XXVII, "The Book of Zhou" 周書, *The Shoo King*, p. 591.

39 These two lines are taken nearly verbatim from the *Book of Poetry*. I follow Legge's translation. See Legge, "Huang yi" 皇矣, "Wen wang zhi shi" 文王之什, Da ya 大雅, *The She king*, p. 453.

They tore through [the enemy like] rotten and withered wood.	摧朽拉枯
[They] were an awesome host.	烈烈轟轟
Once the caitiff chieftains had been annihilated,	虜酋既殲
the Cuan and Bo [of the southwest] were all pacified.	爨僰悉平
Near and far all come in submission to our superior transformative power;	遐爾歸化
all within the four seas have thus been made tranquil.	四海繇以寧[40]

The exiled Hanlin scholar Wang Jing 王景 (1336–1408) composed "Ode to the Pacification of Yunnan" 雲南頌.[41] His preface paints a scene of complete Ming military domination over the Mongols.

> Valorous officers and men numbered in excess of three hundred thousand. They announced [Vajravarmi's] crimes and undertook a campaign of chastisement. The towering ships blanketed the river and the war pennants filled the sky. They sped by like shooting stars as they advanced together in separate columns ... They were as fleet as blowing winds and falling rain, triumphing in every direction they headed. The Yuan troops huddled together like hives of bees and hills of ants; none dared oppose our forces.

---

40 Wang Shen, "Ni Da Ming rao ge gu chui qu shi er shou bing xu" 擬大明鐃歌鼓吹曲十二首 並序, in He Qiaoyuan, compiler, *Huang Ming wen zheng*, 6.6b–7a (*Siku Quanshu cunmu congshu, ji* 328, pp. 159–60). Other early Ming writers also composed additional military tunes to celebrate the military prowess of the imperial throne. Yang Weizhen 楊維楨 (1296–1370) wrote a series of thirteen such tunes entitled "Da Ming nao ge gu chui qu shisanpian" 大明鐃歌鼓吹曲十三篇, while Yang Shiqi 楊士奇 (1365–1444) wrote one to commemorate the Xuande emperor's skirmishes against a Mongol contingent. Yang Shiqi, "Ping hu nao ge gu chui ci you xu" 平胡鐃歌鼓吹辭, in *Huang Ming wen heng, juan* 2, p. XX. Educated men were fully familiar with the genre. As a young man, Song Lian had composed military tunes celebrating the rise of the founding Song emperor, Zhao Kuangyin 趙匡胤 (927–76), in twelve sections. Much of it was devoted to the Song founder's martial prowess and generalship. See Song Lian, "Song nao ge gu chui qu" 宋鐃歌鼓吹曲 in *Zheng ji ke ji bu* 鄭濟刻輯補, in *Song xue shi wen ji*, vol. 3, pp. 1868–72.

41 According to one funerary inscription, Wang Jing composed twenty military tunes 鐃歌 and one paean 頌 on Yunnan "to promulgate [the emperor's] sage virtue in order to celebrate his vast accomplishments" 鋪敭聖德以潤色鴻業. See Chen Lian, "Hanlin xue shi feng zheng da fu Chang zhuai Wang gong Jing mu zhi ming" 翰林院學士奉政大夫常齋王公景墓碑銘, in Jiao Hong, compiler, *Guo chao xian zheng lu*, 20.30a, vol. 2, p. 806.

> 虎狡之士，三十餘萬，聲罪致討，樓船蔽江，旌旗亙天，星流電邁，分道並進， 疾若風雨，所向克捷，元兵蜂屯蟻聚， 毋敢抗我師者。[42]

Wang Jing stresses that in contrast to all previous dynasties from the Han to the Yuan, which had imposed only "loose rein" governance on Yunnan, the Ming now "treated it as equal to the inner lands;" that is, it would be subject to the same administrative and cultural standards applied to the rest of the Ming polity. Such an "accomplishment surpasses that of antiquity," gushes Wang Jing. "True kings," Wang Jing reminds his readers, "consider nothing as external" 王者無外也.[43] Wang Jing here refers to a classical vision of rulership that highlights differences between the Chinese and barbarians yet holds that ultimately those barbarians would be integrated into the Chinese polity.[44] As we shall see again in the following section, Wang Jing and like-minded men frequently depicted Ming military success as the march of civilization against the benighted forces of savagery and ignorance.

The Yongle Emperor's Court

During the Yongle emperor's reign, the production and dissemination of literary celebrations of war with the Mongols appears to have increased. Such an impression is due in part to the larger number of surviving works from the early fifteenth century and to changing literary fashions at court, most noticeably the rise of the so-called Towers and Pavilions Style 台閣體. A large number of poems celebrated the presentation of tribute (especially exotic animals such as giraffes, lions, elephants) by foreign envoys and auspicious signs (such as Sweet Dew, propitious grains, the waters of the Yellow River running clear) as evidence of the emperor's superior virtue, universal recognition of the dynasty's legitimacy, and Heaven's support.[45] As Liu Ji's poem on the auspicious stalk of wheat discussed above makes clear, such themes were not

---

42 Wang Shen, "Ping Yunnan song" 平雲南頌, in Cheng Minzheng, compiler, *Huang Ming wen heng, juan* 20; He Qiaoyuan, compiler, *Huang Ming wen zheng*, 19.11b–15b (*Siku quanshu cunmu congshu, ji* 328, pp. 601–603).

43 The expression comes from the *Gongyang Commentary* 公羊傳 on the *Spring and Autumn Annals*. See the first year of Duke Yin 隱公元年.

44 The *Gongyang Commentary* observes, "The True Monarch wants to unify All under Heaven, so why talk of internal and external." Cited in Yuri Pines, "Limits of All-under-Heaven: Ideology and Praxis of Great Unity in Early Chinese Empire."

45 Ye, *Mingdai zhongyang wenguan zhidu*, pp. 51–80; Robinson, *Martial Spectacles*, pp. 76–82.

unprecedented, but the volume and variety of such celebratory poems does seem to have increased during the reign of the Yongle emperor. Perhaps most striking is the large corpus of poems and other celebratory accounts devoted to war from the Yongle reign.[46] Due to space limitations, below I offer a single illustrative example commemorating the Yongle emperor's first steppe campaign in 1410 against the powerful eastern Mongolian leader Arugtai, who ostensibly exercised power on behalf of his Chinggisid lord, Bunyashiri. "Ode to Pacifying the Northern Horsemen" 平胡頌 was composed by Yao Guangxiao 姚廣孝 (1335–1418), one of the Yongle emperor's most influential political advisors.[47] Yao first provides an extended preface that offers a political, military, and rhetorical contextualization of the campaign, its background, its highlights, and its triumphant conclusion. He then recapitulates the main points in a series of tripartite stanzas.

> Your minister has in the past heard that the Grand Progenitor, the August Emperor on High Who Unified Heaven and was of Great Filiality, Who was sagely in his Civil Accomplishment and Divine in his Martiality, Whose Reverence and Intelligence Inaugurated a New Era, and Who was of Overweening Virtue and Accomplished Merit[48] received Heaven's

46 Chen Xu 陳循 (1385–1462), Gao Deyang 高德暘 (1352–1420), Hu Guang 胡廣 (1370–1418), Hu Yan 胡儼 (1361–1443), Jin Shan 金善 (1371–1439), Wang Fu 王紱 (1362–1416), Yang Rong 楊榮, Yang Shiqi 楊士奇 (1365–1444), Zeng Qi 曾棨 (1372–1432) and others composed poems to celebrate the Yongle emperor's wars with the Mongols. See Robinson, *Empire's Shadow: The Ming Court in Eurasia*.

47 Yao Guangxiao 姚廣孝, "Hu Ping song" 胡平頌, in Chen Zilong, compiler, *Huang Ming jing shi wen bian*, 13.4a–7a, vol. 1, pp. 92–94. For the career of Yao Guangxiao (also known by his monastic name Daoyan 道衍), see Eugen Feifel and Hok-lam Chan in Goodrich and Fang, *The Dictionary of Ming Biography*, pp. 1561–65. The term *hu* 胡 may also be translated as foreign, foreigner, barbarian, northern barbarian, etc. In the context of the early Ming court's discussions of the steppe, *hu* was often used to refer to the Yuan ruling house and its descendants. "Ode to Pacifying the Northern Horsemen" is not included in Qing-period manuscript copies of Yao Guangxiao's poetry such as *Tao xu zi shi ji* 逃虛子詩集 held at Nanjing Library (*Siku quanshu cunmu congshu, ji* vol. 28) or *Tao xu zi shi bu yi* 逃虛子詩補遺 (*Xuxiu Siku quanshu, ji*, vol. 1326). Nor is it included in the Ming edition of *Du an wai ji xu gao* 獨庵外集續稿 (rpt. in the Liaoningsheng tushuguan guben shanben congkan 遼寧省圖書館孤本善本叢刊 series, rpt. Beijing: Xianzhuang shuju, 2003).

48 The Grand Progenitor 太祖 was a posthumous title for the Hongwu emperor. It was a common posthumous title for dynastic founders in East Asia. Many of the various attributes noted in the passage had their origins in classical works such as the *Book of History* but contemporary understanding of such terms needs further research. For instance, where I have translated the passage 聖神文武 "Who was sagely in his Civil Accomplishment and

intentions and ascended the throne. He pacified [all within] the four seas and accomplished the great unification. He invested territory to his sons so that they might serve as palisade princes for the royal family.[49] Oh! Our Grand Progenitor saw that His Majesty the Emperor early on possessed great wisdom and was imposing and decisive beyond other men and thereupon invested him in Yan.[50] The Grand Progenitor once told his ministers, "With Our prince now holding fast against the boreal steppe, We will have no worries from the north." For more than four decades, the heavens were clear and the earth was tranquil. That there was no dust flying from hooves of the northern horsemen was all due to the labors of the Emperor. In the *wuyin* year of the Hongwu reign (1398), when the Grand Progenitor became a guest of Heaven, the emperor succeeded to the grand throne.[51] He obeyed Heaven and followed the people; neighboring kingdoms of the four quarters looked up in admiration and were transformed. The nine barbarians came in submission.[52] They traversed mountains and crossed the seas;[53] not a day at court went by without someone presenting rhinoceros horn and ivory or offering precious stones and jade. The Three Armies and the myriad surnames were harmonious and bright. It was like the age of Tang and Yu.[54] Heaven and earth, spirits and deities, even insects and plant—there was none that was not pleased. His Majesty regularly resides within the nine-fold palace.[55] He expels the villainous and advances the worthy. He exalts virtue and believes in the Way. He takes the *Books of Poetry* and *History* as his palace; rites and music as his gardens; elegances of ceremony as his cap

Divine in his Martiality," Legge renders the original and slightly fuller articulation as "It is sagely, spirit-like, awe-inspiring, and adorned with all accomplishments" 乃聖乃神乃武乃文." "It" in the original passage refers to the virtue of Di, the High God. See Legge, "The Counsels of the Great Yu" 禹謨, Book II, Ch. I, 4, *The Shoo king*, p. 54.

49 Chen Zilong 陳子龍 (1608–47), the editor, comments at this point in the text, "He drew appropriately from the institutions of the previous dynasty."

50 Yan refers to the area in and around today's Beijing. Zhu Di was granted his investiture there in 1370 and took up residence there in 1380.

51 "became a guest of Heaven" is a euphemism for the emperor's death.

52 In this case, the nine barbarians was a generic reference to neighboring polities and peoples rather than nine specific groups.

53 I.e. they traveled great distances and endured great difficulties to present themselves at the Ming court.

54 Tang and Yu were two sage rulers of distant antiquity.

55 The nine-fold palace refers to the imperial palace.

and gown; benevolence and righteousness as his heart.[56] He is courteous and self-restrained, profoundly silent. He rectifies himself and faces southward.[57] The worthy kings of antiquity fall far short [of him]. Only these remnant horseriders of the north, these leftover villains obstinately refuse to be civilized and fail to present themselves at court. [Instead] they remain savage in the wastelands, brutally murdering each other with wild abandon. The emperor said, "Alas, these northern horserider caitiffs are born in the steppe, befuddled and ignorant. They have never heard a single good word or witnessed a single good deed.[58] Thus they fall in with the recalcitrant and are nourished by repugnant action. They simply wish to destroy this mandate. Deeply pitying them, We dispatched an envoy bearing an edict to pacify and instruct [them], wishing them to look into themselves, to change their repugnant ways, and to bring life to its fullness. Who could have anticipated that the northern horsemen thieves would not obey [Our] orders [but instead] detained and murdered Our envoys and plundered Our frontiers?" The emperor could not but be furious and thus told the court ministers, "The northern horsemen thieves are beast-like people. They do not understand rites and righteousness. They devote themselves exclusively to a perverse course. Their crimes cannot be pardoned. It is appropriate that We personally lead the Six Armies to attack them." The assembled officials thereupon bowed their foreheads to the ground and said, "These insignificant little north-

56 The *Book of History* and the *Book of Poetry* were two classical works familiar to all educated men. The expression *shi shu* 詩書 could also be read as a more generic reference to poems and letters.

57 The text as preserved in the *Huang Ming jing shi wen bian* reads 正已 *zheng yi*, which I take as a scribal error for 正己 *zheng ji*. As used by Mencius, the expression often carries the implication that by rectifying himself the superior man also rectifies others. "There are those who are great men. They rectify themselves and others are rectified." 有大人者，正己而百物正者. See Legge, "Jin xin shang" 盡心上, *The Works of Mencius*, Bk. VII, Pt. I, Ch. XX, p. 458; D.C. Lau, *Mencius*, Book VII, Part A, p. 185.

58 Mencius uses identical language to draw out the difference between the sage Shun and "the uncultivated man of the mountains." When Shun "heard a single good word, witnessed a single good deed, it was like water causing a breach in the dykes of the Yangtse or the Yellow River. Nothing could withstand it." 聞一善言，見一善行，若決江河，沛然莫之能禦也。See D.C. Lau, *Mencius*, Book VII, Part A, pp. 184–85. One possible reading would be that when placed in an inhospitable environment utterly devoid of good words or deeds, even a sage like Shun would seem little different from the uncultivated man of the mountains.

ern horsemen caitiffs are a villainous ilk;[59] they noisily posture in the inhabited territory. How could they understand the expanse of all under Heaven? If [Your Majesty] raises an army to attack them, how could they withstand our fearsome generals? We would that Your Majesty formulate strategy from within the nine-fold palace to secure victory ten thousand *li* away. This is sufficient unto itself. Given that frozen valleys and snow drifts are what people cannot endure, would it be appropriate for us to subject His Highness to such travails and to fatigue the royal person?" The emperor said, "Oh! What you ministers say is to love me over much. Have you not heard of Xuanyuan's victory over Chi You at Zhuolu?[60] We only know [that We must] kill rebels to bring peace to the realm. How could We mind the travails of campaign? Do not speak of this again." Thereupon he ordered the commanders to ready their armies and order the troops, regulate the beat of the drums that signal attack, prepare the ritual of stationing the feathered pennants at encampments, bore throughout mountains and to open roads, rush the delivery of grain and fodder, and when every single thing is prepared, select a day to set out. Thereupon on a spring day in the second lunar month of the *gengyin* year of the Yongle reign (1410), with a gentle eastern breeze, His Highness departed the nine-fold city and mounted the Six Dragon chariot.[61] The multitudinous deities led [the chariot] in front, and the ten thousand riders protected [the emperor] in the rear. The golden shields and carved dagger axes flashed against the sun. Feathered pennants and multi-colored banners blocked out the sky. How valiant the tiger soldiers! How grand the fish-scale formation! Once an order was issued, the soldiers competed to be the first to obey. They were careful to carry out assignments. They were unrushed but swift. In less than a month, they had already arrived in caitiff territory. The evil ones clamored and shouted; they had no place to flee. We occupied their dens and warrens and exterminated their foul kind. The number of captured horses, camels, cattle, and sheep was incalculable; we swept the boreal desert and washed clean the grassy wilds. The soldiers rolled up their armor, and the troops did not bloody their blades.[62]

---

59 Literally, "the category of foxes and pigs" 狐豕之類.

60 Xuanyuan was the personal name of the Yellow Emperor, a sage ruler of antiquity who defeated Chi You, depicted in many classical writings as a rebel, at Zhuolu, located south of today's Zhuolu County, Hebei Province. On the complex relation of the Yellow Emperor and Chi You, see Lewis, *Sanctioned Violence in Early China*, pp. 165–212.

61 The dragon was often closely associated with the emperor.

62 The soldiers rolled up their armor here means that the Mongols surrendered in defeat.

It was in truth the army of a true king.[63] It was without precedent in all antiquity. The edict of victory was issued, and the imperial chariot turned back. The mountains and streams were bright and clear; the elders and the black haired people competed to offer obeisances along the road. The moans and groans of the past were all transformed into songs of praise. The emperor mounted his belled chariot.[64] He ascended the Heavenly Gate. He took the axial position.[65] He reported at the Altar of Earth and the Ancestral Shrine.[66] Heaven moves in compliant order and sun is auspicious; deities and man and all celebrate. [When] in the past the Grand Progenitor invested the emperor in Yan to defend against the boreal steppe, who knew that there would be such clear proof [of his wisdom] today? In this way, how can the spirit of the Grand Progenitor in Heaven not be comforted and pleased? Your Majesty, such is your divine accomplishments and sagely virtue, that they should be recorded in historical annals, set to stringed instruments and song, and inscribed in stone and metal in order to pass down for ten thousand years. This is your minister's first duty. Your minister Guangxiao is ashamed to hold a post of letters. Although meager of talent and shallow in learning, without sufficiency to fully communicate magnificent accomplishments, how could I simply remain silent? Thereupon [I] composed an ode, which I present with one hundred obeisances. The ode reads:

> 臣昔聞太祖聖神文武、欽明啟運、俊德成功、統天大孝高皇帝，繼天立極，平定四海，成大一統，分封諸子，以蕃王室。繄我太祖，見皇帝陛下蚤具大智，雄武英斷，出於人上，遂封於燕。太祖嘗謂群臣曰：「吾王坐鎮朔漠，朕無北顧之憂矣。」四十餘年，天清地謐，胡塵不飛者，皆皇帝之力也。洪武戊寅，太祖賓天，皇帝繼登大寶，應天順人，四國仰化，九夷來歸；梯山航海，貢犀象而獻寶玉者，庭無虛日。三軍萬姓，雍和緝熙，若唐虞之世。天地神明，至於昆蟲草木，罔不喜豫。陛下端居九重，退奸進賢，崇德信道；以詩書為宮室、禮樂為園苑、文章為冠裳、仁義為心腑，恭儉淵默，正已南面，古之賢王，遠不　及矣。惟此殘胡遺孽，梗化不庭，跳踉草野，肆虐讎殺。皇帝曰：「籲！此胡虜者，生於沙漠，昏憒無知，而未嘗聞一善言、見一善行，所以從逆滋惡，徒欲殞厥命耳，朕

63 I.e. an army that conquered without needless bloodshed.

64 A variety of chariot adorned with small bells.

65 I.e. he took the imperial throne.

66 Emperors or their representatives frequently reported on important political and military events to their ancestors and deities.

甚憐之。且遣使齎敕書以撫諭，欲其自省，改惡而全生也。」豈意胡賊反不順命，拘殺我信使，寇擾我邊陲，皇帝不得不怒，乃謂廷臣曰：「胡賊禽獸人也，不知禮　義，惟務橫逆，罪不可宥。朕當親率六軍以討之。」群臣載拜稽顙言曰：「蕞爾胡虜，狐豕之類；跳踉呌呶於無人之境，豈知天下之大小也。若舉兵討之，烏足以當我熊虎之將？願陛下運籌于九重之上，決勝於萬里之外，可也。氷穀雪磧。人所不堪，其可枉聖駕，而勞玉體歟。」皇帝曰：「籲！卿等所言，愛朕之過也。豈不聞 軒轅氏之戰蚩尤於涿鹿乎？朕但知殺賊以安天下，何恤此行勞苦？爾卿等無載言。」於是即命將帥、整師旅、齊隊伍、節鉦鼓、禡旗纛；鑿山開道，挽粟飛芻。百物畢 備，差日啟行。爰於永樂庚寅二月春日載陽，東風扇和。陛下出九重之城，御六龍之車。百靈導於前，萬騎擁於後。金盾雕戈而耀日，羽旄彩幟以遮天。虎賁之　士，何其勇也；魚麗之陣。何其大也。是侍三大營卒，訓練整肅，故擇日行師，神速如此。號令一出，遵行恐後，奉公惟厪，不速而疾。曾未及月，即抵虜境。群凶嗷嗷，無處 逃命。摟其窟穴，盡其醜類，所獲馬駝牛羊，不計其數。掃淨朔漠，洗清草野，士卒卷甲，兵不血刃，誠為王者之師，自古所無有也。凱奏駕還，山川清明。父老黔黎， 爭拜於道。昔之呻吟者，皆化為謳歌矣！皇帝乘鸞輅、登天門、御宸極、告社廟。天日順祥，神人胥慶。太祖昔封帝於燕，坐鎮朔漠，孰知今日之明驗也如此。太祖在天之靈，寧不慰悅也哉！皇帝陛下，神功聖德，當載之史冊，被之弦歌，勒之金石，以垂萬祀。此臣子之所先務也。臣廣孝，忝在文職，雖短才淺學，不足以發揮盛烈，豈可默默而已乎？遂作頌百拜以獻，頌曰：

Oh, magnificent, our august emperor,	於赫皇帝
Who early on, because of his virile martial power,	蚤以雄武
Received his investiture at Yan.	受封燕兮
He defended against the boreal steppe;	坐鎮朔漠
The dust of the northern horsemen did not fly	胡塵不飛
For forty years, oh!	四十年兮
After Grand Progenitor traveled afar;[67]	太祖陟遐
Our [emperor] mounted the precious throne;	繼登寶位
And he “grasped the auspicious signs of rulership.”[68]	握乾 符兮

67 Another euphemism for the death of the Hongwu emperor.

68 I.e. Zhu Di took over duties as emperor.

[His] way equaled the Three Emperors;[69]	道齊三皇
As children he cared for the myriad surnames;	子養萬姓
And perpetuated his domain.	永蘿圖兮
Licentious sounds, dogs and horses,	聲色犬馬
Pearly gems, gold and money[70]	珠玉金貝
He never considered as precious;	不為寶兮
The *Book of Poetry* and *Historical Documents*,	詩書禮樂
The *Book of Rites* and canons of ritual music	制度文章
Institutions and elegances of ceremonies—	
These are what he enjoyed.	是所好兮
He expels the traitorous and advances the worthy;	退奸進賢
His transforming nurturing spread like water;	化育流行
The realm is in balance!	天下平兮
The northern horsemen caitiffs are ignorant;	胡虜無知
They run rampant over the grassy wild,	猖獗草野
And bully the border settlements.	侮 邊城兮
The emperor blazed in anger;	皇帝赫怒
On that same day he raised the army;	即日舉兵
And personally led a campaign of chastisement.	躬行討兮
The ilk of foxes and hairs;	狐豕之類
How would they dare confront [the imperial army]?	彼惡敢當
It was like crumbling desiccated wood.	若摧槁兮
The Six Armies were resplendent;	六師煌煌
The ten thousand riders were formidable;	萬騎霫霫
They displayed Heaven's wrath!	示天威兮

69 The Three Emperors were sage rulers of antiquity known for such key cultural developments as writing, agriculture, and medicine among others.

70 Rulers were commonly assumed to be keenly interested in beautiful women, precious stones, horse riding, and hunting. Thus a lack of such an interest is here offered as evidence of the Yongle emperor's superior qualities as sovereign.

[He] drove straight into caitiff territory;	直抵虜境
The host of evil ones was thrown into panic;	群凶倉皇
They had no place to go!	無所依兮
He exterminated those who were greatly abhorred;	殲厥大憝
He pardoned their followers;	宥其徒眾
How generous and benevolent is he!	何寬仁兮
The soldiers rolled up their armor;[71]	士卒卷甲
The troops never bloodied a blade;	兵不血刃
As magnanimous as spring!	盎如春兮
The victory reported, the emperor's chariot turned back;	凱奏駕還
He returned the horses [to their pasture] and set the oxen free;[72]	歸馬放牛
They were as numerous clouds!	如雲集兮
The elders gathered around to make obeisance;	父老羅拜
They came to welcome the simurgh chariot;	來迎鸞輿
They sang, they were pleased!	歌且懌兮
[The emperor] made offerings to the mountains and streams;	奠於山川
He reported to the Earth Altar and the Ancestral Shrine;	告于社廟
The spirits and deities assembled!	鬼神會兮

71 The text as preserved in the *Huang Ming jing shi wen bian* reads 七卒 *qi zu*, which I take as a scribal error for 士卒 *shi zu*.

72 The imagery of the horses and oxen is drawn from a passage about the end of the military campaign by King Wu of the Zhou against the Shang dynasty in the *Book of History*. "He hushed all the movements of war and proceeded to cultivate the arts of peace. He sent back his horses to the south Mt. Hua and let loose his oxen in the open country of Taolin, showing to all under Heaven that we would not use them again." See Legge, "The Successful completion of the War or Wu cheng" 武成, "The Book of Zhou" 周書 *The Shoo king*, p. 308.

North and South in a single view; 北南一覽
All submitted to the ruler's transforming moral force; 盡歸王化
In its greatness, there was nothing considered external![73] 大無外兮

His divine accomplishments glow and gleam; 神功烈烈
His sagely virtue is lofty and looming; 聖德巍巍
He equals Heaven! 與天齊兮

Record [his deeds] in the historical chronicles; 紀諸史冊
Inscribe them in metal and stone; 刻之金石
Make them shine on ten thousand generations! 昭萬世兮

Although only brief comments are possible here, a few issues deserve attention. First, like many other such celebratory poems, "Ode to Pacifying the Northern Horsemen" affirms the legitimacy of the Yongle emperor's rule. He is painted as the founding emperor's true successor: he is the Hongwu emperor's favorite and most capable son as seen in his investiture to Yan; he satisfies the classical standards of rulership through his virtue and devotion to governance; he enjoys nearly universal recognition from surrounding polities and peoples who manifest their admiration and approval through the presentation of tribute. Second, Yao Guangxiao takes great pains to justify war with the Mongols, including the emperor's dramatic decision to lead his army into the field. The Mongol leaders' misguided refusal to offer tribute contrasts with the joy all other neighbors felt when the Yongle emperor took the throne. The Mongolian people live in a desperate wasteland of senseless violence and chaos; the emperor's merciful efforts to save them are met with betrayal, murder, and unbending arrogance. Despite concerned ministers' protests, the Yongle emperor's sense of duty does not allow him to remain safely within the walls of the imperial complex; instead he emulates the example of the Yellow Emperor of antiquity to vanquish dangerous rebels. The campaign is depicted as a decisive, inevitable, and irreversible triumph that demonstrates the emperor's martial prowess, his surpassing humaneness, and his army's invincible power. Finally, despite his gestures of humility, Yao Guangxiao positions himself as an

---

73 Yao Guangxiao draws on the language of universality and universal rule. Although he may have had in mind the passage from the *Gongyang Commentary* on the *Spring and Autumn Annal* noted above about nothing considered external, but the specific language comes from the line "In its greatness there is nothing left external" 至大無外 in the "Tian xia" 天下 passage of the *Zhuangzi* 莊子, which describes the Great One or Great Unity 大一. I thank Huang Ch'i-chiang for drawing my attention to this reference.

essential actor in the emperor's magnificence. Only through Yao Guangxiao's literary creation will his ruler's accomplishments secure contemporary praise and lasting historical fame.

Poems like "Ode to the Pacification of the Northern Horsemen" were often more a commentary on the Yongle emperor's moral qualifications as ruler than an analysis of the geopolitical factors that led the emperor into the steppe against the Chinggisid *qaghan*, Bunyashiri. Yao Guangxiao offers a token description of the splendor of the Ming army ("The golden shields and carved dagger axes flashed against the sun. Feathered pennants and multi-colored banners blocked out the sky") but wastes little ink on the depiction of battle, the valor of individual soldiers, or the devastation visited upon the enemy.

Rather than dismiss poems like "Ode to Pacifying the Northern Horsemen" as literary confectionaries, we would do better to understand them as an element of conflict and contestation at the Ming court. Such literary artifacts were attempts by civil officials, including those closely tied to the emperor, to recast certain unpleasant realities. The emperor had in fact repeatedly ignored injunctions from his senior civil ministers against leading his armies into the field. Massive military operations on the steppe siphoned away economic resources from projects that many civil officials felt deserved higher priority, such as the rebuilding of schools. War also distracted the sovereign from essential but less exciting tasks of daily governance and put political capital and influence in the hands of potential political rivals such as military commanders, including Mongol and Jurchen leaders who had recently joined the Ming dynasty. Yao Guangxiao had little choice but to satisfy the demands of his patron, the emperor, for literary celebration of his martial glory, but Yao highlighted rulership and virtue, the clash between civilization and a barbaric steppe, while omitting less lofty facets of the campaign such as strategic calculation, the prominence of military commanders, and the general irrelevance of senior civil officials. As an educated man, the Yongle emperor doubtless understood Yao's motives, but as a ruler keen to win acceptance of his wars from an influential portion of his subjects, the literati, he likely felt that Yao's representation of the steppe campaigns neatly served his interests.

Concluding Remarks

Over the decades, Prof. Rossabi has consistently stressed the need to cut through the dense thicket of Chinese political and moral rhetoric that surrounds nearly all Sinitic narratives of the Mongols, including their relations with the Ming dynasty. Such rhetoric systematically understates Mongolian agency, obscures economic self-interest, and privileges key cultural ideals such as benevolence, civilization through education, and the inherent superiority of Chinese civilization. Prof. Rossabi's revisionist interpretations have opened the way to a more even-handed, nuanced, and human understanding of the complex relation between Mongolia and China. This essay is offered as the gentlest of reminders that such rhetoric reveals much about contemporary political and cultural concerns. If viewed as a conscious form of self-representation, such rhetoric can enhance our understanding of how educated Chinese observers perceived Mongols and sought to integrate them into their world.

CHAPTER 8

Flank Contact, Social Contexts, and Riding Patterns in Eurasia, 500–1500

Pamela Kyle Crossley

The history of the way any society in Eurasia and North Africa (henceforward, Eurasia) used the horse is basic to that society. Across the continent, horse technologies have not been developed in isolation for any prolonged period. Well-traveled regions have had access to the full range of materials, skills, and techniques known to others on the continent. That being the case, it is a historical problem that in practice horse technologies have not been evenly used through all regions of Eurasia, and vary in basic ways among regions that resemble each other in climate and in general economic organization. To be more specific: Throughout North Africa, Western and Central Eurasia the flank of the horse has been consistently exposed to the rider, and in eastern Eurasia there developed a tendency to minimize contact between the leg of the rider and the flank of the horse by the use of thick barriers. This corresponds to a disparity not only in the social role of horse riding but also in the deployment of the horse in battle. This essay is a short introduction to the basic principles involved.

Materials extant today[1] suggest that while horse management was considered a relatively open endeavor in which workers and managers could be

1 For a general background on East Asian writing on horse medicine see Paul Buell, Timothy May and David Ramey, "Greek and Chinese Horse Medicine: *Déjà vu* All Over Again" in Sudhoff's Archiv 94:1 [2010]: 31–56. They review the *Zhouli*, *Zhuangzi*, Dunhuang fragments; *Qijin yaoshu* (of the 6th century CE) on veterinary recommendations including for horses. A compendium of 1384, *Simu anji ji* 司牧安驥集; includes studies on acupuncture, especially the "Bo Le" equine acupuncture tradition. After the fourteenth century, East Asian writings on horse care generally referenced the Korean work of 1399—*Simbyeon jipseong ma'ui bang* 신편집성마의방 (新編集成馬醫方—in large part drawn from *Simu anji ji*; published in China in 1634, and later in Japan, but originally published in Korea, in 1399. By the late seventeenth century it was partly superseded by *Yuan Heng Liaoma ji* 元亨療馬 集. first published in China in 1608. (Buell et al., *op.cit.*, 16–26). See also Buell, May, and Ramey, "Chinese Horse Medicine: Texts and Illustrations," http://www.researchgate.net/profile/Paul_Buell/publication/49810777_Greek_and_Chinese_horse_medicine_dj_vu_all_over_again/links/odeec538dac50dd97c000000.pdf. On Mongol horse training in general see also

© KONINKLIJKE BRILL NV, LEIDEN, 2017 | DOI 10.1163/9789004343405_010

guided by reference texts, riding itself was only cryptically represented in written materials and depended upon closed, personal training by teachers working largely with oral, tightly schooled traditions. In the case of Xenophon (430–354 BCE), certainly, riding advice was offered not to common cavalry but to elite men training to ride horses both in war and in the periodic festivals and games that featured horse tricks based on battle tactics. In East Asian languages, the management issues are treated in equal detail to the early European texts, but there is virtually nothing on riding; in context, this suggests either closed traditions of personal instruction, or access to riding so wide that instruction in writing was regarded as unnecessary.

On the basis of present evidence it appears that people rode horses for between two and four thousand years (very roughly between 5000 and

---

Ruth Meserve, "An Historical Perspective of Mongol Horse Training, Care and Management: Selected Texts" (doctoral dissertation, Department of Uralic and Altaic Studies, Indiana University, 1987). For Manchu manuals on horse management and medicine see Marta E. Hansen, "On Manchu Medical Manuscripts and Blockprints: An Essay and Bibliographic Survey" in *Saksaha: A Review of Manchu Studies* 8 [2003]:1–33. See also Sare Arcanli, "Plurality in Qing Imperial Medicine: Examining Institutional Formations Beyond the Imperial Medical Bureau." *Asia Pacific Perspectives* Fall/Winter 2013–2014: 83.

The scope of western Eurasia writing on horse management and training before the sixteenth century is reviewed in Donald F. McMiken, "Ancient Origins of Horsemanship." *Equine Veterinary Journal* 22:2 [Mar 1990]: 73–78. He cites Mesopotamian inscriptions of 2000 BCE; the Hittite horse expert Kikkuli's instructions on the care and feeding of chariot horses and Ugarit veterinarian texts of the fourteenth century BCE; Xenophon's text (incorporating some of an earlier work by Simon of Athens) of 400 BCE. A collection of Greek manuscripts on horse management and medicine were collected as the *Hippiatrica* (including ostensible redactions of fragments of the work of Simon of Athens) in the fifth or sixth century CE; see Anne McCabe, *A Byzantine Encyclopedia of Horse Medicine: The Sources, Compilation and Transmission of the Hippiatrica*. Oxford: Oxford University Press, 2007. In the sixteenth century a European explosion in social and gender coding related to horsemanship produced texts by John Astley, Federico Grisone, Pascale Caracciolo, Claudio Corte, followed by the iconic authorities Antoine de Pluvinel and William Cavendish, the last of whom is regarded as the predecessor of modern horse training. They were followed by various schools of thought on horsemanship and horse management from the eighteenth century to the present. See also the discussion in Elizabeth Pope Simmons, "The Rejection of the *Manège* Tradition in Early Modern England: 'Equestrian Elegance at Odds with English Sporting Tradition'," doctoral dissertation, University of North Florida, 2001, pp. 10–11 on the exclusive oral transmission of riding knowledge in medieval Europe (quoting Luigi Gianoli). On related traditions in the Islamic world see Housni Alkhateeb Shehada, *Mamluks and Animals: Veterinary Medicine in Medieval* Islam (Leiden, 2012), pp. 4–18, historiography.

1000 BCE)[2] with no saddles, and even after the appearance of the saddle the most spectacular riding continued without it. Bare-back riding at its highest level of achievement permits maximum agility for horse and rider. The near-total involvement of the rider's legs in communication with the horse allows lateral as well as forward maneuvering and the greatest precision in the balancing of the rider on the horse (including a head-on encounter with an enemy). At the same time, lack of a saddle allows the greatest speeds because of the minimal load the horse must carry. But the cost of the highest achievements of agile horsemanship is the restriction of such riding to small segments of society. In the case of the Plains societies of North America, for instance, blanket or bareback riding at the level required for the bison hunt, horse theft or the military vanguard was limited to men of proven riding skills, who monopolized the ownership of stallions and breeding; common riders owned mares and brought up the rear in battle.[3]

An Early Eurasian Complex of Saddle, Loose Legs and Flank Exposure

The earliest known depiction of a saddle is on a colored felt wall hanging found in the early graves at Pazyryk,[4] dated to the fifth century BCE (roughly contemporary with Xenophon). The saddle represented has a single girth (the strap going under the horse's abdomen to secure the blanket or saddle), no fenders (leather or heavy textile coverings protecting the side of the horse), and a distinct pommel as well as cantle (see illustration 1). It appears likely that the Pazyryk saddle has undergone a considerable degree of change through a

2 All evidence for the dates of the emergence of riding, the later development of fighting or shooting from horseback, and the development of the saddle to stabilize much greater numbers of riders is subject to interpretation. Robert Drews, *Early Riders: The Beginnings of Mounted Warfare in Asia and Europe* (London, 2004) includes succinct summaries of the arguments on both points, and in his case tends toward later estimates than, say, Marija Gimbutas, who tends to make them earlier.

3 Pekka Hämäläinen, "The Rise and Fall of Plains Indian Horse Cultures." *Journal of American History* (2003) 90 (3): 833–862.

4 Assumed to be a Skythian burial site in a dry valley opening on the Bolshoy Ulagan River valley in Kazakstan. The site consists of five large and nine smaller burial mounds and dates from about the 5th to the 3rd century BC, It was excavated in 1929 and 1947–49. The best single source is Sergei I. Rudenko [M.W. Thompson, trans.], *Frozen Tombs of Siberia: The Pazyryk Burials of Iron Age Horsemen* (Berkeley and Los Angeles, 1970). See also Drews, *op.cit.*, pp. 64–65.

long line of earlier models, since one would expect saddles evolving from padded blankets to develop first a cantle, subsequently such specialized features as the pommel and ultimately the tree.[5] The high cantle and pommel steady the rider during rapid forward motion, and the pommel provides support in the case of a sudden halt, as well as for travel over long distances, when the rider can lean on it for comfort. The importance of securing the rider during rapid shifts in both speed and trajectory are also suggested by the breastplate and crupper (see illustration 1), both of which may have been made of either hemp or leather. The rider appears to be wearing leggings of animal hide, which would have increased friction and stability, especially in contact with the horse's flanks. The saddle depicted may have been covered with felt or woven textiles; two complete such covers were found at Pazyryk and are now at the Hermitage, along with fragments of riding blankets (always with an opening for the rider's leg to touch the horse) or wool caparisons (a light textile for protection or for emblematic display). This covering would have the advantage of providing friction to help steady the rider, and of enhancing the padding that was incorporated into the saddle's interior design. Though the rider can enjoy the stabilizing effects of the saddle and its well-developed cantle and pommel, his lower legs are in contact with the horse, and he retains the option of making efficient lateral movements while riding (see Illustration 1).

This basic design principle—a modest saddle seat with no fender but possibly laid over a pad or caparison—dominated all Eurasian saddle design until about 400 CE or a bit earlier. It strongly accords with classical Greek depictions of mounted warriors and commanders; though they were often represented as bare-legged (which would have a similar, if reduced effect of friction as hide leggings), their legs hang in the same toe-down position as the Pazyryk rider. Xenophon had recommended this in order to keep the lower leg loose and avoid impact injuries that could occur from stiffening the leg.[6] Like the representations of riders in Greek art, the Pazyryk rider's feet hang well below the flank of the horse. The height of riding horses in most parts of Eurasia before the sixth century BCE is accepted to have been in the range of 13 hands

5 This seems to be evident in an Egyptian tomb of the fifteenth century BCE, excavated in 1935, in which an apparent saddle blanket of linen had been augmented with rear supports of leather, forming an early cantle; the blanket also had sewn-in girths. See Thornton Chard, "An Early Horse Skeleton" in *The Journal of Heredity* 28:9 [September 1937]:317–319, esp. p. 317. This was later called the "Buhen horse," see Harold B. Barclay, "Another Look at the Origins of Horse Riding" in Anthropos 77 [1982]:1/2:244–249, esp. p. 248.

6 See Xenophon [H.G. Dakyns, trans.], "On Horsemanship," Project Gutenberg http://www.gutenberg.org/ebooks/1176, location 334.

(approximately 132 centimeters) or less, which today would be considered a pony; by 500 CE or a little later, European mounts may have commonly stood at 14 hands, which today would still be a pony. A rider intending to make contact with the sides of his horse for speed or positioning would normally contract his leg, bring up his toes to better expose his heel to the horse's flank, and in the same action enlarge his calf as a second means of signaling to the horse.

Roman cavalry units—in the early period a mix of commoners and noblemen, in the later period aristocrats (*equites*) and foreign auxiliaries (*ala*)—used a small rectangular saddle with wooden infrastructure and leather covering, without fenders but often laid over a light textile covering that prevented excessive wear on the rider's leggings (see Illustration 2). Most were secured by a single girth around the horse's abdomen, but surviving metal from some sites suggests additional girthing or at least the addition of a breastplate to stabilize the saddle during rapid acceleration. The rider was held in place by four projections, or horns, one at each of the rectangle's corners.[7] These horns rose up and curved inwards, designed to grasp the rider by his thighs and hips. It was peculiarly well designed to stabilize a rider engaging in combat with *mêlée* weapons (such as sword, lance or mace) from horseback. Combined with the hide leggings which would have generated considerable grip of the rider's legs against the horse, the saddle would have permitted extraordinary lateral agility for riders who were adept fighters but perhaps not sufficiently expert to use no saddles at all.

This saddle opened war riding to a much greater variety of soldiers than the highly specialized bareback and leather-pad riding of the Republic era. But the saddle was difficult to mount and its potential to injure the rider was spectacular. Moreover it was not able to accommodate a stirrup, which encourages the rider to rise frequently from the saddle, while the horns of the Roman saddle required him to stay closely seated. Later introduction of the iron stirrup would have obviated the purpose of this saddle (though it may have persisted in a modified form among the Sassanians), since riders could afterward stabilize themselves from the feet up and did not need the saddle horns. This Roman saddle was a deviation from the basic course of Eurasian saddle design. Nevertheless it had traits that subsequently became important in all Eurasian

7 See Peter Connolly, "A Reconstruction of a Roman Saddle" in *Britannia* 17 [1986]: 353–355. Ann Hyland's reconstruction and riding demonstration is described in Jeremiah B. McCall, *The Cavalry of the Roman Republic*, London: 2001). pp. 47–49. Earlier, Roman cavalrymen probably rode bareback; the idea of the saddle may have come from the Celts or Germans, who may have got it from Skythian Central Asia (the general direction of Pazyryk). See also Ann Hyland, *Equus: The Horse in the Roman World*, (New Haven: 1990), esp. pp. 85–192.

saddle design: Its leather covering was shock-absorbing, durable, and repairable, and it was built on the rigid wooden infrastructure that would become the universal Eurasian saddle tree.

In East Asia during the Han period, saddle development exhibited some features that differed from its Roman counterpart, while retaining the most basic notions of saddle function derived from the style depicted at Pazyryk. The saddles represented in the terracotta figures from the tomb of Qin Shihuang, buried in 210 BCE and discovered in 1974, clearly show a small treeless saddle that permits contact with the horse's flank from the rider's thigh to heel, while the riders wear leggings similar to those of the Roman *ala*, maximizing friction between leg and flank.[8] The mounted figures are all riding in the toes-down, loose-legged style depicted at Pazyryk and recommended by Xenophon a couple of centuries earlier. But the saddles are secured with two and, infrequently, three slender girths (see Illustration 3). The saddle is perhaps best characterized as permitting roughly the same maneuverability as the Roman saddle, but by means of more secure girthing rather than the specialized horns of the Roman variant.

By about 400 CE, the ensemble of unfendered saddle with cantle and pommel had become universal throughout Eurasia; within a century the iron stirrup was common across central Eurasia, and by 800 CE at the latest was generally used from Europe to East Asia. The riding principle expressed through this general design was also universal: The rider balanced himself in the saddle by means of friction of his leg (with or without covering) against the horse, and used his heel and knotted calf against the exposed flank of the horse when necessary to move forward or to the side. The critical interplay of leg stasis, clarity of communication with the horse, and balance was noted by Xenophon and his predecessors well before the stirrup was introduced.

A linen, wool or silk caparison could be and was added to this basic saddle configuration without altering its functions. Such a skirt was of a thin material and often extended below the rider's calf, but never so far as his heel. This practice is widely represented in the art of northern Europe, Central Asia, and eastern Eurasia during classical times (1500 BCE–500 CE). The functional neutrality of the skirt suggests that it would have been most practical to restrict its use to ceremonial occasions, but a more coarse version might have been useful

8 Similar riders, unarmored, are portrayed in the ceramic funeral army discovered in 1965 at Yangjiawan 杨家湾 in Xianyang Country, Shaanxi province, and now in the Xianyang country museum. They come from the tomb of General Zhou Bo and his son Zhou Yafu, and are depicted in 中国陶瓷全集 *Zhongguo taoci quanji*, vol 3. (Shanghai, 2000), plates 72, 74, 82, and 88.

for riders who wished to avoid chafing of the leg while travelling. It should also be remembered that since the saddle's purpose was to extend horseback transport to greater numbers of people who would otherwise not have been able to ride, ostentatious bedecking of horses—always a feature of artistic horse representation and doubtless a ubiquitous element in the real world—would quickly have affected both the use and the representation of such skirts. They are unrelated to truly protective gear such as the chains used by Romans to protect the horse's neck (now known as the *crinière*) and rump, or the lacquered leather plates used across Eurasia for the same purpose.

The open flank of the horse, the high saddle, light armor and especially the spur—which emerged not later than Roman times—all mark the continuing fixation on facilitation of lateral or rotating motion of the horse. What evidence we have suggests that there was great variability in the degree of lateral movement learned and its application on the battlefield. This has been famously captured in Tacitus's general description of the German cavalry as employing a large encirclement as a battle tactic, which he said continued in one direction (usually to the right, or clockwise). He contrasted it to the rapid *uariare* [*variare*] *gyros*, a movement by which the Greeks and Romans pivoted their horses to the right or left, even reversing course. Greek and Roman riders initiated this reeling *gyros* from the horse's hind feet—that is, the weight was thrown onto the back feet in the moment before the front was pivoted right or left. It was an essential movement for fighting from the saddle with *mêlée* weapons, whether against a standing infantryman (who could be encircled and trapped with such moves) or against a mounted opponent, who could use *gyros* movements as extensions of the thrust and parry movements of a weapon.[9] Xenophon addresses the question of reversing the horse and executing the simple turn (*volte*) repeatedly, and the science of turning the horse was a focus of classical training. Using the reins to rapidly turn the head of a speeding horse was likely to result in a fall and injury for both horse and rider. In the *gyros*, the horse shifts its center of gravity in response to signals against its flank, and the head remains largely in line with the body. The rider also remains balanced, and in

9 Ernst A. Ebbinghaus, "Germania VI, 10: Germanic Cavalry Manoeuvre" in Mohammad A. Jazayery, ed., *Historical and Comparative Linguistics*. Tacitus uses *gyros* twice to describe or contrast German cavalry moves; in one instance it appears to mean a large circle used by a troop of horsemen to surround an enemy group; and in another it means reversing the horse by means of pivoting on the hind legs; the latter of these Tacitus explicitly said that the Germans did not use (*sed nec variare gyros in morem nostrum docentur*). Duane Reed Stuart, trans. and ed., Tacitus [Duane Reed Stuart, trans. and annotation], *The Germania with Introduction and Notes* (New York, 1916), esp. pp. 39–40.

command of his weapon. The use of *gyros*-based movements became, especially after the introduction of the stirrup, the hallmark of military riding (and display riding, later dressage) across Central Asia, the Middle East, northern India, North Africa and Europe between 500 and 1500.

With large encirclement at one end of the spectrum and the reeling *gyros* at the other, the degrees of manoeuverability of the horse from its flank is sometimes represented in early narratives as a point of distinction between imperial armies, such as those of Rome and Han, and the so-called "barbarian" armies they confronted. The circling that Tacitus described as part of the German cavalry tactics is reminiscent of two Han-period encounters with Xiongnu cavalry who successfully and literally rode circles around Han troops, the first involving the Emperor Gaozu (Liu Bang) in 200 BCE[10] and the second resulting in the capture of General Li Ling in 99 BCE.[11] Both occurred within a window of the Han transition (very roughly coincident with the Roman transition) from chariot to cavalry warfare, a time when mounted warrior casualties in confrontation with infantries were high. In reference to later periods (in fact, generally the time that Tacitus was complimenting the Roman forces on their fancy riding), Han historians would claim that Han cavalry tactics were refined enough to be better than the Xiongnu against infantry; where the Xiongnu (like the Germans) used large cavalry encirclements, the Han (like the Romans) used lateral movement and highly disciplined horses.

From Roman times at the latest, iron spurs (which may have had bone or wood predecessors) were used at the back of the rider's boot to enhance signals to the horse. As in the case of the saddle, spurs would have compensated (as they do today) for mediocre or poor riding skills, allowing greater numbers of riders to control horses during herding or battle. We have now many spurs that show the marked European enthusiasm for using large, heavy, sharp objects to facilitate communication of heel commands to the horse's flank. Some of the size is undoubtedly attributable to relative encumbrances of European armor in the fourteenth and fifteenth centuries, as well as the growth of European war horses of the charger and destrier categories. The increase in spur size was paralleled by more severe bits, suggesting that the larger horses needed for bearing heavy cavalry were not easy for the riders to control. And the argument for a lower level of riding skill is reinforced by the enlargement and elaboration of cantle and pommel, as well as the tendency toward harsh bits,

10 In the Xiongnu chapter of Ban Gu 班固, *Han shu* 漢書·匈奴傳: 冒頓縱精兵三十餘萬騎，為高帝于白登七日。

11 In Li Guang and Su Jian biographical chapter of the *Han shu*: 李廣蘇建傳.

double reins and martingales.[12] The implication is that, in medieval Europe, skills in horsemanship were lower priorities than the need to get landed men onto horses—an irony, given the fact that casualties among knights who fell from their horses were extremely high, and a probable explanation for the fact that very heavy armor used on extremely powerful horses prevailed for only a very brief period, after which the cavalry techniques of earlier times returned. Though European horse tackle of this period impeded the maneuverability of the horse on all fronts, there remained a distinct concern that lateral mobility be retained to some significant degree—an essential element in fighting with *mêlée* weapons from the saddle. Whether the long textile caparisons worn ceremonially, or the long coats of armor (metal or lacquer) provided for protection of the horse,[13] there was always the accommodation of a slit or a cut-away to allow the spurred boot of the rider to contact the bare flank of the horse.

This insistence on using the flank of the horse is a strong indication that Europe follows the traditional stream of Central Asian horsemanship (and the post-stirrup type of bare-flank riding is today most purely represented in the European polo saddle). The openness of the flank bespeaks the enduring importance in European riding of highly trained communication between horse and rider, the significance placed on horse breeding (including the establishment of imperial stud facilities) to produce the temperament necessary to endure the training and deployment, and the resulting association in European history of horsemanship with elite status.[14]

Dropped Reins, Soft Boots and Closed Flank Riding

Like their Central Asian predecessors and their European contemporaries, Mamluk riders fitted their horses out with prominent pommel, cantle, breastplate and crupper, and used a complex girth. This suggests the fundamental importance of *mêlée* fighting from the saddle, illustrated in Mamluk manuscripts. The Mamluks also emphasized a version of the *gyros*, used for lance fighting

12 For very vivid examples see Gaston Phoebus (1331–1391), *Le Livre de chasse*, Bibliothèque nationale de France. The work has been in print since 1507 and facsimiles are now widely available.

13 The development of whole-body armor (cataphract) for horses is a separate topic, but also with a Eurasia-wide history. Because of space it cannot be dealt with here.

14 On the last phenomenon see the interesting work by Patricia M. Franz, "The Horseman as a Work of Art: The Construction of Elite Identities in Early Modern Europe, 1550–1700." doctoral dissertation CUNY, 2006.

between mounted warriors.[15] Accordingly, the Mamluks used small spurs to magnify the effect of signals against the horse's flank (see Illustration 4). This complexity of this system suggests that, as in classical times, riding, and particularly battle riding, was the preserve of highly trained professionals with dedicated military or ritual functions. This is reinforced by what is found in the massive Mamluk literature of *furusiyya* culture, which included not only skills encompassing every aspect of horse war, but also games, etiquette and values.

Mamluk riders were trained not only to fight from the saddle, but also to shoot arrows from speeding horses. In this respect they represented—rather than initiated—a transition from riding focused on close control of the horse's lateral movements by signaling against an open flank to riding specifically designed for horseback archery and accessibility to common soldiers. Their saddles show evidence of well-developed knee-rolls, allowing the rider to raise his knees for better gripping of the horse and better front-to-back stability. Their manuals describe the steps in the training of a rider to learn to use a bow and arrow, including the training of the horse to keep a steady onward pace when the reins were dropped. The Mamluks are the link to the style of riding for which the Mongols were later the best known practitioners.

The medieval presentation of mounted archery as it became widespread throughout eastern Eurasia depended upon covering the flank of the horse with material stiff enough to prevent the rider's feet from contacting the flank. Mounted archery did not depend upon the ability to make a rapid lateral or circular movement; on the contrary, it virtually required that the horse run primarily in a straight or moderately curving trajectory. In theory, riders could be trained to give the horse no signals via the flank, but a much more efficient method was simply to isolate the rider's foot and lower leg from the horse and give up the use of the spur. This also greatly simplified the training of the

15 On the training and varied status of Mamluk riders see David Ayalon, "Notes on the Furusiyya Exercises and Games in the Mamluk Sultanate" in *Scripta Hierosolymitana* 9 [1961]; Ulrich Haarmann, "The late triumph of the Persian bow: critical voices on the Mamluk monopoly on weaponry" in Thomas Phillipp and U. Haarmann, eds., *The Mamluks in Egyptian Politics and Society* (Cambridge, 2007): 174–187; H.A. Shehada, *op. cit.*, 28–31; Reuven Amitai, "The Logistics of the Mongol-Mamlûk War, with Special Reference to the Battle of Wādī'l-Khaznadār, 1299 C.E." in John Prior, ed., *Logistics of Warfare in the Age of Crusades* (Surrey, 2006): 25–42. The best-known Mamluk illustrated manual on horsemanship *Nihāyat al-su'l wa-al-umnīyah fī ta'allum a'māl al-furūsīyah* (not later than 1348) has been put online by the Qatar Digital Library. http://www.qdl.qa/en/archive/81055/vdc_100000000044.0x0003ca. Use of the gyros is seen in several illustrations, for example 97r.

horses used in this kind of riding. Instead of spending years teaching horses the meaning of a variety of flank signals, the horses could be taught to be steady and not to swerve. The result for any society using such a method was the ability to get the greatest number of mounts and remounts into service, and the greatest number of expert archers into the saddle.

Long fendering evolved slowly. The antecedents are clearly seen in a mural from the Muyong tomb, dated to the fifth century. This is now in Jilin province, China, but in the fifth century was part of the territory of the Goguryeo kingdom.[16] We know from remarks in the historical records that Goguryeo warriors were adept in the same skills of fighting with sword, lance and mace from the saddle as their contemporaries across Eurasia.[17] But here we have a good depiction of the emergence of mounted archery using an adaptive saddle apparatus—a long, thick fender extending below the rider's heel. In the Goguryeo tomb murals, riders still have small, blunt spurs on their boots. Their very loose trousers extend nearly to the ankle, indicating that the basis of rider stability are the stirrups rather than the rider's grip on the horse's flank (see Illustration 5). The context here of Goguryeo culture in general and horse technologies in particular suggests that this style of mounted archery must have been widespread in Korea and Japan (where riding was beginning) in the east, and during the Northern Wei (386 to 534 CE) dynasty of the Tagbach people, who neighbored Goguryeo in the northwest; Northern Wei terracotta figurines show that long-fender riding was common among hunters and warriors. From these points in particular, it is reasonable to believe that the technology was communicated across Manchuria and Mongolia.

Cumulatively the art relating—contemporaneously or in retrospect—to the Tang empire (618–906 CE) suggests a style of saddle similar to the saddle used

16 The Goguryeo tombs now found in Jilin and at various sites in Korea depict many aspects of horse management and riding, including the feeding of horses and the use of horse armor of long metal plates, reaching far below the rider's feet and uncut on the flanks. The best illustrated report is probably Preservation of the Koguryo Kingdom Tombs (UNESCO, 2005) and for background see Yonson Ahn, "The Contested Heritage of Koguryo/Gaogouli and China-Korea Conflict" in *Japan Focus: The Asia-Pacific Journal* 2631 (http://www.japanfocus.org/-Yonson-Ahn/2631/article.html).

17 Goguryeo is legendary in Korean history for its horsemanship, and is regarded as the source for the enduring subculture of the *hwarang* 화랑 花郞. Though the *hwarang* are often compared to the individual Mamluk troopers or to European knights with their chivalric code, this is probably an unwise comparison; *hwarang* culture was not originally based primarily upon horsemanship or cavalry service. See also Yun Myeong-chol 윤명철, *Mal tago Goguyeo kada: Goguryeo munha yujeog josa* 말 타고 고구려 가다: 고구려 문화 유적 탐사기 (Seoul 1997).

by Mamluk cavalry—a rounded saddle with moderate fendering, padding in the knee area, and a generous caparison, which may be seen singly or in combination in images such as the tomb fresco of Tang Taizong (599–649) or the Qianling mausoleum of Tang Gaozong (628–683) and his family. It may mean that Central Asian, or Turkic, influence on Tang military riding was stronger than that of northeastern Asia. Tomb art and ceramic figurines suggest, however, that long caparisons or long fenders may have been in use by women and civil elites employing horses for travel or leisure. Classic representations include the painting of female riders, usually with the title "Spring Outing by the Tang Court," by Zhang Xuan 張萱 (713–755)—copied by Li Gonglin 李公麟 (1049–1106)—and the painting by Zhao Yan (d. 923) showing male riders.

During the Song through Ming periods, long-fendered riding was usually represented in connection with aristocrats, women, civil officials and archers; it was a tool available to them to offer them easier access to horse riding (see Illustration 6). Riders are frequently shown applying a crop to the rear of the horse to increase speed, an alternative to using the spur in the absence of contact between foot and flank; to have one hand engaged in this way would also be no particular hindrance, since in the period before 1500 the custom of using one hand (the left) to control the reins was more or less universal across Eurasia. Open-flank riding and the saddles permitting it were still in use by herders, couriers, and *mêlée*-oriented cavalry. Liao art—particularly from the Kitan painters Li Zanhua 李贊華 [Yelu Bei 耶律倍] (899–936), Hu Gui 胡瓌 (907–960) and Hu Qian 胡虔[18]—is an invaluable guide, along with tomb murals, to the variety and uses of saddles in this period. They range from small saddles with short blankets—reminiscent of those used by Northern Qi and Zhou-period military riders—to cutaway saddles allowing access to the horse's flank as desired, to extravagantly large and thick furnishings completely covering the flank. A very finely detailed mural in a tomb believed to be that of Xiao Quli (a son-in-law of Abaoji) shows a leather leg-guard sewn into a stiffened leopard pelt reaching well below the stirrup (see Illustration 7). Riders wear loose trousers or robes, and large, soft, shapeless boots. A courier[19] in a

---

18 For interesting commentary on this see Irene S. Leung, "Felt Yurts Neatly Arrayed, Large Tents Huddle Close" in Nicola di Cosmo and Don J. Wyatt, *Political Frontiers, Ethnic Boundaries and Human Geographies in Chinese History* (Routledge, 2005): 192–219.

19 This painting has been variously titled as depicting a "nobleman" or an "archer." The man is carrying a bow and displaying an arrow, but everything in the painting points to a depiction of a courier. The arrow was a conventional item of authenticity, being the mark of the leader for whom the courier was working. The horse sports red pompoms, probably a mark of the status of the courier's superior, and a working saddle with long, narrow skirts

painting by Li Zanhua has a cutaway saddle with limited flank exposure but no spurs, while a hunter in a Hu Gui painting seems to have two very long and thin needles protruding from the rear of his boots, perhaps as an extreme means of communicating with the horse's flank in the event of a tiger charge. Riders anticipating few similar emergencies, or none, are shown equipped with long, fan-like crops to urge their horses forward.

It is possible that the rich visual representations of Liao-period horsemanship creates the illusion that their use of the horse was not only more specialized in some sectors but also more various than that of the Mongols; what can be said is that evidence from art and archeology suggests an overwhelming Mongol preference for the long, rigid fender. Depictions available today range from the very clear detail of the paintings of Chen Juzhong 陈居中 (fl.1201–1204) to the much less detailed representations in Persian miniatures and Russian sketches. Archeology provides examples of ceremonial and funeral saddles, including one attributed to Chinggis. The consistencies are strikingly evident through all the varieties of media. Mongol saddles show a prominent pommel and cantle and a dual-circle fender that by the twelfth century was widespread throughout eastern Eurasia; we can note, too, soft boots, stirrups, and an absence of spurs (see Illustration 8). This is representative of the mounted archer (as contrasted to the shooting rider), with discernable lines of development back to Goguryeo and Northern Wei.

The seriousness with which the Mongols isolated the horse's flank from contact with the rider is vividly illustrated in a sketch by Zhao Mengfu 赵孟頫 1254–1322) of a Mongol tightening the girth on his horse—with his elbow the man holds his entire fender straight up in the air. Such rigidity would have been best accomplished with layering of leather, felt and sheepskin. This should be related to two broad characteristics of Mongol society and warfare—the involvement of a maximum number of men and boys in mounted warfare, and the large number of remounts (by statute, seven though some sources specify three to five) that could be brought to the campaign because of the minimal training needed for their tasks. It is also related to the lack of elaborate horse breeding and training programs in medieval eastern Eurasia. The Mongols

made of tiger hide. The horse has a luggage roll, and most distinctive is the saddle. Its skirt is long but very narrow. Working saddles of this sort must have been in common use among herdsmen, couriers, and possibly some cavalry. The saddle afforded the comfort of a long-skirted saddle for distance riding, but on occasion could also permit the contact with the flank of the horse that could urge it forward or push it laterally. This saddle was effective enough to remain in continuous use, has a direct modern descendant in the Mongolian herding saddles today, and a close relative in the modern endurance saddle.

represented the ultimate development of a regional riding style that brought to their general population the ancient arts of shooting from horseback as practiced by specialists among the Parthians. But the consistency of form and function in Mongol riding should not suggest, particularly to analysts of military history, that strongly marked priorities in horse technologies meant exclusion of other horse battle skills. The Mamluks emphasized horseback *mêlée* fighting in their technologies and training, but could use range weapons from horseback as an auxiliary skill. The Mongols emphasized range weapons but could fight from horseback as an auxiliary skill. "Horsemanship" as an absolute cannot be reasonably factored into battle analysis without the differentiation of riding styles as products of society, environment, and technological exchange.

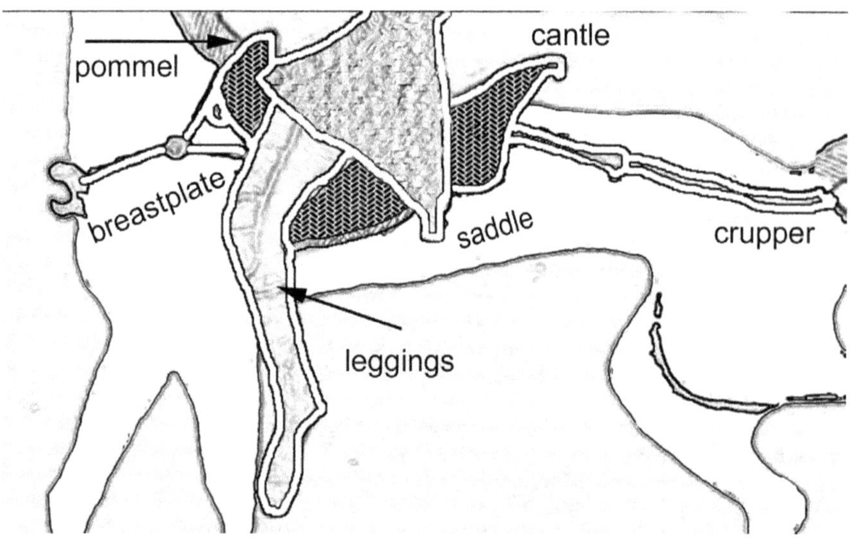

FIGURE 8.1 *Early Eurasian riding: Based on: the saddle decoration from Pazyryk (c. 500 BCE) shows the leg covered for maximum friction against the open flank of the horse; pommel, cantle, crupper and breastplate (breastgirth) help to stabilize the rider during rapid starts and stops.*

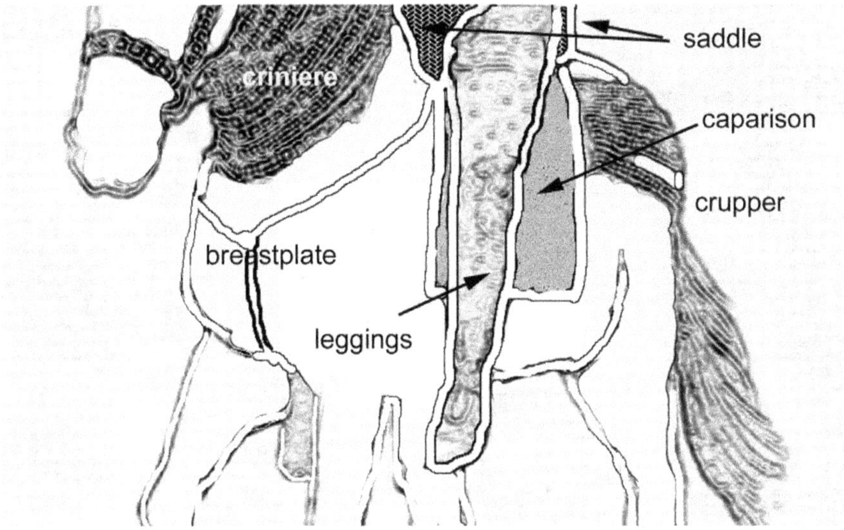

FIGURE 8.2 *Roman adaptation of standard Eurasian style for mounted infantry: open flank, hide leggings, toes down (spurs often added for amplifying signals to the flank). Based on: Michael P. Speidel,* Riding for Caesar: The Roman Emperor's Horse Guard, *2002.*

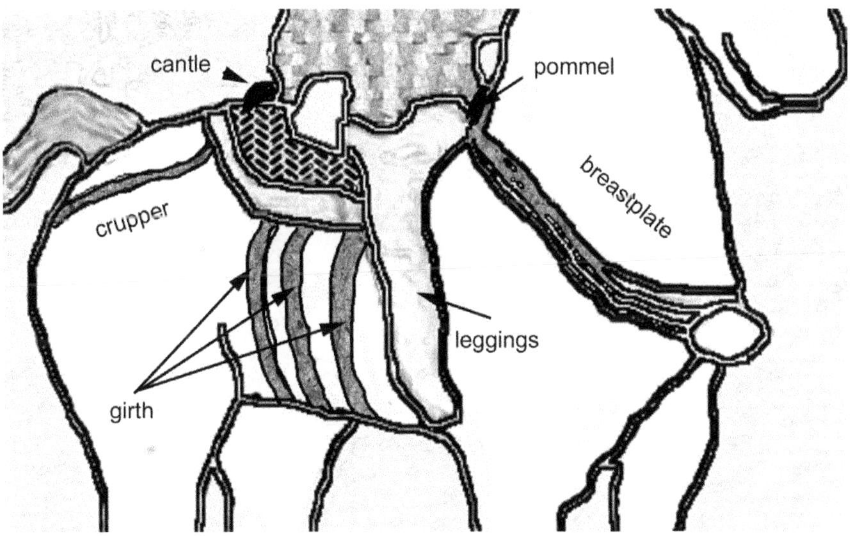

FIGURE 8.3 *Later Han period Chinese adaptation of standard Eurasian style for mounted infantry: open flank, hide leggings, toes down; multiple girthings for added stability. Based on: Ceramic figures from the Yanjiawan tomb excavations, Shaanxi province.*

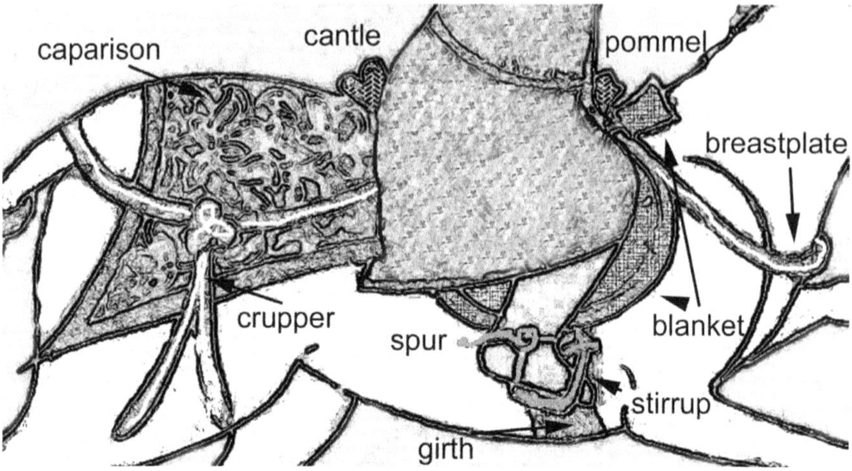

FIGURE 8.4 *Mamluk adaptation of standard Eurasian style, for mêlée fighting from horseback: the flank of the horse is open, and the rider uses small spurs on soft riding boots to accentuate signals for forward or lateral movement. Based on: color illustrations from Muḥammad ibn ʿĪsá ibn Ismāʿīl al-Ḥanafī's* Nihāyat al-su'l wa-al-umnīyah fī taʿallum aʿmāl al-furūsīyah, *fourteenth century.*

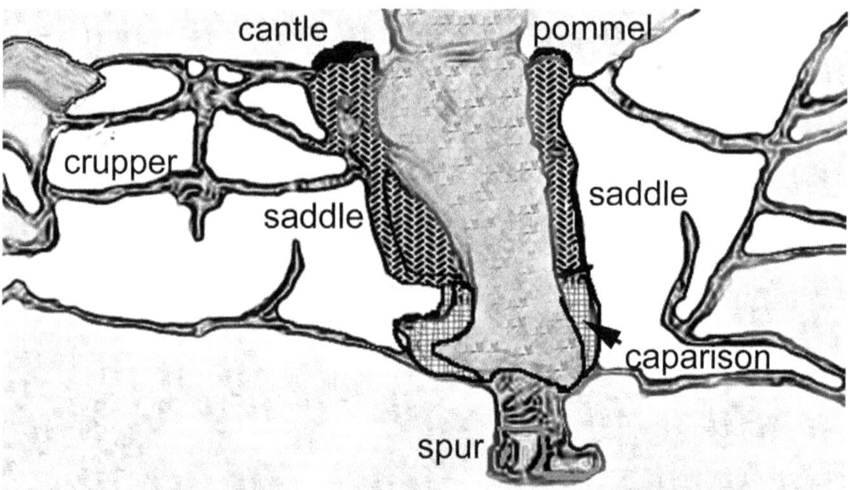

FIGURE 8.5 *Early representation of emerging East Asian style of closed-flank riding by mounted archers: Stiff covering prevents casual contact with the flank, but rear segment open for signals for forward speed. Based on: Wuyong tomb paintings (Jilin province, China) from the period of the Goguryeo kingdom, fifth century.*

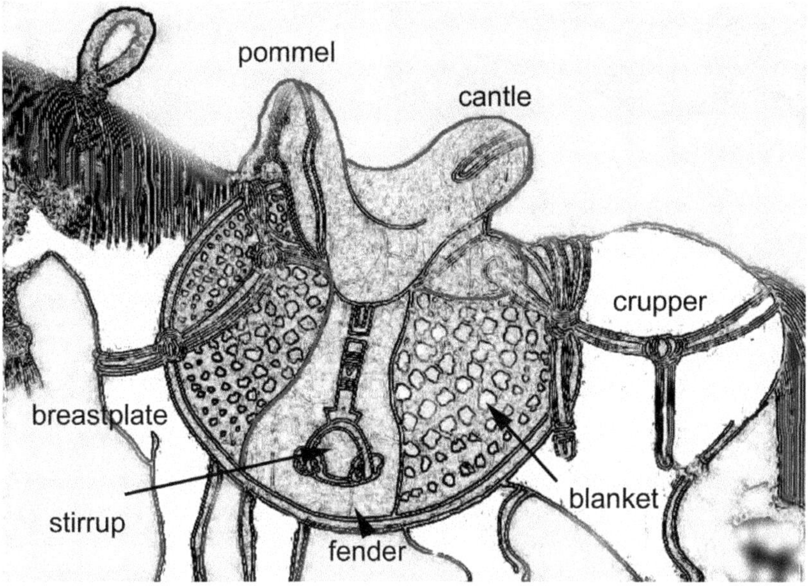

FIGURE 8.6 *Kitan adaptation of East Asian style, using a stiff animal hide, reinforced for the entire length of the leg, preventing flank contact. Crupper and breastplate stabilize the rider during rapid forward movement and deceleration. Based on tomb mural from Aohan, Inner Mongolia, dated to c. 1000* BCE.

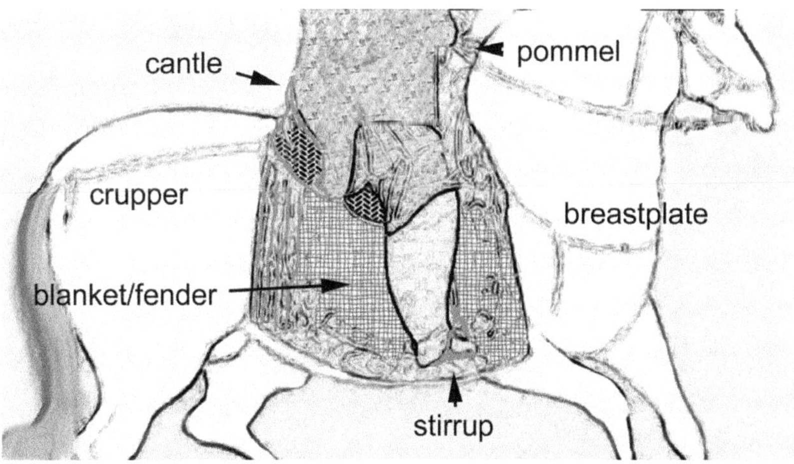

FIGURE 8.7 *Tenth and eleventh-century Chinese adaptation of East Asian covered flank riding, in this case pleasure riding by civilians, using heavy brocade to prevent signals being transmitted from the foot and leg. The rider wears soft boots and uses no spurs. Based on paintings by Zhao Yan (born 923) and Li Gonglin (1049–1106).*

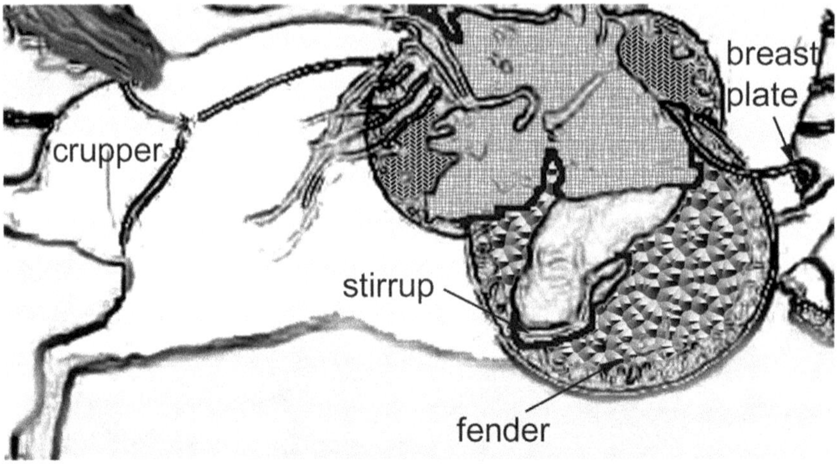

FIGURE 8.8 *Mongol adaptation of East Asian covered flank riding for use by mounted archers. An inflexible animal hide covers the entire flank, the rider wears soft boots with no spurs. Based on: Chen Juzhong's painting of a Mongol archer, early thirteenth century.*

CHAPTER 9

Modern Origins of Chinggis Khan Worship: The Mongolian Response to Japanese Influences

Yuki Konagaya

Introduction

In 2006, which marked the 800th year since Chinggis Khan's coronation in 1206, Mongolia celebrated the "800th Anniversary of the Establishment of Statehood." According to its related websites,[1] some 60 events had been planned to take place during the period from January 1 to December 31, 2006. This means, of the 365 days of the year, one out of five days or a total of 70 days were devoted to festivals. On July 15, for example, a large-scale show was held with the participation of 800 *morin khuur* (two-string horse-head fiddle) players and 800 singers. Another *morin khuur* song concert was scheduled for November 19. Many international conferences were also held. On September 18 a "Miss Mongolia" contest took place, followed by an international research conference on September 20.

Some of these events were organized by Japanese advertising companies. One example of such events was the "Chinggis Khan's Cavalry Ride," a two-hour show performed a total of 31 times from July to September. Those who wanted to see the show were required to make a reservation through certain designated agencies. To coordinate the whole project, an organization called the Executive Committee of the 800th Anniversary of the Establishment of Mongolian Statehood, Limited Liability Cooperative Association, was founded in Japan. This indicates that Chinggis Khan is a cultural resource for international business (Shimamura, 2008), and also that Japan's involvement in this grand-scale festival honoring Chinggis Khan's accomplishments was considerable

Interestingly, this series of events was also recognized internationally as an effort to promote the Global Agenda for Dialogue among Civilizations during the UN General Assembly held in November 2005. The year-long festival, which was initially supposed to be a purely domestic affair, gained international recognition as part of the UN agenda thanks to the historic significance and

1 http://www.mongolia800.mn.

 | DOI 10.1163/9789004343405_011

ecological importance of nomadic civilization.[2] These developments attest to Mongolia's outstanding diplomatic skill.

In Mongolia, preparations for the festival honoring Chinggis Khan had been under way since the previous summer. In August 2005, the mausoleum in Sükhbaatar Square [the principal square in the capital city] which symbolized socialism, was demolished, and the bodies of Sükhbaatar and Choibalsan, the two leading figures in the socialist era, that had been kept inside were cremated. And on the 6th of October, Prime Minister Elbegdorj performed the ceremony of groundbreaking for the State guesthouse and mausoleum for Chinggis Khan. Meanwhile, Bat-Ochir, a Mongolian scholar, asserted that Chinggis Khan was born on July 11, 1162.[3] The date coincides with the National Day, on which the country's annual *naadam* festival is held. If I may use the analogy of a keyboard, what Mongolia has done is like erasing the definite recent past by pressing the "Delete" key, while pressing the "Backspace" key to go backward and fix an indefinite remote past. In other words, the country is explicitly "rewriting history." In this rewriting or reforming of Mongolian history, nationalism has become conspicuous (Kaplonski, 2005), and that nationalism has indeed risen as a solution to the identity crisis of the post-socialist society (Pleines, 2008).

The 2006 festival invites comparison with the one in 1962, when Mongolia was still a People's Republic, and planned to celebrate the 800th anniversary of the birth of Chinggis Khan. At that time, it was assumed that he was born in 1162, and the festival marking the 800th year of his birth was about to take place. Prime Minister Tsedenbal ordered Tömör-Ochir, a Politburo member whom he regarded as a potential rival, to organize this event. Because Tömör-Ochir followed the order and organized activities concerning Chinggis, he was denounced as a "nationalist" and was banished to the provinces of Bayankhongor and Khövsgöl, and was later assassinated (Boldbaatar, 2004, 269–71).

Under the socialist regime, the 800th anniversary of Chinggis Khan's birth might have been a trap designed by some Mongolian politicians as a handy tool to gain approval from Moscow and to drag down their political rivals. In other words, the 1962 event was more of an internal political conflict than an affair of national significance. However, since nobody dares to emphasize the intra-Mongol struggle, or perhaps in order to downplay the intra-Mongol conflict, the event has been retold as part of a history of Soviet Russian repression of Mongolian nationalism.

With the start of the democratization process, the 1962 political incident began to be remembered as the epitome of oppression by the socialist regime.

2 United Nations General Assembly Agenda A/60/L.7.

3 http://www.montsame.mn (Mongolian National News Agency) 2005.08.16.

For example, a rock group called *Khonkh* (meaning "bell") contributed to the furtherance of the pro-democracy movement by winning the hearts and minds of the people with the song in which they apologized to Chinggis Khan for not having paid him due respect.[4]

These kinds of cultural movements created the illusion that the general public in Mongolia had had a voluntary and genuine sense of reverence towards Chinggis Khan before the socialist era. A large number of college graduation theses written in the 10 years immediately after democratization took up "national identity" as a subject. A faculty member disclosed that almost all these theses addressed the subject of Chinggis Khan or Tibetan Buddhism. This phenomenon illustrates the fact that the fall of socialism brought about an identity crisis and that Chinggis Khan was a character readily available to those who seek a symbol for their national identity.

Thus widespread reverence for Chinggis Khan in Mongolia has been described as a revival, based on two assumptions. One is that, in the Soviet era, worship of Chinggis Khan was prohibited. The second is that, before the Soviet era, people revered Chinggis Khan. These assumptions are part of today's master narrative. However, the true situation is not at all clear, and a partial modification of these simplistic assumptions has begun.

In this paper I will simply offer a few examples of cases that contribute to the revision of these assumptions. I suggest that the portraits of Chinggis Khan and the military song of Chinggis Khan confirm the modern origin of Chinggis Khan worship as, in large part, inspired by Japan (Bulag, 2010).

I use the word "worship" here to mean ordinary people's reverence for the historic figure of Chinggis Khan; I do not deal with the "Chinggis Khan Ritual" that was built up historically by rulers at the royal court. In other words, I focus on the secularization process of Chinggis Khan in modern times.

The Worship of Chinggis Khan in 1940's Inner Mongolia

At the beginning of the twentieth century, the Qing Dynasty collapsed, and East Asia began changing dynamically. While Outer Mongolia declared its autonomy, Inner Mongolia sought independence or autonomy under much more complicated international circumstances.

After the Japanese takeover of Manchuria in 1931, the eastern part of Inner Mongolia became part of the newly created Manchukuo (満州国) State. In

4 The words of the song "Chinggis Khaan" appear in the book which a Japanese ambassador to Mongolia has written after his retirement (Takase, 1992).

this puppet State, the Japanese attempted to combine, through formal education, disparate ethnicities into a single new national identity as people of Manchukuo (Li Narangoa 2001). In 1944, the Chinggis Khan Mausoleum was built in the city of Wang Ye Miao (nowadays Ulan Khot), and Chinggis Khan became the symbol of the integration of Mongolians and many other ethnic groups, including the Japanese newcomers.

Outside of the territory of Manchukuo, in 1937 three Mongolian autonomous governments were established, and in 1941 these three governments were integrated into the Mongolian Autonomous Federation (蒙古自治邦). Demchigdonrov, who was the leader of this integrated government, accepted Japanese supervision, especially of the military and educational systems. Imperial Japan founded the Good Neighbor Association in 1934 and started conducting education in the Japanese language at schools set up at local district base stations of this special agency, and also began to admit Mongolian students to schools in Japan (Tuvshin, 1984; Mori 2000).

Thus both inside and outside Manchukuo, Japanese influences in both the military and educational systems were dominant. According to Tanaka, who investigated the process of building the Chinggis Khan Mausoleum, Mongolian intellectuals who had been to Japan were ardent nationalists, and the Japanese made use of their desires and aspirations in building Manchukuo and the Mongolian Federation (Tanaka, 2009). Early in 1937, not only was the mausoleum built, but also the Chinggis Khan calendar was introduced to the Mongolian autonomous governments.

1 *Portraits of Chinggis Khan*

In one of his novels, a Japanese writer who in 1943 had been in Abaga Banner, Shilingol League, an area situated in the present-day Inner Mongolian Autonomous Region of China, wrote about the cultural landscape of that time.. An elderly Mongolian says to the Japanese teacher, “I heard your schools hang a picture of Chinggis Khan on the wall and make the students pray to him every day. I don’t see what sort of benefit will come out of it. Isn’t it more auspicious to put up a picture of Gegen, the Living Buddha?”(Kimura, 1994, 47–50)

This description indicates that, in this particular area near the home territory of Demchigdonrov, schools were built as part of Japan’s cultural promotion policy, and the students were taught to “worship Chinggis Khan.” The custom of daily worship reminds us of the “Emperor worship” practiced throughout Japan in those days.

According to the results of a questionnaire of religious consciousness developed in 1936 at the Military Academy of Wang Ye Miao, only ten students out of 176 mentioned Chinggis Khan as the name of God (Akamatsu, 1941).

This figure also showed the low awareness of Chinggis Khan among ordinary people. "Because the spiritual world of students was dominated by Tibetan Buddhism and Daoism, the Mongolian intellectual elite tried to evoke nationalism through Chinggis Khan"(Tanaka, 2009, 121).

In a blueprint of a girls' school in West Sunit Banner, which happened to be the homeland of Demchigdonrov and the core center of the Japanese agency, two portraits were arranged on the altar in the *khoimor* (north-west corner for gods) of a *ger* (Mongolian tent). One was of Chinggis Khan, and the other was of Demchigdonrov. (Naito, 1943(3), 52–53).[5]

One Mongolian elder remembered that he heard the name of Chinggis Khan for the first time from his cousin who had been to the junior high school, as a Japanese teacher and a Mongolian teacher from Kalgan (Zhangjiakou), using Chinggis Khan's portrait, described his great achievements (Tsuji, 2001, 205).

Unfortunately, it is not clear from these sources exactly which portraits these were. There were two types of images of Chinggis Khan (Charleux, 2009). One was based on the famous portrait held at the National Palace Museum in Taiwan. This type of portrait was used in formal education in Manchukuo (Li Narangoa, 2010). The textbook for second-year students in elementary school gave instructions on how to worship Chinggis Khan by burning incense and making offerings to the portrait. The figure in the handbook published by the Good Neighbor Association (in Japanese, *Zenrinkyokai*) in 1938 (Fig. 1) is one of the variants of this type, with a slightly different beard from the original, and just the same as that in the book of "Images of Chinese Emperors" (Tsutsumi, 2012). The portrait recollected by the Mongolian elder might be this type because "the figure was wearing the traditional costume" (Tsuji, 2001, 205).

The other type is quite different in costume, especially the helmet (Fig. 2). It was printed in the initial issue of *Blue Banner* (Blue Flag), which was published as part of Japan's cultural promotion policy for the Mongolians in Manchukuo after the Nomonhan Incident (or Battle of Khalkhin Gol) between the victors, Mongolia and the Soviet Union, and the loser, Japan, in 1939. The chief editor was a Japanese with a Mongolian name (Hirokawa, 2007, 115). Regarding this modern type, while it is said to have been drawn by a Japanese (Yang,

5 The famous Mongolian poet Saichogt (formerly named Saichinga) was a teacher from 1942 to 1947 at this girls' school. He first learned the Japanese language in 1936, went to Japan from 1937 to 1941, and for a while he was a secretary to Demchigdonrov. Sainchinga wrote a poem called "Descendant of Chinggis" during the 1940's (Nachin, 2011, 380), and in his diary, the entry for 22 August, 1940, mentioned that he hummed the song "The Army of Chinggis." This is a typical case of a Mongolian intellectual who studied in Japan and was an agent of nationalism and/or worship of Chinggis (Na Sainchogt, 1999, 202).

2001, 12), Sayinshiyal claimed, in his book *The Short History of the Chinggis Khan Mausoleum*, that this portrait was drawn by a Frenchman in the nineteenth century and was kept at Chinggis Khan's gravemound in Ordos until it went missing in China's Great Proletarian Cultural Revolution of 1966 to 1976 (Sayinshiyal, 1987, vol.2, 1209). A photo of it was taken in the 1920s by Zhang Xiangwen (張相文), the president of the Geographical Society, and appeared in the journal of this society. I checked the journals and discovered that from 1915 to 1917 Zhang had been to the Ordos four times and reported four times (Zhang, 1915; 1916; 1917a; 1917b); however, I could not find the original photo in these issues of the journal.

This type of portrait traveled north through the translation of Sayinshiyal's book into Russian (Hamayon, 2010, 159–60) and is used nowadays on calendars in the Buryat Republic (Fig. 3). Actually the original calendar printed by the *Blue Banner* publisher for the Mongols in Manchukuo (Fig. 4) was almost the same and can safely be said to be reused again nowadays in Buryatia.

This type of Chinggis Khan portrait must have been renowned in Japan, because it appeared in the best-selling book *Chinggis Khan Is Minamoto Yoshitsune*, written by Oyabe Mataichiro (Fig. 5). In order to confirm the bizarre idea that the defeated Japanese hero and samurai Yoshitsune adopted the name "Chinggis Khan" after moving to the North Asian mainland, Oyabe traveled from Changchung via Harbin to Hairal (Oyabe, 1924, 199) and finally arrived at the Aga Temple 107 km. south-west from Orowiyannaya (Oyabe, 1924, 222). He found this portrait in that temple and wondered why the monks prayed not to the Buddha but to a military officer. Identifying the figure on the helmet as the family crest of the Genji (the family of Minamoto Yoshitsune), he argued that Chinggis Khan was originally Japanese (Oyabe, 1924, 231).

An absurd story was fabricated about Minamoto Yoshitsune (1159–1189), one of the greatest samurai. His name in Chinese characters is pronounced as Gen Gikei, which sounds the same as "Genghis." According to this, Chinggis Khan was really Minamoto Yoshitsune, who, though in reality had died in 1189, allegedly crossed over to the continent (Miyawaki, 2006). This story was designed to develop a psychological climate that would justify Japan's advances into the continent of Asia. It was of course false, but no matter how untrue it was, forging a memory of Chinggis Khan was essential to creating an emotional rationale for promoting Japan's grand design to portray itself as having strong links with the Mongolian people.

Moreover, we can find another case of this type of portrait in a photo album published in 1921 (Hosoo, 1921), which a Russian who had been raised at a Buddhist temple in Ulaanbaatar had purportedly drawn.

Thus the same Western type of Chinggis Khan was found at three different places and attributed to a Japanese, a French, or a Russian artist. We do not have to decide which is an accurate representation.; each expresses the Western influence on this portrait. Similarly, in Japan, a portrait of the Meiji Emperor done in the Western style was used to educate people to revere the emperor as the symbol of modern nationalism. Whoever may have drawn the portrait, this depiction of Chinggis was useful for teaching modern nationalism to Mongolians. Whether in the traditional or military style, the Japanese brought the portraits of Chinggis Khan to Mongolian society to help arouse modern nationalism.

2 *Martial Songs*

Military songs, as well as pictures, were also disseminated under Japan's colonial policy. Of about one hundred songs collected and transcribed into musical notation by Henning Haslund-Christensen, a member of the Northwestern China Expedition team led by the Swedish explorer Sven Hedin, five songs have titles or lyrics referring to Chinggis Khan (Haslund-Christensen, 1943). These are: song number 5, "The Song of Chinggis Khan," recorded in the Jarait Banner; song number 30, "The Father Chinggis" (translated as "Our Ancestor Chinggis Khan"), recorded in the Tosheet Gung Banner; song number 35, "The Song of the Heroic Army of Our Ancestor Chinggis," recorded in the Darkhan Wang Banner; song number 44, "The Father Chinggis" (translated as "Our Ancestor Chingis Khan"); and song number 54, "Khasar Chinggis," recorded in the Zasagt Khan Banner.

The last is a folk song with a slow tempo and might have been inherited as part of an oral tradition. On the other hand, the other four songs are just marches. Numbers 30 and 44 have the same title, and their melody lines are almost the same (Fig. 6). They are similar to the Japanese army song entitled "Brothers-in-the-army", composed by Miyoshi Waki in 1905 (Fig. 7).

This Japanese military song in its original form tells a long story about a wounded soldier who became the chief of a village. Ordinary people enjoyed singing it as a sad melody in a short version, which includes phrases about the loss of friends. Although the army banned it because of its sad melody, people continued to sing it in the period of the Second World War, and after the War it became the most popular of the nostalgic martial songs. This song is not an official military song, but soldiers love it nevertheless. Hattori pointed out that the Japanese military song "Subaltern Ogawa" was also widely known in Inner Mongolia (Hattori, 1977, 90), and it might have the same melody as song number 48, "Beauty of the Togol River" (Haslund-Christensen, 1943, 50).[6]

6 In Outer Mongolia, too, through the Japanese community, the Japanese "Song of the Railroad" became the Mongolian "Song for Women" (Futaki, 1985).

In addition to these songs, some Japanese collected and transcribed songs entitled "The Song of Chinggis' Army" (Fig. 8) or "The Song of Saint Chinggis" (Fig. 9). The one we call simply "The Army of Chinggis" is the same song. Variants of the melody have been reported (Takeda, 1940, 149), and this song was also recorded and distributed in Japan by the Columbia Records company in 1938 (Taki, 1938, 75). The same song is referred to in the novel mentioned above (Kimura, 1994, 51), which describes schools' practice of marching in the afternoon. If there were onlookers, they would sing along.

The memoir of a Japanese national who came back to Japan from the continent says, "We spent months and years in Inner Mongolia. And the first thing we learned by heart was this song of Chinggis Khan. We used to sing it on many occasions in our daily lives."[7] At least, it is clear from such memories that Japanese people sang the Chinggis Khan song and worshipped him much more than the Mongolians did.

It also seems likely that some Japanese nationals were involved in the composition of "The Army of Chinggis," It is undoubtedly not a folk song, with its note intervals clearly different from those of other local folk songs. In lyrics such as "let us conquer Asia, conquer north and south, suppress Europe, and subjugate China and Tibet," the sense of advancing across the Asian continent and the optimistic mood of the imperial Japanese were vividly expressed.

The evidence offered above concerning the modern worship of Chinggis Khan in Inner Mongolia may be rested in this way.

(1) The Japanese side initiated rites for the worship of Chinggis Khan.
(2) The Japanese community admired Chinggis Khan.
(3) Mongolian intellectual elites developed the rituals for the worship of Chinggis Khan.
(4) Ordinary Mongolians believed in Tibetan Buddhism and did not admire Chinggis Khan.

The truth of (1) and 3) has long been well known, and with regard to (2) the historical change has been pointed out already (Elverskog, 2006, 85–89). In this paper I have produced some minor but tangible evidence of (2) and (4).

7 Mr. Kitagawa gave me not only the musical notation and the words of this song but also described the memories of the people living there.

Conclusion

Educational and military systems often shape modernization. In the northeastern part of China in the mid-20th century, Japan established new schooling and military systems to promote modernization among the Mongolian people, and the worship of Chinggis Khan was also developed and disseminated as part of this process.

In Japan, the legend of Yoshitsune imagined a community between Japan and Mongolia. This "imagined community" (Anderson 1983), together with the worship of Chinggis Khan as an "invented tradition" (Hobsbaum 1983), created a "fictitious community" that cast a net over a society with a totally different legal framework and culture. Historically, the absurd story of Yoshitsune crossing the sea was created long ago, in the Edo period (Morimura, 2005); in modern times an essay in English re-created the legend (Miyawaki 2006); and in 1924 Oyabe Mataichiro's book paved the way for the idenitification of Yoshitsune with Chinggis Khan.

After the collapse of imperial Japan, Japanese use of Chinggis Khan followed a different course from that in Mongolia. In Japanese literature, the wounded man, or the man with a defect, who would go on to be a success was an important theme, and so Chinggis Khan, too, became a hero whose defect was that he was not a legitimate son. Specifically, in Inoue Yasushi's best-selling Japanese novel about Chinggis Khan, titled *Gray Wolf* (1959), he created a new pseudo-historical story that Chinggis was not a legitimate son, just as Chinggis' alleged son Jochi was not a legitimate son of Chinggis Khan's. Chinggis determined to overcome the defect of his birth by striving to conquer the world (Konagaya, 2008). The Japanese–Mongolian film based on this Japanese novel has gained a bad reputation, and been greeted with protest demonstrations at the Japanese embassy because the Mongolians were upset by the story. Nowadays the "imagined community" of the past could not exist.

Acknowledgements

This is an abridged translation from a paper in Japanese published in 2013 in the Bulletin of the National Museum of Ethnology, 37(4), 425–447. Originally the paper was based on the oral report "The Modern Sources of the Chinggis Khan Cult in Mongolia" presented at the international symposium "The Image of Powers in Asia" held in Paris, 22–27th March, 2006, and was developed for the international symposium "Chinggis Khan and Mongolia in the 21th century" held in Tokyo, 20th May, 2012. I wish to thank the organizers for giving me the opportunity to present my views. Moreover, I deeply appreciate the valuable advice I received from many researchers at the two symposia, and also I thank Mr. Kitagawa and Mr. Tsuzuku for providing the musical material I cited in this essay.

FIGURE 9.1 *Portrait of Chinggis Khan (Good Neighbor Association, research division, 1938).*

FIGURE 9.2 *Portrait of Chinggis Khan (Yang, 2005).*

FIGURE 9.3 *Portrait of Chinggis Khan (Hamayon, 2010).*

図1 満洲国 新京 青旗報社のカレンダー (大阪大学外国学図書館石濱文庫蔵)

FIGURE 9.4 *Calendar from Blue Banner Publishers (Tsutsumi, 2012).*

成吉思汗之肖像

原圖蒙古首府喇嘛總本山秘藏

（圖中の蒙古文字は大聖成吉思汗と譯す）

FIGURE 9.5 *Portrait of Chinggis Khan (Oyabe, 1924).*

FIGURE 9.6 *The two songs entitled "Father Chinggis" (Hasslund-Christensen, 1943).*

戦友

FIGURE 9.7 *The melody line of the Japanese martial song, "A Fellow Soldier." However, the sorrow of the melody had disappeared.*

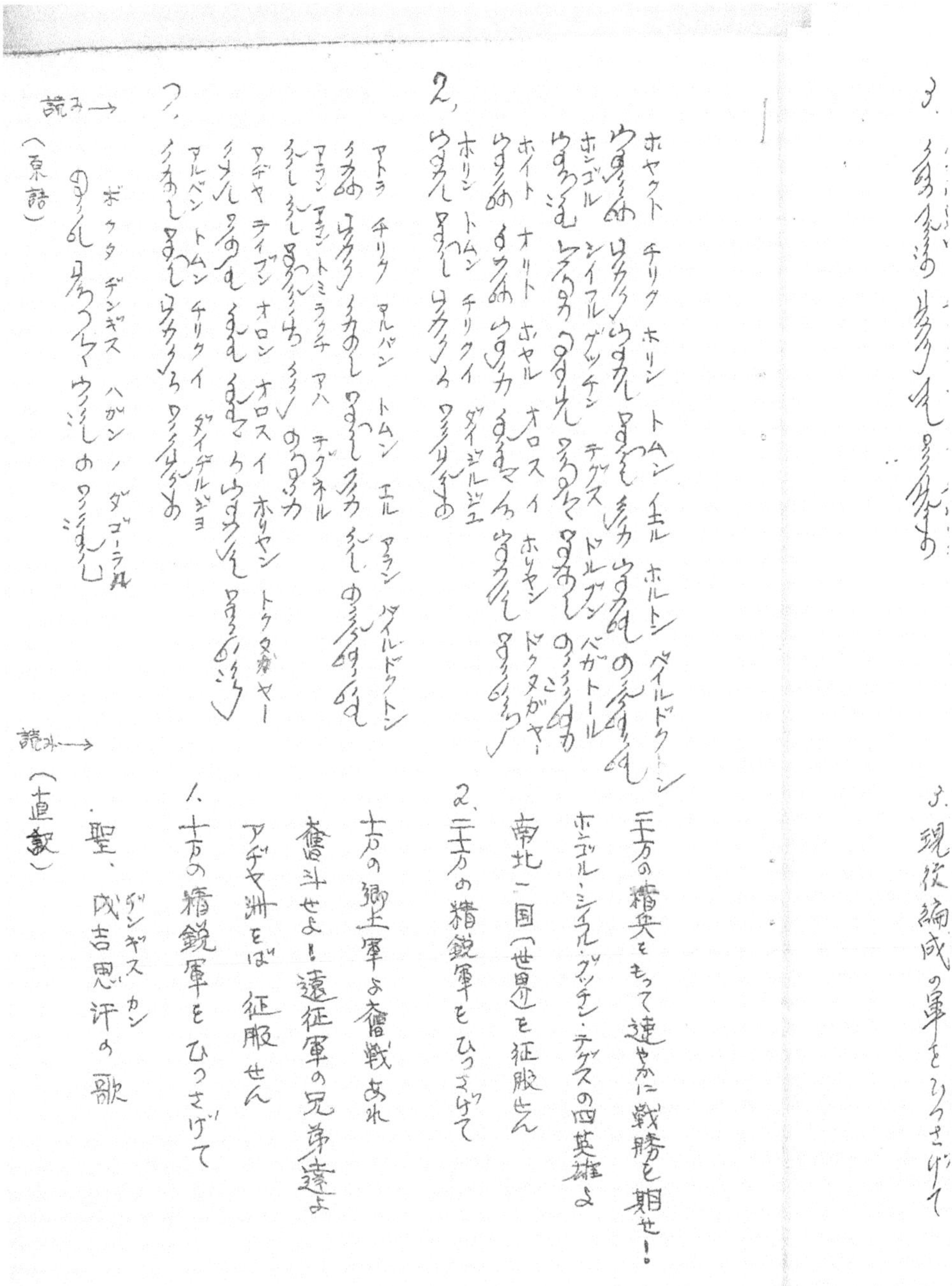

FIGURE 9.8 *The lyrics of the song "Bogd Chinggis Khan" (supplied by Kitagawa Masashi).*

FIGURE 9.9 *The score for the song "The Launch of Chinggis Khan" (supplied byTsuzuku Muneo).*

CHAPTER 10

Mongolia: Addressing the Risks and Promises of the Nuclear Age

Enkhsaikhan Jargalsaikhan

Introduction

Mongolia's Foreign Policy Challenges

In many respects, and certainly in foreign relations and diplomacy, Mongolian policies are affected above all by its geographical location and reflect the main events of a particular time period. In many cases, its policies can be understood as reactions to the events occurring in neighboring Russia and China, in their relations with each other as well as with other major powers. That is why Mongolia tries, within the limited possibilities and means at its disposal, and when circumstances allow, to play an active part in trying to influence events, either to avoid harm or to its advantage.

After the disintegration of the Mongol Empire, Mongolian tribes engaged in internecine wars, while Russia and China expanded their territories. By the beginning of the twentieth century, Mongolia found itself sandwiched and squeezed between the still aggressively expanding Russia and China. Isolated and with nowhere else to turn (in 1911–13 Mongols tried to gain support from the United States, Japan, and some other influential countries but without success) and mindful of China's historical interest in absorbing its territory, Mongolia decided to seek Russia's protection from the probable encroachments of China. This coincided with the period of revolutionary changes in Russia. Close relations with Soviet Russia took its toll. Mongolia had to toe the Soviet line in both its internal and foreign policies.

In the socialist period (1924–90), the notion of the nation's interest was supplanted by that of "class interest," which in reality meant Soviet/Russian interest and virtual Soviet domination. This "class interest" transcended all domestic and foreign policy interests. Because of the "class" approach to all issues, including internal opposition to sovietization of Mongolian society, even national security came to be seen through the prism of "class interest" and "class struggle." This approach divided Mongolian society into oppressed and oppressors. Hence, by the early 1930s the country was in a state of virtual civil war. This led to wave after wave of purges and repressions, and resulted

 | DOI 10.1163/9789004343405_012

in the physical elimination of tens of thousands of Mongolians, especially the elites, the clergy, and independent-minded people. Thus, until 1990 Mongolian society was heavily under the influence of the Soviet Union, while its "class struggle" approach to foreign policy and virtual self-isolation hampered its ability to acquire friends and develop cooperation with other countries.

The end of World War II and establishment of pro-Soviet states in Central and Eastern Europe, in China and the DPRK, were welcome developments for Mongolia since they to some extent reduced its isolation. However, it had to wait for 15 years to be admitted to the United Nations, which gradually reduced its ideological and political isolation. In the 1950s and 1960s Mongolia worked hard to overcome political isolation and develop normal relations with non-socialist countries. India was one of these to recognize Mongolia and establish diplomatic relations with it. The United Kingdom recognized Mongolia in 1963 and became the first Western country to establish diplomatic relations and open up its embassy. Establishment of the long-awaited diplomatic relations with the United States in 1987 signaled the end of Mongolia's diplomatic and political isolation.

The next logical foreign policy goal was to promote mutually beneficial trade, economic and cultural relations with countries other than its neighbors or fellow socialist countries. This period coincided with the break-up of the Soviet bloc and disintegration of the Soviet Union itself. This in turn led to the fundamental reorientation of the country from socialist authoritarianism towards a democratic multiparty system and market economy. In foreign policy its priorities were to promote its own national interests as perceived and defined by Mongolians themselves and reflected in the new 1992 post-Cold War Constitution, and then in greater detail in three important policy-setting interrelated documents: the Concept of National Security of Mongolia, the Concept of Foreign Policy and the Fundamentals of the Military Doctrine of Mongolia. These documents, passed in 1994 by the State Great Khural (parliament) of Mongolia, set forth the following as the country's foreign and security policy goals:

- Pursue a pragmatic, open, multi-track[1] and multi-pillar[2] foreign policy;
- Ensure a favorable external security environment primarily by political and legal means;

1 Multi-track foreign policies are policies in political, economic, social, science and technology, cultural and other areas.

2 A multi-pillar policy is a Mongolian policy that gives priority to Mongolian relations with its immediate neighbors and the "third neighbors". Other pillars are relations with the Asian countries, the United Nations and other international organizations, and other countries with which it had or has closer relations.

- Follow a policy of non-alignment, political realism, and pursuit of vital national interests, while at the same time respecting the legitimate interests of its partners;
- Accord top priority to balanced good-neighborly relations with its immediate neighbors, maintain neutrality in their disputes unless they affect Mongolia's vital interests, in which case she would follow those interests;
- Pursue the policy of greater openness and acquiring "third neighbors," i.e., Eastern or Western democracies, international organizations, or other stakeholders that support Mongolia's democratic development. In doing so special emphasis is placed on fostering the long-term economic interests of the major industrial powers and their companies in Mongolia.

Looking back over 25 years of Mongolia's political-economic development and foreign policy, one could say that the major goals of democratic development and introducing a market economy, as well as broadening its foreign relations, have been achieved. Thus today Mongolia maintains diplomatic relations with almost all the members of the United Nations. With its immediate neighbors it has no territorial or border problems and maintains relations of strategic partnership. All three have agreed not to allow the use of their territories to harm the interests of the other two. The neighbors have agreed to respect Mongolia's choice of its political and socio-economic development. They have also tacitly agreed to its "third neighbor" policy as long as it did not infringe their vital national interests.

Mongolia and Nuclear Issues

Mongolia's location between two nuclear-weapon states and lack of direct free access to other countries or world markets makes it imperative, *inter alia*, to specifically address the issues of nuclear security, whether military or connected with the peaceful uses of its nuclear energy. Mongolia could choose either to be passively affected by the perils of the nuclear age or to try to play an active role, as far as possible, in shaping its future, promoting its national interests and enjoying, as much as possible, the benefits and dividends of the peaceful atom.

The three distinct issues that it needs to address are:

1. nuclear-weapon-related threats;
2. safety of nuclear facilities located near Mongolia; and
3. benefiting from the peaceful uses of nuclear energy.

Nuclear-Weapon-Related Threats

During the Cold War period Mongolia was involuntarily subjected to double Cold War pressures: East-West and Sino-Soviet. As a Soviet ally, from 1967 it hosted Soviet bases on its territory.

In the late 1960s, at the height of the Sino-Soviet ideological dispute, Mongolia found itself involuntarily involved in its two immediate neighbors' ideological and political polemics and by implication in their virtual nuclear stand-off, although it did not have any intention of getting involved. When China successfully developed nuclear weapons in the late 1960s, the Soviets either entertained the idea of making a preemptive nuclear strike against its fledgling nuclear-weapon facilities so as to bring to a halt or at least delay as far as possible such a development, or made believe to China, the United States and other countries that it seriously entertained such an idea. When archive materials are made available in those countries, it will be possible to know whether that was the actual intention or a bluff designed to scare and pressure China. A preemptive strike would surely have had a devastating effect on Mongolia since the Chinese side was aware of Soviet bases near its borders and the dual-use weapons therein. That is why in 1992, when the Cold War came to an end and the Soviets/Russians withdrew their troops and armaments from Mongolia, President P. Ochirbat went to the United Nations General Assembly and declared the country a single-state nuclear-weapon-free zone (NWFZ) and pledged to have that status internationally guaranteed. Since then, Mongolia has been working hard to realize that grand goal.

In June 1994 the State Great Khural adopted the National Security Concept of Mongolia as a strategy to ensure Mongolia's security in the post-Cold War period. That concept envisioned the country's nuclear-weapon-free status as an important element in the strengthening of its security by political means.

The Nuclear-Weapon-Free Status of Mongolia

The gist of the proposal was to declare that it did not have nuclear weapons on its territory and to make sure that henceforth it would be nuclear-weapon free so that, unlike during the Cold War, no country near or far would train its nuclear weapons on Mongolia. This policy also meant that no nuclear-weapon threat to others would emanate from the vast Mongolian territory. Reference to international guarantees meant that the five nuclear-weapon states (P5), including its two immediate neighbors, would recognize Mongolia's nuclear-weapon-free status and would commit to respect it and not involve Mongolia in their geopolitical calculations or nuclear doctrines and policies, thus ensuring predictability and stability in that part of the region. Subsequent events, including US destabilizing policies of renouncing the AMB treaty[3] and developing national or regional missile defenses, have shown the timeliness of Mongolia's policy of turning its territory into an internationally recognized NWFZ to avoid being drawn into increasing Russia-West confrontation.

The international community has widely supported Mongolia's initiative. In 1998, the United Nations General Assembly welcomed Mongolia's policy, its support for Mongolia's good-neighborly and balanced relations with its neighbors being an important element in strengthening regional peace, security and stability. The resolution also invited member states, including the P5, to cooperate with Mongolia in taking the necessary measures to consolidate and strengthen its "independence, sovereignty and territorial integrity, the inviolability of its borders, its economic security, its ecological balance and its nuclear-weapon-free status, as well as its independent foreign policy".

On the basis of wide international support for its initiative, in February 2000 the Mongolian parliament adopted a special law that defined the country's NWF status at the national level and criminalized acts that would violate that status. Thus the law reaffirmed Mongolia's commitments, undertaken by the Treaty on the Non-Proliferation of Nuclear Weapons, not to produce or otherwise obtain nuclear weapons and, in addition, it outlawed the stationing and transit through its territory of nuclear weapons by any means. Reflecting the importance of the issue for the society as a whole, the law enables non-governmental organizations and individuals, within the mandate provided by the legislation, to exercise public oversight of the implementation of the law and submit proposals thereon to government authorities.

Following up on the General Assembly resolution and mindful of its legislation, in October of that year the P5 made a joint statement providing Mongolia with negative[4] and positive[5] security assurances. Mongolia welcomed this joint statement as an initial step in institutionalizing its status. At the same

3 The ABM treaty is a treaty between the United States and the Soviet Union on the limitation of the anti-ballistic missile (ABM) systems to defend areas against ballistic missile-delivered nuclear weapons in their respective countries.

4 Negative security assurance is a pledge provided by a nuclear weapon state to a non-nuclear-weapon state that under certain conditions it would not use or threaten to use nuclear weapons against the latter.

5 Positive security assurance is a pledge provided by a nuclear weapon state to a non-nuclear-weapon state that it would provide assistance should the latter become a victim of nuclear attack.

time it informed the P5 that since the joint statement was political, it lacked legal force and could not serve as a viable security assurance: it could be rescinded by a subsequent joint statement. Content-wise, Mongolia thought that it was made in a Cold War spirit by virtually enumerating conditions under which the P4 (not including China, which provided unconditional assurances to Mongolia) would not use or threaten to use nuclear weapons against it. Mongolia believed that this was in stark contrast with the good-neighborly relations that it enjoyed with its neighbors and the remaining P3. Though the P5 was reluctant to admit that their one-size-fits-all approach to the issue was not appropriate in Mongolia's case, they were clearly unwilling to admit this reluctance since doing so would embarrass them.

Between 2000 and 2012 Mongolia held a number of bilateral, trilateral and multilateral meetings with the P5, which led to an agreement to adopt parallel P5 joint declaration and Mongolian declaration in which the terms of Mongolia's nuclear-weapon-free status would be clearly defined and whereby the P5 would provide Mongolia with more practically useful and credible assurances. In its declaration Mongolia reaffirmed its commitment not to allow nuclear weapons to be stationed on, or transported through, its territory. For their part the P5 not only reaffirmed their 2000 negative and positive security assurances, and welcomed the passage of Mongolia's law in 2000, but also pledged to respect the status and not contribute to any act that would violate it. In practical terms that meant that none of the P5 would involve Mongolia in their nuclear strategies, including the establishment of a nuclear missile defense system, global or regional, or basic elements of a possible counter system on its territory. In that sense the joint P5 declaration is in the national interest of Mongolia as well as that of regional stability and confidence.

There is a saying in Mongolia that "a duck is calm when the lake is calm". In other words, Mongolia's interests are best served when the regional security environment is stable. That is why it tries to play an active positive role in the region, especially since it has no territorial issues or border problems with any country and maintains good-neighborly relations with all the countries of the region, including the DPRK. With respect to the latter, it believes that engagement rather than isolation of the DPRK is a key to addressing the region's security-related issues. That is the main purpose of the Ulaanbaatar security dialogue in Northeast Asia proposed by President Ts. Elbegdorj in 2013, so as to provide a space and platform for track 1.5 or 2 meetings and to discuss the issues under the so-called Chatham House rules. Two such meetings have been held since, which contributed to a more informal atmosphere for the discussion of issues that cannot be carried on in the formal Six Party Talks format. Referring to regional security through the establishment of a Northeast Asian

NWFZ, President Elbegdorj has expressed Mongolia's readiness to promote informal meetings on the issue. Two such informal meetings have been held in Ulaanbaatar in which it was possible to focus on the essential issues that need to be addressed if there is to be a serious discussion of the issue.

Silent Nuclear Threats

Nuclear-Weapon Tests and Their Impact

We are living in a nuclear age with its enormous promises as well as hidden perils. In the past half-century, the world has witnessed escalation of the dangerous nuclear arms race and a race to "perfect" nuclear weapons through tests. Out of 2,050 registered nuclear weapons tests conducted in the world, 760 (or about one third) have been conducted by Russia and China. The Soviet Union has conducted 207 atmospheric and 508 underground tests, most of them at the Semipalatinsk test site not far from Mongolia.[6] Geographically, Mongolia is "downwind" from Semipalatinsk, with all the ensuing consequences.

China has conducted 23 atmospheric and 22 underground tests at Lop Nor test site that is also not far from Mongolia.[7] So far the health and environmental impact of these tests on the Mongolian population and the environment have not been assessed. Hence, as a country that has witnessed over 500 nuclear-weapon tests on its doorsteps, and as a member of the Conference on Disarmament, Mongolia took an active part in the negotiations of the Comprehensive Test Ban Treaty (CTBT) and was one of the first countries to have signed and ratified the treaty. It advocates early entry into force of the CTBT and hosts duly certified primary seismic, infrasound and radionuclide stations of CTBT's International Monitoring System.

Since Mongolia enjoys good relations with both of its neighbors, it needs to raise the issue of assessing, together with relevant international organizations or experts, the impacts of nuclear-weapon tests on the Mongolian people living in the areas situated near test sites. When raising this issue with its neighbors, it should underline the importance of this for the second and third

6 According to the IAEA report Estimation of Global Inventories of Radioactive Waste and Other Radioactive Materials (IAEA-TECHDOC-1591, p. 39, 2007) nuclear weapon testing at Semipalatinsk generated the widespread dispersion of ${}_{90}$Sr 3.5 E3 TBq (i.e. terabyte or 10^{12} bequrel radioactivity), ${}_{137}$Cs 6.6 E3 TBq, ${}_{239}$Pu<1.0 E2 TBq.

7 According to the IAEA, the material available shows that nuclear weapon testing at Lop Nor (as of 1989) left the site a certain amount of ${}_{239}$Pu, which has been estimated to amount to about 6.7 E1 TBq.

generation of affected people; and not necesssarily for the purpose of asking for belated compensation. Most of the countries that have been affected by nuclear weapon tests have addressed the issue and have taken appropriate, though perhaps belated, measures. This is the least that the Government can do, even belatedly, to the children and grandchildren of the victimized people.

Border Area Security

With the virtual cessation of nuclear-weapon tests, one of the challenges that Mongolia is facing today, besides nuclear weapons and such weapon-related facilities as are located not far from the Mongolian territory, is also over 30 nuclear facilities used for so-called peaceful nuclear activities. There are no nuclear power plants or nuclear reactors (except for a nuclear power plant to be built at Kurchatov in the eastern region of Kazakhstan). China and Russia are the two *de jure* nuclear weapon states[8] that, along with the US, UK and France, have a special status not only within the United Nations Security Council or the NPT, but also at the IAEA. The safeguards regime that is applied for other states does not fully apply to them. Hence, instead of concluding a comprehensive safeguard agreement (CSA) with the IAEA, they have agreed to voluntary offer safeguard agreements (VOA). The agreement is based on the discretion of the nuclear-weapon states, whereby they offer for inspection a list of nuclear materials and/or facilities from which the Agency and its inspectors may select those subject to safeguards, on condition that the P5 may withdraw the offers or exempt those they consider to have national security significance. So the Agency implements safeguards in the P5: (i) to test innovative safeguards methods, or to provide the Agency with experience that it might not otherwise gain in safeguarding advanced nuclear fuel cycle facilities; and/or (ii) to fulfill the expectations of non-nuclear-weapon states that some facilities in nuclear-weapon states should be subject to safeguards. The safeguards are also applied as a result of legal obligations arising from other safeguards agreements and for reasons of efficiency. Thus the Russian list consists of 30 facilities for the possible application of the Agency's safeguards.

Hence the dilemma that Mongolia faces is that most Russian and Chinese civilian nuclear facilities are not accessible to IAEA inspectors and thus their nuclear security and safety are not transparent to assure the prevention of

8 *De jure* nuclear weapon states are the five nuclear weapon states that had declared and tested nuclear weapons before 1967 and have thus been designated as such in the 1968 Treaty on the Non-Proliferation of Nuclear Weapons.

possible accidents that could affect adjacent areas, in this case Mongolian territory, especially the people in that particular border area. Knowing well that, as long as there are nuclear weapons, the military bases and nuclear-weapon-related facilities will be off limits, it is important to delineate clearly nuclear-weapon-related facilities and facilities for peaceful uses of nuclear energy and to open all the latter facilities, without exception, for nuclear inspections by the IAEA. This would ensure that the safety standards are observed at all civilian nuclear facilities and that these are open for random inspection if necessary.

Nuclear Waste

Disposal of nuclear waste is one of the most challenging issues facing not only the international scientific community but the world in general. The world's 443 nuclear reactors in 30 countries have produced around 300,000 metric tons of spent nuclear fuel (SNF). At present there are over 250,000 tons of spent nuclear fuel waiting for permanent disposal. Annually, 10,000–12,000 tons of "new" waste are produced that will eventually need permanent disposal as well.

Today Mongolia runs the risk of becoming sandwiched between its two immediate neighbors' enormous nuclear waste repositories, with all the ensuing potential long-lasting health and environmental consequences. Russia, with 34 nuclear reactors, is number 3 and China, with 27 reactors, is number 5 of top nuclear energy producers which create enormous amounts of nuclear waste. Russia is building 10 additional reactors and planning 14 more in the next decade. China, for its part, is planning to build an additional 27 reactors and adding 32 more in the future. According to the understandings reached, Russia is expected to accept nuclear wastes from countries that are using Soviet/Russian-built nuclear reactors and nuclear fuel for those reactors. Though China is a newcomer in the business of exporting nuclear power plants, what arrangements it would have for the disposal of nuclear waste from its exported reactors, let alone its own nuclear waste, is still unknown.

At present, the share of nuclear power in overall electricity production is about 16 percent. Despite the 2011 Fukushima nuclear accident, the number of power stations being built would practically double the share of nuclear-generated electricity to almost 30 percent by 2030. With the possible increase of nuclear waste produced nationally as well as internationally, there has even been some talk of building a global nuclear waste repository (also known as a multinational nuke waste repository) in Russia. According to Russian nuclear experts, the country has already accepted for permanent disposal nuclear wastes from Romania, Bulgaria, Libya and some other countries. Russia's national operator for radioactive waste management, NO RAO, has completed the design documents for an underground research laboratory to study the feasibility of final disposal of solid high-level radioactive waste (HLW) and solid medium-level long-lived wastes in Nizhnekansky granitoid rock massif in Zheleznogorsk, in the region of Krasnoyarsk. The waste is expected to be stored at a depth of 450–525 meters. Russia's Krasnokamensk, in the Chita region adjacent to Mongolia, is also a potential site for a permanent nuclear waste repository.

Another development that could affect Mongolia's nuclear environment is the establishment in Angarsk, part of the Irkutsk region bordering on Mongolia, of an International Uranium Enrichment Center (IUEC). The center has become operational and maintains guaranteed a reserve of LEU[9] for countries willing to develop nuclear power generation. Mongolia needs to know if Russia would be ready to take back the spent nuclear fuel of the enriched uranium used in client states' nuclear power plants (which is the accepted international practice), and, if yes, where and how the spent fuel would be stored.

As to China, information on its nuclear weapons facilities and waste is scarce and virtually inaccessible. What is known so far is that China's 26 nuclear reactors produce about 20 GWe. By 2020 it is expected that it will have the third largest number of nuclear power generating units after the United States and France, producing about 58 GWe. In the past decade China has become almost self-sufficient in reactor design and construction and is looking forward to exporting nuclear technology. It has a number of enrichment centers that would be able to produce fuel that would be used for their export-oriented nuclear reactors.

It is natural that China, which is struggling to bring down coal consumption, should be turning to nuclear energy and even working to export nuclear power plants. However, for Mongolia the question is how and where China will be disposing of the nuclear waste. According to Chinese nuclear experts, at present the country has two sites for disposing of medium and low radioactive wastes: in Yumen of Gansu Province (part of Inner Mongolia, bordering on Mongolia) and in Beilong in Guangdong Province on the southeast coast.

As to the highly radioactive nuclear waste, China does not yet have a permanent disposal site. However, Beishan, also in Gansu Province—not far from Mongolia—has been designated as the best place, since it is believed to have a granite bedrock and stable tectonic activity. Hence, an underground laboratory for the Beishan nuclear waste disposal storehouse would be built by 2025 and

9 LEU is low-enriched uranium, i.e. uranium that has lower than 20% concentration of ^{235}U.

by 2040 the Beishan disposal storehouse for highly radioactive nuclear waste could be completed and made operational. According to China's Commission for Science, Technology and Industry for National Defense, so far there would be only one permanent disposal storehouse for highly radioactive nuclear waste that has a designated life of 10,000 years; no other such storehouse would be built in the next 100–200 years.

For its part, Mongolia cannot ignore these serious nuclear developments in Russia and China simply because they are taking place in other countries. Though it cannot directly blame its neighbors for their policies and choices, nevertheless there is little doubt that they pose a potential threat. This is why Mongolia needs to bring up these issues with its immediate neighbors and ask for irrefutable assurances that these long-term repositories would not affect people's health and the environment in surrounding areas. Real good-neighborly, lasting relations and mutual confidence cannot be based on mistrust and suspicion. Mongolia should raise these issues before final decisions are taken in China and Russia. If Mongolia feels that it lacks expertise in this area, it can and should ask for expert advice from its neighbors, the IAEA, or other relevant sources. Once such fateful decisions are taken in Moscow or Beijing, it will be impossible for Ulaanbaatar to have them reversed.

Promises of the Peaceful Uses of Nuclear Energy

The third area of interest for Mongolia is the peaceful use of nuclear energy, which has enormous potential for generating environmentally clean electricity. Despite the Chernobyl, Three Mile Island and Fukushima Daichi nuclear accidents, interest in nuclear power as a source of energy is increasing. Also, radioisotopes and radiation have many useful and ever-increasing applications in agriculture, medicine and healthcare, industry, mining and other areas.

In agriculture, nuclear science helps to better manage and use fertilizers that increase crop variety and help food preservation. Isotope hydrology enables accurate tracing and measuring of underground water resources and provides effective analytical tools to manage and conserve water, and to identify new sources of water. Radiation and radioisotopes are also increasingly used in medicine both for diagnoses and for therapy.

As to uranium, Mongolia is estimated to have around 74.000 tU, while its reserves are estimated to be around 1.47 mln. tU, if not more. Thus uranium would allow it to produce nuclear energy, making it much less dependent on imported oil and electricity. However, because of its small population, enormous territory, and lack of a well-developed national power grid, a nuclear power plant is not economically viable at this stage. The question of when to start uranium production and in what form its products could be either used in the country or exported is still being studied and discussed. Export of unprocessed uranium ores or those processed only as yellow cake does not seem to be a commercial option. Russians are interested in importing Mongolian uranium since they are a nuclear power and also have a uranium enrichment facility in Chita, not far from the Mongolian border. But at present Mongolia need not be in a hurry to build a nuclear power plant or export uranium, since the market value and price will surely increase with time. Also, internationally there are a number of projects under way to build smaller and safer nuclear power plants to meet the needs of small developing countries or smaller developed communities. Therefore Mongolia may, within two or three decades, need to develop and produce its own nuclear energy. That is why, until then, more effort is needed to develop renewable sources of solar and wind energy, especially as Mongolia is known for the vast number of sunny and windy days it has. At present, instead of plans to build a nuclear power plant, there is talk of building a research reactor for training purposes, and to carry out non-destructive tests on materials and produce radioisotopes as well as isotopes for medical and industrial use. Working with a research reactor will gradually build and instill a safety culture that is crucially important in the nuclear industry.

In the non-energy area, Mongolia is rightly focusing on the following three issues: training of personnel, diagnosing and treating cancer, and addressing the challenges connected with an outbreak of foot and mouth disease, sheep and goat pox and other transboundary animal diseases.

In the past four decades, in close cooperation with the IAEA, Mongolia has been able to train people in such areas as nuclear and atomic physics, nuclear chemistry and radiochemistry, the application of isotopes and radiation in food and agriculture, and radiation medicine. However, the level of development is such that some trained people cannot fully practice what they have learned. In some cases there is no possible practical application for the knowledge their training has given them. The research reactor and its applications would provide such opportunities.

The area of heightened interest for Mongolia today is nuclear medicine, especially cancer prevention, diagonosis and treatment, since cancer is spreading at a high rate and almost three quarters of those diagnosed with cancer learn about it at the third or even the fourth stage, known as the terminal stage.[10] That is why more emphasis needs to be placed on awareness-raising,

10 Today cancer is the cause of 22 % of the total population mortalilty. It is the second main cause after cardiovascular diseases.

preventive measures, correct diagnosis and effective treatment. However, that is easier said than done—Mongolia is a vast country, while cancer can be fully diagnosed only in Ulaanbaatar. Moreover, not everyone can afford to make long trips to Ulaanbaatar for the sole purpose of a check-up and diagnosis. The lack of equipment to diagnose cancer or give radiotherapy further complicates the situation. In short, state-of-the-art nuclear medical equipment, quick diagnosis and effective treatment are the goals in nuclear medicine. IAEA support has been crucial for Mongolia in building gamma-beam radiation protection and X-ray calibration systems to support the country's cancer control, diagnosis and treatment programme. Yet, that is not enough. If it wants to improve the situation, the Government needs to broaden the scope of its activities and reach out for assistance and cooperation to countries with a well-developed nuclear medical sector and experience.

The third area is animal husbandry, which until recently has been the backbone of the country's economy and still produces about a fifth of its GDP. This traditional sector of the economy has from time to time been devastated by outbreaks of foot and mouth and other transboundary animal diseases. According to the World Organisation for Animal Health (OIE) Mongolia needs to have a better equipped lab and knowlegeable personnel to speedily determine the serotype of the animal disease. Knowing whether the disease is a serotype A or O, for example, would help determine the appropriate, and hence effective serotype and vaccine. Also, Mongolia needs to set up a vaccine production facility that can produce and provide without unnecessary delay the required type of vaccine. In all these areas nuclear science plays an important role. Clearly much still needs to be done by Mongolia to make the best use of the promises that nuclear energy offers.

Some Concluding Thoughts

With regard to the issues of nuclear-weapon-related threats, Mongolia was able to have the P5, including its two immediate neighbors, recognize its unique nuclear-weapon-free status, commit to respect it, and refrain from any act that would violate it. At this stage that is the most, as they say, that the P5 can deliver without setting a precedent for others. Though Mongolia is not fully satisfied with a political pledge, despite it being provided in the form of a jointly signed declaration, it can live with that, bearing in mind the good-neighborly relations that it maintains with the P5 and especially with its immediate neighbors. It knows full well, and the Ukrainian case has reinforced this, that no security assurance would be credible in practice if the great powers felt threatened by a situation that might affect their vital or long-term interests. Hence Mongolia's policy should be to make sure that no such threat emanates from its territory or policy. Bearing that in mind, Mongolia should move from the P5 declaratory assurances to a more structural prevention; i.e., to making Mongolia's nuclear-weapon-free status an organic part of Northeast Asian security structure. This means that Mongolia's neutral stance in a possible Sino-Russian conflict should be maintained and its policy of not allowing the use of its territory to harm the strategic interests of others should become a norm of international law and practice.

As to the silent nuclear threats, they are not direct threats but rather risks that cannot be ignored and should be addressed in a manner that is non-provocative for Mongolia's neighbors. To do justice to the people that have been affected by the enormous number of nuclear-weapon tests, an objective study needs to be made using the internationally accepted methods employed in assessing the residual radiation fallout from the tests in Kazakhstan and the Russian Republic of Altai on human health and the environment.

Of the silent nuclear threats, the most sensitive, which might have long-lasting effects, is the issue of nuclear waste. Mongolia needs to address it without delay by approaching its neighbors and demanding to be provided with credible, scientifically based evidence that indeed the establishment of permanent nuclear repositories in Zheleznogorsk (the Krasnoyarsk region, Russia) and Beishan (the Gansu region, China) would not negatively affect Mongolia, its people or the environment. According to the principles of state responsibilities, a state should make sure that any act within its territory will not negatively affect, directly or indirectly, the sovereignty of third states and their well-being.

Nuclear energy is a double-edged sword. It can be threatening, but it can also serve as a factor to promote economic and social development and improve people's lives. This article has tried to show the areas where nuclear energy can and should help Mongolia to address the issues of its socio-economic development. One of its major peaceful uses is in the generating of nuclear power. In Mongolia's case, I believe the time is not ripe to talk about a nuclear power plant; rather, it would be better to start by building a research reactor and make the most use of it, including the training of nuclear engineers. In this situation prudence and patience are important. In the meantime Mongolia should concentrate on such valuable concerns as making the most of nuclear medicine for the prevention, early diagnosis and effective treatment of cancer, employing nuclear technology to increase crops in Mongolia's particular environmental and climatic conditions, making the best use of its water resources, and fighting foot and mouth and other animal diseases.

Note

As author of this paper, I am honored and privileged to have been asked to contribute to this Festschrift for Professor Morris Rossabi, a renowned and highly respected scholar in Mongolian and Chinese studies, Distinguished Professor of History at the City University of New York and Adjunct Professor at Columbia University. He has not only studied and researched extensively the histories of China, Mongolia and Inner Asia, but taught and lectured on the history of this part of the world to thousands of students and researchers. He is also author of many important works of history, both ancient and contemporary, such as *Khubilai Khan, Voyager from Xanadu, The Mongols, The Mongols and Global History, Modern Mongolia: From Khans to Commissars to Capitalists*, some of which have been translated into Russian, Korean, Chinese, Mongolian and other languages.

A strong believer in the role of the arts and culture in understanding peoples and bringing them closer together, Professor Rossabi has written many scholarly works and articles on their role in relation to China, Inner Asia and Mongolia. An appreciation of his knowledge in this under-researched area has led to Professor Rossabi being invited to help organize exhibitions at the Metropolitan Museum of Art, the Cleveland Museum of Art, the Asian Art Museum of San Francisco, and he has produced invaluable reference books both for academics and for the general public. He also worked with the Mongolian Government in organizing, with much success, the first Mongolian art exhibitions in San Francisco, New York and Houston. Professor Rossabi's lectures and teaching have earned him such honors as Distinguished Professor of History and Distinguished Visiting Scholar. In 2009 he was awarded an honorary doctorate by the National University of Mongolia.

His writings about contemporary Mongolia, the successes and challenges of the country's at times painful transition to democratic governance and a market economy are well known. However, the one area of Mongolian studies which he has not yet researched is contemporary, post-Soviet Mongolia's foreign policy. I believe that an understanding of the country would not be complete without an understanding of its foreign policy, its challenges and what is being done to address them. For this reason, I have decided to contribute in Professor Morris Rossabi's honor by writing about one important, yet little-researched area of Mongolian foreign policy which addresses the risks of the nuclear age.

Bibliography

Akamatsu, Chijyo. "Religious consciousness of modern Mongolian youth" in Akamatsu Chijyo and Akiba Takashi eds. *Ethnicity and Religion in Manchukuo and Mongolia.* Tokyo: Osakaya goshoten, 1941, pp. 289–296.

Akasaka Tsuneaki 赤坂恒明. *Juchi-ei shoseiken shi no kenkyū* ジュチ裔諸政権史の研究. Tokyo: Kazama-shobo, 2005.

Allsen, Thomas T. "Prelude to the Western Campaigns: Mongol Military Operations in the Volga-Ural Region, 1217–1237." *Archivum Eurasiae Medii Aevi* 3 (1983), pp. 5–24.

Allsen, Thomas T. "The Mongols and the North Caucasus." *Archivum Eurasiae Medii Aevi* 7 (1987–1991), pp. 5–39.

Allsen, Thomas T. *Commodity and Exchange in the Mongol Empire.* Cambridge: Cambridge University Press, 1997.

Allsen, Thomas T. "Sharing Out the Empire: Apportioned Lands under the Mongols." In Anatoly M. Khazanov and André Wink. eds. *Nomads in the Sedentary World.* Richmond, Surrey: Curzon Press, 2001, pp. 172–190.

Allsen, Thomas T. *Culture and Conquest in Mongol Eurasia.* Cambridge: Cambridge University Press, 2001.

An Shuangcheng, et al., eds. *Man-Han da cidian.* Shenyang: Liaoning chubanshe, 1993.

Anon. *Huang Ming benji* 皇明本紀. In Deng Shilong 鄧士龍, compiler, *Guo chao dian gu* 國朝典故. Beijing: Beijing daxue chubanshe, 1993 rpt., vol. 1.

Atwood, Christopher P. "The Date of the *Secret History of the Mongols* Reconsidered." *Journal of Song-Yuan Studies* 37 (2007), pp. 1–48.

Atwood, Christopher P. "Informants and Sources for the *Secret History of the Mongols.*" *Mongolian Studies* 29 (2007), pp. 27–39.

Atwood, Christopher P. "Some Early Inner Asian Terms Related to the Imperial Family and the Comitatus," *Central Asiatic Journal* 56 (2012–13), pp. 49–86.

Atwood, Christopher P. "The Uyghur Stone: Archaeological Revelations in the Mongol Empire." In Florin Curta and Bogdan-Petru Maleon. eds. *The Steppe Lands and the World beyond Them: Studies in Honor of Victor Spinei on his 70th birthday*, ed. Iaşi: Editura Universităţii "Alexandru Ioan Cuza, 2013, pp. 315–343.

Atwood, Christopher P. "Manuscript Families of Rashīd al-Dīn and Their Affiliations: Survey of Japanese Scholarship and Evidence from Mongolian And Chinese Transcriptions." Paper given at the "Association of Central Eurasian Students Conference." Central Eurasian Studies Department, Indiana University, Bloomington, IN, 2015.

Aubin, Françoise. "Les sanctions et les peines chez les Mongols," *Transactions of the Bodin Society for Comparative Institutional History, LVIII, Punishment, Non European World.* Brussels: De Boeck University, 1991.

Aubin, Françoise. "Some Characteristics of Penal Legislation among the Mongols (13th–21st Centuries)." In Wallace Johnson and Irina Popova. eds. *Central Asian Law: A Historical Overview: A Festschrift for the Ninetieth Birthday of Herbert Franke*. Lawrence, Kansas: Society for Asian Legal History, 2004.

Bartlett, Beatrice S. *Monarchs and Ministers: The Grand Council in Mid-Ch'ing China, 1723–1820*. Berkeley and Los Angeles: University of California Press, 1991.

Benson, Douglas. *The Mongol Campaigns in Asia*. Chicago: The Author, 1991.

Bernard, Elizabeth. "The Qianlong Emperor and Tibetan Buddhism." In James Millward et al. eds. *New Qing Imperial History: The Making of Inner Asian Empire at Qing Chengde*. London: RoutledgeCurzon, 2004.

Biran, Michal. *Qaidu and the Rise of the Independent Mongol State in Central Asia*. Surrey: Curzon, 1997.

Birge, Bettine. "Chu Hsi and Women's Education" in Wm. T. de Bary and J. Chaffee. eds. *Neo-Confucian Education: The Formative Stage*. Berkeley: University of California Press, 1989.

Birge, Bettine. "Levirate Marriage and the Revival of Widow Chastity in Yuan China." *Asia Major* 8:2 (1995), pp. 107–146.

Birge, Bettine. *Women, Property, and Confucian Reaction in Sung and Yuan China (960–1369)*. Cambridge: Cambridge University Press, 2002.

Birge, Bettine. "Women and Confucianism from Sung to Ming: The Institutionalization of Patrilineality" In Paul Smith and Richard von Glahn. eds. *The Song-Yuan Ming Transition in Chinese History*. Cambridge, Mass.: Harvard University Press, 2003.

Birge, Bettine. "Law of the Liao, Chin, and Yuan and Its Impact on the Chinese Legal Tradition" in Liu Liyan. ed. *New Perspectives in Chinese History, Legal History: The Formation and Transformation of Traditional Chinese Legal Culture*. Taipei: Academia Sinica Lianjing, 2008.

Bodde, Derk and Clarence Morris. *Law in Imperial China*. Cambridge, Mass.: Harvard University Press, 1967.

Boldbaatar, Ch. *Statesmen in struggle in 20th century Mongolia*. Ulaanbaatar, 2004.

Bretschneider, Emil. *Medieval Researches from Eastern Asiatic Sources*. London: Kegan Paul, Trench, Trübner, & Co., 1910.

Buell, Paul. "Early Mongol Expansion in Western Siberia and Turkestan (1207–1219): A Reconstruction." *Central Asiatic Journal* 36 (1992), pp. 1–32.

Buell, Paul. *Historical Dictionary of the Mongol World Empire*. Lanham, MD and Oxford: The Scarecrow Press, 2003.

Bulag, Uradyn, E. *Collaborative Nationalism; The Politics of Friendship on China's Mongolian Frontier*. Lanham, Boulder, New York, Toronto, Plymouth: Rowman & Littlefield Publishers, 2010.

Chan Hok-lam. "The Demise of Yuan Rule in Mongolian and Chinese Legends." In Géza Bethlenfalvy and Alice Sárközy. et al., *Altaic Religious Beliefs and Practices*. Budapest: Akademiai Kiao, 1992, pp. 65–82.

Chan Wing-tsit, trans. *Reflections on Things at Hand: The Neo-Confucian Anthology*. New York: Columbia University Press, 1967.

Chan Wing-tsit. "Chu Hsi and Neo-Confucianism." In Hok-lam Chan and Wm. Theodore de Bary, eds. *Chinese Thought and Religion under the Mongols*. New York: Columbia University Press, 1982.

Charleux, Isabelle. "Chinggis Khan: Ancestor, Buddha or Shaman?" *Mongolian Studies*, 31 (2009), pp. 207–258.

Chen Gaohua 陳高華, "Lun Yuandai de junhu" 論元代的軍戶. *Yuanshi luncong* 元史論叢1 (1982), pp. 72–90.

Ch'en, Paul Heng-chao. *Chinese Legal Tradition under the Mongols*. Princeton: Princeton University Press, 1979.

Chen Zilong 陳子龍. compiler. *Huang Ming jing shi wen bian* 皇明經世文編. Pinglu tang 1638; Beijing: Zhonghua shuju, 1962 rpt.; third printing 1997.

Cheng Minzheng程敏政 compiler. *Huang Ming wen heng* 皇明文衡. 1527 edition; Taibei: Shijie shuju, 1962 rpt.

Chu Hung-lam. "Intellectual Trends in the Fifteenth Century." *Ming Studies* 27 (1989), pp. 1–33.

The Ch'un Ts'ew with the Tso chuen. In *The Chinese Classics*. Oxford: Oxford University Press, 1893–95; rpt. Taibei: Southern Materials Center, 1983. 4 vols.

Crossley, Pamela K. "Review Article: The Rulerships of China." *American Historical Review* 97: 5 (1992), pp. 1468–1483.

Crossley, Pamela K. *The Manchus*. Oxford and Cambridge, Mass., 1997.

Da Ming lü jijie fuli 大明律集解附例. Wanli ed. Taipei: Taiwan xuesheng shuju, 1970.

Da Yuan shengzheng guochao dianzhang 大元聖政國朝典章 [called *Yuan dianzhang*] (Photo reprint of 1322 Yüan edition). Taipei: Gugong bowu guan, 1976.

Dardess, John W. *Conquerors and Confucians: Aspects of Political Change in Late Yuan China*. New York: Columbia University Press, 1973.

Dardess, John. "Did the Mongols Matter? Territory, Power, and the Intelligentsia in China from the Northern Song to the Early Ming," In Paul Smith and Richard von Glahn, eds. *The Song–Yuan–Ming Transition in Chinese History*, ed. Cambridge, Mass.: Harvard University Press, 2003, pp. 111–134.

Das, Sarat Chandra. *A Tibetan–English Dictionary*. Calcutta: Bengal Secretariat Book Depot. New Delhi: Guarav Publishing House, 1991 rept.

de Bary, Wm. T. *Neo-Confucian Orthodoxy and the Learning of the Mind and Heart*. New York: Columbia University Press, 1981.

de Rachewiltz, Igor. "The Dating of the *Secret History of the Mongols*—A Re-interpretation." *Ural-Altaische Jahrbücher*, new series, 22 (2008), pp. 150–84.

Demchigdonrov. *Autobiography of Demchigdonrov; Dream and Failure of a Mongol Revival*. trans. By Mori Hisao. Tokyo: Iwanami shoten, 1994.

Deng Shilong 鄧士龍, compiler. *Guo chao dian gu* 國朝典故. Beijing: Beijing daxue chubanshe, 1993 rpt..

Dongdu shilüe 東都事略, by Wang Cheng 王稱. Taibei: Wenhai chubanshe, 1967.

Drevnetiurkskii slovar', ed. V.M. Nadeliaev, D.M. Nasilov, E.R. Tenishev, and A.M. Shcherbak. Leningrad: Nauka, 1969.

Duli Cunyi 讀例存疑, comp. Xue Yunsheng 薛允升, 5 vols., 1907; rpt. Taibei: Chinese Materials and Research Aids Service Center, 1970.

Elman, Benjamin and Theodore Huters. "Maga'erni shituan, houxiandai zhuyi yu jindai Zhongguo shi: ping Zhou Xirui dui He Weiya zhuzuo de piping." *Ershiyi shiji* (Twenty-first Century) 44 (1997), pp. 118–30.

Elverskog, Johan. "The Story of Zhu and the Mongols of the 17th Century," *Ming Studies* 50 (2004), pp. 39–76.

Elverskog, Johan. "Sagang Sechen On the Qing Conquest." In Stéphane Grivelet, Ruth Meserve, Àgnes Birtalen, and Giovanni Stary, eds. *The Black Master: Essays on Central Eurasia in Honor of Professor György Kara on His 70th Birthday*. Wiesbaden: Harassowitz Verlag, 2005, pp. 43–56.

Elverskog, Johan. *Our Great Qing: The Mongols, Buddhism, and the State in Late Imperial China*. Honolulu: University of Hawaii Press, 2006.

Elverskog, Johan. "The Legend of Muna Mountain, *Inner Asia* 8:1 (2006), pp. 99–122.

Ershiwushi bubian. Shanghai: Kaiming Shudian, 1955.

Esherick, Joseph. "Cherishing Sources from Afar." *Modern China* 24:2 (April, 1998), pp. 135–161.

Esherick, Joseph. "Tradutore, Traditore." *Modern China* 24: 3 (July, 1998), pp. 328–332.

Farmer, Edward. *Zhu Yuanzhang and Early Ming Legislation: The Reordering of Chinese Society Following the Era of Mongol Rule*. Leiden: E.J. Brill, 1995.

Farquhar, David. *The Government of China Under Mongolian Rule*. Stuttgart: Franz Steiner Verlag, 1990.

Fragner, Bert. "Iran under Ilkhanid rule in a world history perspective." In Denise Aigle, ed. *L'iran face à la domination mongole*. Louvain: Institut français de recherche en Iran, 1997.

Franke, Herbert. "Jurchen Customary Law and the Chinese Law of the Chin Dynasty." In Dieter Eikemeier and Herbert Franke, eds. *State and Law in East Asia: Festschrift Karl Bünger*. Wiesbaden: Otto Harrassowitz, 1981.

Franke, Herbert. "Chinese Law in a Multinational Society: The Case of the Liao." *Asia Major* 3rd Series 5:2 (1992).

Franke, Otto and B. Laufer. *Epigraphische Denkmäler aus China 1. Theil, Lamaitische Kloster-Inschriften aus Peking, Jehol und Si-Ngan, mit Unterstützung der Hamburgischen Wissenschaftlichen Stiftung.* Berlin: D. Reimer, 1914.

Futaki, Hiroshi. "The Japanese Song of the Railroad to Mongolia." *Mongolika* 1 (1985), pp. 29–32.

Gammer, Moshe. "Russia and the Eurasian Steppe Nomads: An Overview." In Reuven Amitai and Michal Biran, eds. *Mongols, Turks, and Others: Eurasian Nomads and the Sedentary World.* Leiden and Boston: Brill, 2005.

Gao Wende, ed. *Zhongguo minzushi renwu cidian.* Beijing: Zhongguo shehui kexueyuan, 1990.

Geertz, Clifford. *Negara: The Theatre State in Nineteenth-Century Bali.* Princeton: Princeton University Press, 1980.

Gökhel, Ahmet. "Kipchaks and Kumans." In Hasan Cell Güzel, C. Cem Oğuz, and Osman Karatay, eds. *The Turks.* Ankara: Yeni Türkiye, 2001, Vol. 1, pp. 643–659.

Golden, Peter B. "Cumanica II: The Ölberli (Ölperli): The Fortunes and Misfortunes of an Inner Asian Nomadic Clan." *Archivum Eurasiae Medii Aevi* 6 (1988 [1986]), pp. 5–29.

Golden, Peter B. "The Qipčaks of Medieval Eurasia: An Example of Stateless Adaptation in the Steppes." In G. Seaman and D. Marks, eds. *Rulers from the Steppe: State Formation on the Eurasian Periphery.* Los Angeles: Ethnographics Press, 1991.

Golden, Peter B. "Nomads and Their Sedentary Neighbors in Pre-Činggisid Eurasia." *Archivum Eurasiae Medii Aevi* 7 (1987–1991), pp. 41–82.

Golden, Peter B. *An Introduction to the History of the Turkic Peoples.* Wiesbaden: Otto Harrassowitz, 1992.

Goodrich, L. Carrington and Chaoying Fang, eds. *Dictionary of Ming Biography 1368–1644.* New York and London: Columbia University Press, 2 vols., 1976.

Gugong Bowuyuan, ed. *Qingdai gongting huihua.* Beijing: Wenwu chubanshe, 1992.

Halperin, Charles J. "The Missing Golden Horde Chronicles and Historiography in the Mongol Empire." *Mongolian Studies* 23 (2000), pp. 1–15.

Halperin, Charles J. "The Kipchak Connection: the Ilkhans, the Mamluks, and Ayn Jalut." *Bulletin of the School of Oriental and African Studies* 63:2 (2000), pp. 229–245.

Hamayon, Roberte, N. "The Joint Making of Illusion and Disillusion: Chinggis Khan on a Buriyat Calendar." In I. Charleux, G. Deplaplace, R. Hamayon, and S. Pearce eds. *Representing Power in Modern Inner Asia: Conventions, Alternatives and Opposition.* Bellingham, Washington: Center for East Asian Studies, Western Washington University, 2010.

Hambis, Louis. *Le chapitre CVIII du Yuan Che.* Leiden: E.J. Brill, 1954.

Han i araha ubaliyambuha duin bithe / Yuzhi fanyi sishu. Matsumura Catalog no. A8, Library of Congress, Asia section. 1755.

Haneda Tōru. *Man-Wa jiten*. Kyoto, 1937.

Haslund-Christensen, H. *The Music of the Mongols*, The Sino-Swedish Expedition Publication 21, Stockholm: Trycieri Aktiebolaget Thule, 1943.

Hattori, Ryutaro. *Mongolian Folksongs*, Tokyo: Kaimei shoin, 1977.

Hauer, Erich. *Handwörterbuch der Mandschusprache*. Wiesbaden: Otto Harrassowitz, 1952–55.

He Qiaoyuan 何喬遠, compiler. *Huang Ming wen zheng* 皇明文征. *Siku quanshu cunmu congshu* 四庫全書存目叢書, *ji* 集 328. 1631 edition Jilin Provincial Library. Jinan: QiLu shushe, 1997 rpt.

Hedin, Sven. *The Chinese Lama Temple: Potala of Jehol*. Chicago: Lakeside Press, 1932.

Hedin, Sven. *Jehol, City of Emperors*. London: Kegan Paul, Trench, Trübner & Co., 1932; New York: E. P. Dutton, 1933.

Henan Chengshi yishu. In *Er Cheng quanshu* 二程全書 (Sibu beiyao ed.)

Hevia, James. *Cherishing Men from Afar: Qing Guest Ritual and the Macartney Embassy of 1793*. Durham: Duke University Press, 1995.

Hevia, James. "Postpolemical Historiography: A Response to Joseph W. Esherick." *Modern China* 24: 3 (July, 1998), pp. 319–327.

Hirokawa, Saho. "Traces and development of Mongolian Periodical Publications," *Japan-Sea Rim Studies Annual Report* 14 (2007), pp. 104–126.

Holmgren, Jennifer. "Observations on Marriage Practices in Early Mongol and Yüan Society." *Journal of Asian History* 20:2 (1986).

Hosoo, Moichi. *Mongolian Photo Album*, Tokyo: Moukokyoukai shuppanbu, 1921.

Hsiao Ch'i-ch'ing. *The Military Establishment of the Yüan Dynasty*. Cambridge, Mass.: Harvard University Press, 1978.

Hu Zengyi, ed. *Xin Man-Han da cidian*. Urumchi: Xinjiang renmin chubanshe. 1994.

Huang Ming zhishu 皇明制書, 6 vols. Taibei: Chungwen chubanshe, 1969 rpt.

Huang Qinglian 黃清連, *Yuandai huji zhidu yanjiu*元代戶計制度研究. Taibei: Guoli Taiwan daxue, 1977.

Hummel, Arthur W. et al. *Eminent Chinese of the Ch'ing Period (1644–1912)*. 2 vols. Washington: U.S. Government Printing Office, 1943–44; Reprint, 2 vols. in 1. Taipei: Ch'eng-wen, 1970.

Jackson, Peter. "The Dissolution of the Mongol Empire." *Central Asiatic Journal* 22 (1978), pp. 186–244.

Jackson, Peter, with David Morgan, trans. and ed. *The Mission of Friar William of Rubruck: His Journey to the Court of the Great Khan Möngke, 1253–1255*. 1990; rpt. Indianapolis: Hackett Publishing, 2009.

Jia Jingyan 賈敬顔. (乙未 [1955], error for己未 [1979]). *Shengwu qinzheng lu jiaoben* 聖武親征錄校本. Beijing: Minzu University mimeograph, 1979.

Jiang Yonglin, trans. *The Great Ming Code: Da Ming lü*. Seattle: University of Washington Press, 2005.

Jiao Hong 焦竑. *Guo chao xian zheng lu* 國朝獻徵錄. 1594–1616. Taibei: Xuesheng shuju, 1965 rpt.

Jinshi 金史. Beijing: Zhonghua shuju, 1975 rpt.

Jones, William, trans. *The Great Qing Code*. Oxford: Clarendon Press, 1994.

Juvaini, 'Ala-ad-Din 'Ata-Malik, trans. John Andrew Boyle. *The History of the World Conqueror.* Manchester University Press, 1958, 2 vols.

[Jūzjānī] Minhāj-ud-Dīn, Abū-'Ūmar-i-'Uṣmān Siraj, trans. Major H.G. Raverty. [1881] *Ṭabaḳāt-i-Nāṣirī: A General History of the Muhammadan Dynasties of Asia, Including Hindustan; from A.H. 194 (810 A.D.) to A.H. 658 (1260 A.D.) and the Irruption of the Infidel Mughals into Islam.* Calcutta: Asiatic Society, 1995 rpt.

Kaplonski, Christopher. "The Case of Disappearing Chinggis Khaan: Dismembering the Remembering," *Ab Imperio*, 4 (2005), pp. 147–173.

Kara, György. "The Bush Protects the Little Bird." *Acta Orientalia Academiae Scientiarum Hung.* 48: 3 (1995), pp. 421–28.

Kimura, Tetsuyuki. *Sainshinga's family on the Mongolian Steppe*. Fukuoka: Ashishobo, 1994.

Konagaya, Yuki. "Chinggis Khan as a Resource for Japanese Literature." *Human Culture* (*Bulletin of Shiga Prefecture University Faculty of Human Culture*) 24 (2008), pp. 87–98.

Kovalevskii, Osip. *Mongols'sko-russko-francuzskii slovar' / Dictionaire Mongol-Russe-Français.* Kasan: Imprimerie de l'universite', 1844; Reprint, New York: Paragon Reprint Corp., 1964.

Lam, Joseph. *State Sacrifices and Music in Ming China: Orthodoxy, Creativity, and Expressiveness*. Albany: State University of New York Press, 1998.

Lane, George. *Early Mongol Rule in Iran: A Persian Renaissance*. London: Routledge, 2003.

Langlois, John. "The Hung-wu Reign." In Denis Twitchett and Frederick Mote, eds. *Cambridge History of China, volume 7, The Ming Dynasty Part One*, Cambridge: Cambridge University Press, 1988, pp. 107–82.

Lau, D.C.. *Mencius*. New York: Penguin Books, 1970; rpt. 1988.

Le Strange, G., trans. *The Geographical Part of the Nuzhat-al-Qulūb Composed by Ḥamd-allāh Mustawfī of Qazwīn in 740 (1340)*. 1919; Frankfurt am Main: Johann Wolfgang Goethe University, 1993 rpt.

Legge, James. *The Shoo king*. In *The Chinese Classics*. Oxford: Oxford University Press, 1893–95; Taibei: Southern Materials Center, 1983 rpt. 4 vols.

Legge, James. *The Four Books.* Taipei: Wenxing shudian, 1965 rpt.

Lessing, Ferdinand D. et al. *Mongolian–English Dictionary.* Berkeley and Los Angeles: University of California Press, 1960. Third reprinting, Bloomington: The Mongolia Society, 1995.

Lewis, Mark. *Sanctioned Violence in Early China*. Albany: State University of New York Press, 1990.

Li, Gertraude Roth. *Manchu: A Textbook for Reading Documents.* Honolulu: University of Hawai'i Press, 2000.

Li Narangoa. "Educating Mongols and making 'Citizens' of Manchukuo." *Inner Asia* 3 (2001), pp. 110–126.

Li Narangoa. "Mongol Education under the Japanese Occupation." 11th International Conference on Education Research (ICER), Seoul National University, 2010.

Li Zhiting. "'Xin Qing shi': 'xin diguozhuyi' shixue biaoben." In *Zhongguo shehui kexuebao*. 4 April 2015. http://sscp.cssn.cn/xkpd/zm_20150/201504/t20150420_1592234.html.

Liaoshi 遼史 (Beijng: Zhonghua shuju, 1974).

Liddell, Henry George and Robert Scott, comps. *A Greek–English Lexicon* 8th ed., rev. New York: American Book Company, 1897.

Ling, T.O. *A Dictionary of Buddhism.* New York: Charles Scribner's Sons, 1972.

Liu Ji 劉基. *Liu Bo wen ji* 劉伯溫集. Hangzhou: Zhejiang guji chubanshe, 2011.

Liu, Lydia H. *Translingual Practice: Literature, National Culture, and Translated Modernity—China, 1900–1937.* Stanford: Stanford University Press, 1995.

Liu Yingsheng. "War and Peace Between the Yuan Dynasty and the Chaghadaid Dynasty (1312–1323)." In Reuven Amitai and Michal Biran, eds. *Mongols, Turks, and Others: Eurasian Nomads and the Sedentary World.* Leiden and Boston: Brill, 2005, pp. 339–358.

Ma Dazheng and Ma Ruheng. *Piaoluo yiyu de minzu: 17 zhi 18 shiji de Tu-er-hu-te Menggu*. Beijing: Zhongguo shehui kexue chubanshe, 1991.

Ma Juan. "Yuandai Chincha Yesn Tiemuer shiji kaolun," *Yuanshi Luncong* 10 (2003), pp. 98–106.

Ma Zuchang. "Gu zhenjie zeng Rongguo furen Safalishe beaming" in *Ma Shitian Wenji* in *Yuanren Wenji zhenben congkan*. Taibei: Xinwen feng chubanshe, 1985.

Matsuda, Kōichi. "The Number of Military Households in the Yuan." In *Neilu Yazhou lishi wenhua yanjiu: Han Rulin xiansheng jinian wenji* 内陆亚洲历史文化研究—韩儒林先生纪念文集, ed. Nanjing Daxue Yuan shi yanjiu shi 南京大学元史研究室, Nanjing: Nanjing University Press, 1996, pp. 268–295.

Matsuda, Kōichi. "The Fief (Appanage) Allotment System in North China under Mongol Rule." Paper presented at the conference "Family and the State in Chinggisid and Post-Chinggisid Central Eurasia." Research Institute for Inner Asian Studies, Indiana University, Bloomington, IN, 2008.

Matsuda, Kōichi. "The Fief (Appanage) Allotment System of the Mongol Empire after the Enthronement of Qubilai, focusing on the Eastern Domain of Hülegü." Paper presented at the conference "The Diplomacy of the Mongol Empire and its Legacy." Kreddha and the Austrian Academy of Sciences, Vienna, Austria, 2010.

Matsumura Jun. *A Catalogue of Manchu Materials in the Library of Congress: Xylographs, Manuscripts, Archives.* Tôhoku Ajia bunken kenkyû sôsho, 1. Tokyo: University of Tokyo Press Production Center, 1999.

Melville, Charles. *The Fall of Amir Chupan and the Decline of the Ilkhanate, 1327–37: A Decade of Discord in Mongol Iran.* Bloomington: Indiana University Research Institute on Inner Asian Studies, 1999.

Millward, James A. *'Beyond the Pass': Economy, Ethnicity and Empire in Qing Xinjiang, 1759–1864.* Stanford: Stanford University Press, 1998.

Millward, James A. "Qing Inner Asian Empire and the Return of the Torghuts." In Millward et al., eds. *New Qing Imperial History: The Making of Inner Asian Empire at Qing Chengde.* London and New York, RoutledgeCurzon, 2004.

Millward, James A, Ruth Dunnell, Mark Elliott and Philippe Forêt, eds. *New Qing Imperial History: The Making of Inner Asian Empire at Qing Chengde.* London and New York, RoutledgeCurzon, 2004.

Ming huidian 明會典. Wanli edn.; Beijing: Zhonghua shuju, 1989 rpt.

Möllendorff, P.G. von. *A Manchu Grammar with Analyzed Texts.* Shanghai: American Presbyterian Mission Press, 1892.

Ming Taizu shilu 明太祖實錄 in *Ming shilu* 明實錄. Facsimile reproduction of Guoli Beiping tushuguan cang hongge chaoben 國立北平圖書館藏紅格抄本. Taibei: Zhongyang yanjiuyuan lishi yuyan yanjiusuo 1961–66, 133 vols.

Miyawaki Junko. "The Japanese Origin of Chinggis Khan legends." *Inner Asia* 1 (2006) pp. 123–134.

Morgan, David. "The decline and fall of the Mongol Empire." *Journal of the Royal Asiatic Society*, 3rd series, 19:4 (October, 2009), pp. 427–437.

Mori, Hisao. *The Study of Demchigdonrov*, Tokyo: Sodosha, 2000.

Morimura, Munehuyu. *The Legend of Yoshitsune and the Japanese*, Tokyo: Heibonsha 2005.

Mosca, Matthew W. *From Frontier Policy to Foreign Policy: The Question of India and the Transformation of Geopolitics in Qing China.* Stanford University Press, 2013.

Mote, Frederick. "The T'u-mu Incident of 1449." In John K. Fairbank and Frank Kierman, Jr., ed. *Chinese Ways in Warfare*. Cambridge, Mass.: Harvard University Press, 1974, pp. 243–272.

Mote, Frederick. "Yüan and Ming." In K.C. Chang, ed. *Food in Chinese Culture*, ed. New Haven: Yale University Press, 1977, pp. 195–257.

Mote, Frederick. *Imperial China 900–1800*. Cambridge: Harvard University Press, 1999.

Munkh-Erdene, L. "Selling of Good Father's Name: Legitimacy, Pride and Commodity." *Human Culture* (*Bulletin of Shiga Prefecture University Faculty of Human Culture*) 24 (2008), pp. 35–46.

Na Sainchogt. *Na Sainčoγtu-yin Büren Zohiol.* Kökhot: Öbör Mongγol-un ard-un keblel-ün qoriy-a, 1999.

Nachin. *Na Sainčoγtu-yin Sudulul.* Beijing: Ündüsüten-ü keblel-ün qoriy-a, 2011.

Naito, Shiokuni. "Arguing Mongolian education and culture." *Koua Kyoiku* 2–9 (1943), pp. 41–46, 2–10 (1943), pp. 17–29, 2–11 (1943), pp. 51–56.

Nasawī: consulted in the following editions:

en-Nesawi, Mohammed, trans. O. Houdas. *Histoire du Sultan Djelal ed-Din Mankobirti.* Paris: Libraire de la Société asiatique, 1895.

an-Nasavī, Shikhāb ad-Dīn Muḥammad. Trans. Z.M. Buniiatov. *Sīrat as-Sulṭān Dzhalāl ad-Dīn Mankburny* (*Zhizneopisanie Sultana Dzhalal ad-Dina Mankburny*). Moscow: "Vostochnaia literatura" RAN, 1996.

Norman, Jerry. *A Concise Manchu–English Lexicon.* Seattle and London: University of Washington Press, 1978.

Ouyang Xuan 歐陽玄. [1470–1473] "Gaochang Xie shi jiazhuan 高昌偰氏家傳." In *Guizhai ji* 圭齋集, *juan* 卷 11, 3a–13a. Chenghua era blockprint; Shanghai: Commercial Press, 1922 rpt.

Ouyang Xuan 歐陽玄 ed. Tang Rui 湯銳. In *Ouyang Xuan quanji* 歐陽玄全集, vol. 1, *juan* 卷 11, 321–336. Chengdu: Sichuan University Press, 2010.

Oyabe, Mataichiro. *Genghis Khan is Minamoto Yoshitune* (*Gen Gikei*). Tokyo: Oyama shobo, 1924.

Pleines, Heiko. *Crises and Conflicts in Post Socialist Societies: The Role of Ethnic, Political, and Social Identity,* Stuttgart, Hannover: Ibidem-Verlag, 2008.

Qi Jingzhi. *Waiba miao beiwen zhuyi.* Beijing: Zijincheng chubanshe, 1895.

Rashid ad-Din, trans. By L.A. Khetagurov, ed. A.A. Semenov. *Sbornik letopisei.* Vol. I, part 1. Moscow: Academy of Sciences Press, 1952.

Rashid ad-Din, trans. By O.I. Smirnova, notes by B.I. Pankratov and O.I. Smirnova, ed. A.A. Semenov. *Sbornik letopisei.* Vol. I, part 2. Moscow: Academy of Sciences Press, 1952.

Rashīd al-Dīn, trans. by John Andrew Boyle. 1971. *Successors of Genghis Khan.* New York: Columbia University Press, 1971.

Rashīd al-Dīn Faẕl Allāh ed. Bahman Karīmī. *Jāmiʿ al-Tawārīkh.* Tehran: Iqbāl, 1362/1983–84, 2 vols.

Rashīd al-Dīn Faẕl Allāh Hamadānī, ed. Muḥammad Rawshan and Muṣṭafī Mūsawī, ed. *Jāmiʿ al-Tawārīkh*. Tehran: Nashr-i Alburz. 1383/1994, 4 vols.

Rashiduddin Fazlullah, trans. and ed. By W.M. Thackston. *Jamiʿu't-Tawarikh: Compendium of Chronicles: A History of the Mongols.* Cambridge: Harvard University Press, 1998–1999, 3 vols.

Rásonyi, László, and Imre Baski. *Onomasticon Turcicum: Turkic Personal Names.* Bloomington: Indiana University, 2007, 2 vols.

Ratchnevsky, Paul. "Die Mongolische Rechtsinstitution der Busse in der Chinesischen Gesetzgebung der Yüan-Zeit" in Herbert Franke, ed. *Festschrift für Erich Haenisch zum 80 Geburtstag*. Wiesbaden: Franz Steiner Verlag, 1961.

Ratchnevsky, Paul. *Un code des Yuan.* Paris: Collège de France, Institut des Hautes Etudes Chinoise, 1972–1985.

Rawski, Evelyn S. *The Last Emperors: A Social History of Qing Imperial Institutions.* Berkeley: University of California Press, 1998.

Ren Fangbin 任方冰. *Ming Qing junli yu junzhong yongyue yanjiu* 明清軍禮與軍中用樂研究. Zhongyang yinyue xueyuan chubanshe, 2014.

Richards, D.S., trans. *The Chronicle of Ibn al-Athīr for the Crusading Period from* al-Kāmil fī'l-ta'rīkh, Part 3, *The Years 589–629/1193–1231: The Ayyūbids after Saladin and the Mongol Menace*. Farnham: Ashgate, 2008.

Robinson, David. "The Ming Court." In David Robinson, ed. *Culture, Courtiers, and Competition: The Ming Court (1368–1644)*. Cambridge, Mass.: Harvard University Asia Center, 2008, pp. 21–60.

Robinson, David. *Martial Spectacles of the Ming Court*. Cambridge: Harvard University Asia Center, 2013.

Rossabi, Morris. *China and Inner Asia: From 1368 to the Present Day*. London: Thames and Hudson, 1975.

Rossabi, Morris. "Ming China and Inner Asia." In Frederick Mote and Denis Twitchett, eds. *The Cambridge History of China: Ming: Part 2*. Cambridge: Cambridge University Press, 1998, pp. 221–271.

Rossabi, Morris. *From Yuan to Modern China and Modern Mongolia*. Leiden: Brill, 2014.

Saγang Sečen, *Erdeni-yin tobči* (*Precious Summary: A Mongol Chronicle of 1662*) *Vol. I* ed. By M. Go, I. de Rachewiltz, J.R. Krueger and B. Ulaan. Canberra: Australian National University, 1990.

Sayinshal. *Chinggis qaγan-u tobciyan*, Kökhot: Öbör Mongγol-un arad-un keblel ün qoriy-a vol.1, vol.2, 1987.

Schneewind, Sarah. *A Tale of Two Melons: Emperor and Subject in Ming China*. Indianapolis and Cambridge: Hackett Publishing Company, 2006.

SHM: Secret History of the Mongols. Consulted in the following editions, concordances, and translations:

Cleaves, Francis Woodman. *The Secret History of the Mongols*. Cambridge, Mass.: Harvard University Press, 1982.

Rachewiltz, Igor de, trans. and ed. *Secret History of the Mongols: A Mongolian Epic Chronicle of the Thirteenth Century*. Leiden: E.J. Brill, 2004. 2 vols.

Wulan 烏蘭. *Yuanchao mishi* (*jiaokanben*) 元朝秘史 (校勘本). Beijing: Zhonghua shuju, 2012.

Serruys, Henry. "A Mongolian Version of the Legend of the Mongolian Ancestry of the Yung-lo Emperor." In John G. Hangin and Urgunge Onon, eds. *Analecta Mongolica: Dedicated to the 70th Birthday of Professor Owen Lattimore*. Bloomington: Indiana University, 1972, pp. 19–61.

Shimamura, Ippei. "Chinggis Khan used as a Cultural Resource: Comparative study between Japan, China, and Russia." *Human Culture* (*Bulletin of Shiga Prefecture University Faculty of Human Culture*) 24 (2008), pp. 7–34.

Shimamura, Ippei. *Chingis Haan henii baatar ve?* Ulaanbaatar: Admon, 2012.

Song Lian 宋濂. *Song xue shi wen ji* 宋濂全集. Hangzhou: Zhejiang guji chubanshe, 1999.

Ssu-ma Ch'ien. *Records of the Grand Historian of China* trans. By Burton Watson. New York: Columbia University Press, 1961, 2 vols.

Standaert, Nicolas. "Ritual Dances and Their Visual Representations in the Ming and the Qing." *The East Asian Library Journal* 12, no. 1 (2006): 68–181.

Steinhardt, Nancy. "Yuan Dynasty Tombs and Their Inscriptions: Changing Identities for the Afterlife." *Ars Orientalis* 37 (2007), pp. 138–172.

Su Tianjue 蘇天爵, ed. Yao Jing'an 姚景安, ed. *Yuanchao mingchen shilue* 元朝名臣事略. Beijing: Zhonghua shuju, 1996.

Subtelny, Maria. *Timurids in Transition: Politics and Acculturation in Medieval Iran*. Leiden: Brill, 2007.

Takase, Shuichi. *Going to Genghis Khan's Country*, Tokyo: Maruzen, 1992.

Takeda, Chuichiro. "Songs of the Mongols, Notations and Explanation." *Toyo Ongaku Kenkyu*,II:2 (1940), pp. 147–154

Taki, Ryoichi. "Bibliography and News." *Toyo Ongaku Kenkyu* I:4 (l938), p. 75.

Tamura Jitsuzo, et al. *Gotai Shinbun kan yakkai / Wuti Qingwen jian yijie*. Kyoto: Kyoto Daigaku bungakubu and Nairiku Ajia kenkyûjo, 1966–68, 2 vols.

Tan Qian 談遷 (1594–1658). *Guo que* 國榷. Ca. 1653. Beijing: Zhonghua shushu, 1988 rpt. [1958].

Tan Qixiang, ed. *Zhongguo Lishi Dituji*. Shanghai: Zhongguo Ditu chubanshe, 1982.

Tanaka, Tsuyoshi. "Building Chinggis Khan's Mausoleum." *Social Systems in 20th Century China (Report of Research on Modern China)*. Kyoto: Institute for Research in Humanities, Kyoto University, 2009, pp. 113–139.

Tanglü shuyi 唐律疏議. Beijing: Zhonghua shuju, 1983.

Tongzhi tiaoge jiaozhu 通制條格校注, punct. and annot. by Fang Linggui 方齡貴 Beijing: Zhonghua shuju, 2001.

Tsuji, Yuji. "Memory of Ethnic Group; focusing on the Elders' Narratives." *Bulletin of College of Education, University of Ryukyus* 59 (2011), pp. 203–211.

Tsutsumi, Kazuaki. "The Rise and Fall of Chinggis Khan's portrait: the Calendar for Mongolians in the Ishihama Collection." *Inter-disciplinary research of Ishihama Collection (Report of Osaka University)*. Osaka: Osaka University, 2012, pp. 22–37.

Tuvshin (陶布新) ed. *Autobiography of Demchigdonrov, Historical Materials of Inner Mongolia*, vol.13. Hohehot: Chinese People's Political Consultative Conference, Society for Historical Materials of Inner Mongolia, (『徳穆楚克棟魯普自述』内蒙古文史資料第13輯、呼和浩特：中国人民政治協商委員会内蒙古自治区文史資料研究会), 1984.

Ueda Makoto上田信. *Umi to teikoku: Min Shin jidai* 海と帝国：明清時代. In *Chūgoku no rekishi* 中国の歴史, ed. Tonami *Mamoru* 砺波護, et al. Tokyo: Kōdansha, 2005, vol. 9.

Uno Nobuhiro 宇野伸浩. "'Shūshi' dai 1 kan 'Mongoru shi' no kōtei tekisuto wo meguru shomondai."「集史」第１巻「モンゴル史」の校訂テキストをめぐる諸問題. In *Mongoru shi kenkyū: genjō to tenbō* モンゴル史研究：現状と展望, ed. Yoshida Jun'ichi, 44–64. Tokyo: Akashi shoten, 2011, pp. 44–64.

Vásáry, Istvan. *Cumans and Tatars: Oriental Military in the Pre-Ottoman Balkans, 1185–1365*. Cambridge: Cambridge University Press, 2005.

Waldron, Arthur. *The Great Wall of China*. Cambridge: Cambridge University Press, 1990.

Wang Guowei 王國維, ed. "Shengwu qinzheng lu jiaozhu 聖武親征錄校注." In *Menggu shiliao sizhong* 蒙古史料四種. 1926: facsimile rpt. Taiwan: Cheng-chung Press, 1962, pp. 1–220 (1a–107b).

Wang Qi 王圻. *Xu wen xian tong kao* 續文獻通考. 1586.

Wang Shizhen王世貞, compiler. "Bei lu shi mo zhi" 北虜始末志, in *Yanzhou shi liao* 弇州史料.

Wang Xiangyun. "Tibetan Buddhism at the Court of Qing: The Life and Work of lCang–skya Rol-p'ai-rdo-rje (1717–1786)." Ph. D. diss., Harvard University, 1995.

Wang Yun 王惲. "Da Yuan guanglu daifu pingzhang zhengshi Wuliang shi xianmiao beiming 大元光禄大夫平章政事兀良氏先廟碑銘." In Wang Yun王惲, *Qiujian xiansheng daquan wenji* 秋澗先生大全文集, 50.519a–525b. Hongzhi 弘治era; rpt. Shanghai: Commercial Press, 1922.

Weatherford, Jack. *Genghis Khan and the Making of the Modern World.* Crown Publishers, 2004.

Xinjiang kaogu sanshi nian 新疆考古三十年, ed. Xinjiang shehui kexue yuan kaogu yanjiusuo 新疆社会科学院考古研究所, Ürümçi: Xinjiang People's Press, 1983, pp. 458–466.

Xu Quansheng 许全胜, ed. *Hei-Da shilue jiaozhu* 黑韃事略校注. Lanzhou: Lanzhou University Press, 2014.

Xu Yikui 徐一夔. *Da Ming ji li* 大明集禮. Hongwu period. Revised under Li Shi 李時. 1530.

Xuzizhi tongjian changbian 續資治通鑒長編, by Li Tao 李燾 Beijing: Zhonghua shuju, 1980.

Yan Fu 閻復. "Shumi Jurong Wuyi Wang bei 樞密句容武毅王碑." In *Quan Yuan wen* 全元文, ed. Li Xiusheng 李修生. Nanjing: Jiangsu Guji Press, 1999, vol. 9, 295, pp. 265–268.

Yang Haiying. *Mongolian Intellectuals on the Steppe*, Tokyo: Heibonsha, 2001

Ye Qianzhao 葉潛昭, *Jinlü zhi yanjiu* 金律之研究. Taibei: Shangwu chubanshe, 1972.

Ye Xinmin. *Yuan Shangdu Yenjiu.* Hohot: Neimenggu Daxue chubanshe, 1998.

Ye Ye 葉曄. *Mingdai zhongyang wenguan zhidu yu wenxue* 明代中央文官制與 文學. Hangzhou: Zhejiang daxue chubanshe, 2011.

Yosida Jünyiči [Yoshida Jun'ichi], trans. Chenggel. 《*Monggol-un nighucha tobchiyan*》*-u sudulal: Yosida Jünyiči Proféssor-un ögülel-ün tegübüri.* Beijing: Nationalities.

YS: Song Lian 宋濂, comp. *Yuan shi* 元史. Beijing: Zhonghua shuju, 1976.

Zenrinkyokai (the Good Neighbor Association). *Overview of Mongolia*, Tokyo: Kaizosha, 1938.

Zhang Longxi. "Shenme shi 'Huairou yuanren'? Zhengming, kaozheng yu houxiandaishi shixue." *Ershiyi shiji* 45: (Feb. 1998): pp. 56–63.

Zhang Peizi. "Yuandai Tutuhua jiazu tanyan." *Yuanshi Lunzong* 8 (2001), pp. 194–207.

Zhang Tingyu 張廷玉 et al., eds. *Ming shi* 明史. 1736. Reprinted—Beijing:
Zhonghua shuju, 1974.

Zhang Xiangwen (張相文) "Discovering Chinggis Khan's mausoleum." *Geographical Journal* 3 (1915), pp. 7–13

Zhang Xiangwen (張相文) "Discovering Chinggis Khan's mausoleum. "Report on Chinggis Khan's mausoleum," *Geographical Journal* 4–5 (1916), pp. 1–5

Zhang Xiangwen (張相文) "Discovering Chinggis Khan's mausoleum. "Testifying about Chinggis Khan's mausoleum," *Geographical Journal* 8–9 (1917), pp. 1–6.

Zhang Xiangwen (張相文) "Discovering Chinggis Khan's mausoleum. "Rediscovering Chinggis Khan's mausoleum," *Geographical Journal* 10 (1917), pp. 1–15.

Zhang Yisun, genl. ed. *Bod rgya tshig mdzod chen mo / Zang-Han Da cidian* (Tibetan–Chinese Dictionary). Beijing: Minzu chubanshe, 1985, 1993.

[Zhao Gong 趙珙]. Ed. Wang Guowei 王國維. [1926] "Meng-Da beilu jianzheng 蒙韃備錄箋證." In *Menggu shiliao sizhong* 蒙古史料四種, Facsimile rpt. Taiwan: Chengchung Press, 1962, pp. 431–464.

Zhu Xi. *Zhuzi yulei*. Beijing; Zhonghua shuju, 1986.

Zito, Angela. *Of Body and Brush, Grand Sacrifice as Text/Performance in Eighteenth Century China*. Chicago: University of Chicago Press, 1997.

Index

Note: The authors used different transcriptions for foreign terms and names. We have retained their own preferred transcriptions but have identified them together in this Index.

www.ingramcontent.com/pod-product-compliance
Ingram Content Group UK Ltd.
Pitfield, Milton Keynes, MK11 3LW, UK
UKHW022224051026
15624UKWH00002B/331

9 789004 343382